Teaching for Understanding at University

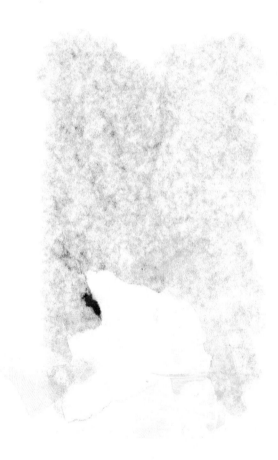

Universities into the 21st Century

Series Editors: Noel Entwistle and Roger King

Further titles are in preparation

Teaching for Understanding at University

Deep Approaches and Distinctive Ways of Thinking

Noel Entwistle

First published 2009 by
PALGRAVE MACMILLAN

Palgrave Macmillan in the UK is an imprint of Macmillan Publishers Limited, registered in England, company number 785998, of Houndmills, Basingstoke, Hampshire RG21 6XS.

Palgrave Macmillan in the US is a division of St Martin's Press LLC, 175 Fifth Avenue, New York, NY 10010.

Palgrave Macmillan is the global academic imprint of the above companies and has companies and representatives throughout the world.

Palgrave® and Macmillan® are registered trademarks in the United States, the United Kingdom, Europe and other countries

ISBN-13: 978-0-230-59385-5   hardback
ISBN-13: 978-0-333-96298-5   paperback

This book is printed on paper suitable for recycling and made from fully managed and sustained forest sources. Logging, pulping and manufacturing processes are expected to conform to the environmental regulations of the country of origin.

A catalogue record for this book is available from the British Library.

A catalog record for this book is available from the Library of Congress.

10 9 8 7 6 5 4 3 2 1
18 17 16 15 14 13 12 11 10 09

Printed and bound in Great Britain by
CPI Antony Rowe, Chippenham and Eastbourne

Contents

Figures and Tables

► Figures

► Tables

Series Editors' Preface

The series is designed to fill a niche between publications about universities and colleges that focus exclusively on the practical concerns of university teachers, managers or policy-makers and those which are written with an academic, research-based audience in mind that provide detailed evidence, argument and conclusions. The books in this series are intended to build upon evidence and conceptual frameworks in discussing issues which are of direct interest to those concerned with universities. The issues in the series cover a broad range, from the activities of teachers and students, to wider developments in policy, at local, national and international levels.

The current pressures on academic and administrative staff, and university managers, mean that, only rarely, can they justify the time needed to read lengthy descriptions of research findings. The aim, therefore, is to produce compact, readable books that in many parts provide a synthesis and overview of often seemingly disparate issues.

Some of the books, such as the first in the series – *The University in the Global Age* – are deliberatively broad in focus and conceptualisation, looking at the system as a whole in an international perspective, and are a collection of integrated chapters, written by specialist authors. In other books, such as "*Teaching for Understanding at University*", the authors look within universities at specific issues to examine what constitutes 'best practice' through a lens of available theory and research evidence.

Underpinning arguments, where appropriate with research-based conceptual analysis, make the books more convincing to an academic audience, while the link to 'good practice and policy' avoids the remoteness that comes from an over-abstract approach. The series will thus appeal not just to those working within higher education, but also to a wider audience interested in knowing more about an organisation that is attracting increasing government and media attention.

NOEL ENTWISTLE
ROGER KING

Author's Preface

The ideas in this book are a product of over 40 years of university teaching and research into student learning, and are intended to provide a conceptual framework for thinking about how university teaching influences student learning. While most books with similar titles focus on the <u>practice</u> of teaching, here the emphasis is on a critical consideration of why certain approaches to teaching are more likely than others to lead students towards a more personally satisfying and accurate conceptual understanding of the subject. The book draws on research specifically focused on student learning that has led to a new way of thinking about university teaching, taking serious account of the differences that exist between disciplines and subject areas within higher education. It suggests that there is an *inner logic of the subject and its pedagogy* that links broad educational aims with the teaching most likely to support student learning in a specific area of study.

In developing the ideas for this book I have drawn substantially on ideas and findings from an interdisciplinary and collaborative research study funded by the British Economic and Social Research Council as part of its extensive Teaching and Learning Research Programme. In our project, groups of researchers worked with teaching staff in 25 different course units from 11 universities to explore the extent to which fine-tuning of the teaching and learning environment could be carried out from analyses of students' ways of studying and their reactions to the teaching they had experienced. I am particularly grateful for the extensive discussions within the research team, and with collaborating colleagues in several university departments, all of which had an important influence on the development of this book. The later stages of writing were supported by the Leverhulme Trust, through the award of an Emeritus Fellowship, which allowed me to interview several prominent researchers to clarify my understanding of their ideas. I am most grateful for this support.

I am particularly indebted to my wife, Dorothy, who worked through successive versions of the book to help me find ways of expressing my ideas more cogently and clearly. She also collaborated in several of the research studies, as did my daughter, Abigail, whose own experiences as a student helped in formulating the ideas on students' understanding that became known as *knowledge objects*.

Thanks also to colleagues who commented on parts of the text as it was developing, including the publishers' reviewers, Piet Janssen and Velda McCune, but particularly my long-time mentor, John Nisbet, who read the whole book and gave valuable support and comments. I have drawn on the many discussions I have had with research colleagues in the projects I've worked on over the years, including Charles Anderson, Dai Hounsell, Paul Ramsden, Hilary Tait, Colin Smith, Velda McCune, Phil Odor, Paul Walker, Don Skinner, and, most recently, David Hay and Max Scheja. I have a debt to many other researchers, including John Biggs, Peter Davies, Hazel Francis, Ola Halldén, Ference Marton, Erik Meyer, David Perkins, Mike Prosser, Keith Trigwell, Lennart Svensson and

Jan Vermunt, all of whose ideas have had a major impact on the development of my thinking. They will recognize where some of the ideas in this book came from.

A special "thank you" also goes to Jenny Hounsell who not only carried out the analyses for Appendix B but also most of those in the whole ETL project. Finally, I would like to express appreciation and thanks to my editor at Palgrave Macmillan, Suzannah Burywood, who has remained supportive and helpful, and above all patient, over the many years it has taken to complete this book.

Acknowledgements for Tables and Figures

I am grateful to the following companies for permission to include the following material from their publications:

British Journal of Educational Psychology, © British Psychological Society. D. Hounsell & J. Hounsell (2007). 'Teaching-Learning Environments in Contemporary Mass Higher Education', in N. J. Entwistle & P. D. Tomlinson (eds), *Student Learning and University Teaching*, Figure 3, p. 101. Leicester: British Psychological Society.

Carfax. N. Entwistle, D. Skinner, D. Entwistle & S. Orr (2000). 'Conceptions and Beliefs about "Good Teaching": An Integration of Contrasting Research Areas', *Higher Education Research and Development*, 19, 5–26.

Kogan Page. N. Eizenberg (1988). 'Approaches to Learning Anatomy: Developing a Programme for Preclinical Medical Students', in P. Ramsden (ed.) *Improving Learning: New Perspectives*, p. 186.

Open University Press. Entwistle, N. J. (1987). 'A Model of the Teaching-Learning Process', in J. T. E. Richardson, M. W. Eysenck, & D. Warren Piper (eds) *Student Learning: Research in Education and Cognitive Psychology*, Figure 2, p. 23.

Orion Fiction and Penguin US. Carlos Ruiz Zafon (2005). *The Shadow of the Wind*, for the use of the epigram introducing Chapter 1.

Routledge. G. Brown (1997). *Assessing Student Learning in Higher Education*, Table 4.3, pp. 46–7.

Scottish Academic Press. F. Marton, D. J. Hounsell & N. J. Entwistle (eds) (1997). *The Experience of Learning*, Table 1.1, p. 19 and Table 5.2, p. 77.

Weidenfeld & Nicholson. C. R. Zafón (2004). *The Shadow of the Wind*.

I am also grateful to Warren Rieutort-Louis for permission to use an extract from his award-winning essay on good teaching for the Engineering Subject Centre of the Higher Education Academy.

1 Teaching for Understanding in a Complex World

He sculpted his sentences neatly, measuring them out with a cadence that seemed to promise an ultimate moral that never came. Years of teaching had left him with that firm and didactic tone of someone used to being heard, but not certain of being listened to.

Carlos Ruiz Zafon, *The Shadow of the Wind*

In spite of the common stereotypes about lecturers, university teachers these days generally care deeply about their teaching. They strive to help students acquire a way of thinking within the discipline or professional area through which the students can look at a problem or an issue and imagine how to set about resolving it. But to decide how best to teach, university teachers need more than a knowledge of the basic teaching techniques; they have to acquire enough pedagogic expertise to be able to think imaginatively about how to present their subject to students. Only then can they understand which methods are most likely to work for the specific purposes they have in mind, and how to adapt to the rapidly changing demands made of them as universities adjust to the new challenges of the twenty-first century.

It is important to be clear what lies at the heart of university education. The eminent educational psychologist, Jerome Bruner, believed that university education should be concerned not so much about the knowledge obtained, but about the *ways of thinking* that leave their mark on students.

> The great disciplines like physics or mathematics, or history, or dramatic forms in literature, were ... less repositories of knowledge than of methods for the use of mind. They provided the structure that gave meaning to the particulars. ... The object of education was to get as swiftly as possible to that structure – to penetrate a subject, not to cover it. You did this by 'spiralling' into it: a first pass to get the intuitive sense of it, later passes over the same domain to go into it more deeply and more formally.
>
> (Bruner, 1960: 20)

The demands of modern society make it imperative that we continue to provide students with the intellectual and other skills necessary for living in a world, which Ronald Barnett argues has *super-complexity*. We are facing problems for which agreed solutions can no longer be expected, and so we have to think for ourselves and adjust quickly to new conditions. Increasingly, knowledge acquired at university can be no more than a springboard for coping with change and complexity in everyday life and the workplace.

Universities have always encouraged students to think for themselves, to develop their own understanding of complex issues and to make the habit of critical thinking part of their make-up. More recently, the emphasis in university education has been shifting towards personal and social skills, and specific employment-related skills, but it is important not to shift the balance too far away from the enduring ways of thinking. Universities have to concentrate on helping students to develop skills, attitudes, knowledge and understanding that will be of maximum value in later life; not just providing an induction into the world of work in a specific profession, but also an effective preparation for life in the twenty-first century. As Diana Laurillard has argued:

> A university education capable of equipping students for the 21st century must pay close attention to the skills of scholarship – keeping abreast of existing knowledge, rigorous argument, and evaluation of evidence – no matter what the discipline. … University teaching must aspire to a realignment of research and teaching and to teaching methods that support students in the generic skills of scholarship, not the mere acquisition of knowledge. … The responsibility of every university [is] to offer its students access to expert teaching informed by current research, to give them the capabilities they need for their own professional lives.
>
> (Laurillard, 2006: 75–6)

The use of research evidence to devise effective teaching methods once seemed straight-forward. In 1926 the psychologist James Ward thought that the relevance of research to teaching was obvious.

> Unless we maintain that the growth of mind follows no law; or, to put it otherwise, unless it be maintained that systematic observation of the growth of (say) a hundred minds would disclose no uniformities; and unless, further, it can be maintained that for the attainment of a definite end there are no definite means, we must allow that if the teacher knows what he wants to do, there must be a scientific way of doing it.
>
> (Ward, 1926: 1)

At that time, psychologists believed that general 'laws of learning' could be established that would generalize to all situations. Now, we know better; there is a host of competing ideas about learning and, even if we identify those most relevant to academic learning, we would still not be able to reach simple conclusions about how best to teach students.

> Too much attention is directed towards finding … 'the best method', even though fifty years of educational research has not been able to support such generalisations. Instead, we should ask which method – or which combination of methods – is best … for which goals, for which students, and under which conditions.
>
> (Dahllöf, 1991: 148)

Panaceas in education, as in medicine, prove illusive. Claims that any one method, whether e-learning or enquiry-based learning, or whatever, is the way to present course material cannot be sustained, either logically or empirically. No single method could ever be equally effective across the whole of higher education, given the range of differing institutions, the contrasts between subject areas, the differences among both students and teachers and the differing views about the purposes of education. What research can offer is a way of thinking about how teaching affects learning and a range of concepts and principles that allow academics to think about pedagogic issues in a more precise way. That is what this book is offering.

▶ Some initial propositions

One main argument running through this book is that there is an *inner logic of the subject and its pedagogy*. There is a logic which holds together the various strands of a discipline or a topic area, and there is a logical connection between the intellectual demands of the subject and how best to teach it. Effective university teaching thus depends on establishing a relationship between the specific subject content and the ways in which students are helped to engage with the ideas, so as to develop their own understanding. In this book, we shall need to keep in mind the necessary diversity of pedagogy in higher education, while establishing general principles that link university teaching with student learning.

The research we shall meet later on shows that university teaching depends, first and foremost, on understanding one's discipline in a sufficiently broad and deep way to be able to make that understanding clear to students. But it also depends on wanting to communicate that knowledge, expressing enthusiasm for the subject being taught and discovering how students come to understand that subject. A recurring theme in the book will be that academic understanding, for students, depends on developing a broad, integrative way of thinking about the topics they are studying, drawing on the explanatory frameworks used within a discipline or professional area and recognizing how evidence is being used to reach conclusions. Effective teaching then depends on staff using their own broad and deep understandings of the subject area to find ways of helping students reach their own integrative academic understandings.

▶ The relationship between teaching and learning

The relationship between teaching and learning is often treated as being straightforward. The teacher presents the information and ideas, which the student then acquires. That view has led to an overemphasis on the *techniques* of presentation, whether through lectures, books, or e-learning. But the effects of teaching on learning are both subtler and more complex. Teaching influences learning directly, not just by making knowledge and ideas available but also by modelling ways of thinking or showing how evidence is used in building up an argument. Teaching also affects learning indirectly by influencing the approaches that students use in tackling their academic work. And this indirect influence comes not just from the act of teaching but also through the assignments set, the additional learning material offered or recommended, the support provided through tutorials and feedback on set work and, perhaps most importantly, what is rewarded through the assessment procedures. The importance of this indirect effect is an unequivocal finding from student learning research over the last 20 years and underpins the main argument being developed in this book.

In traditional university education, much of the face-to-face teaching still involves lectures, which take the form of a logical presentation of information and ideas, and yet often make it difficult for students to maintain interest and attention. There is an important distinction between 'lecturing' and 'teaching', which will become the focus of our later discussion. As one student, interviewed recently, explained:

> I was raised in the US and maybe they do things a little bit differently there. I'd never experienced a lecture before coming here. I had experienced teaching, and to me lectures seemed very, very different, because you'd be sitting in the middle row, sleeping through the whole thing: in teaching that never happened. It was always a case of the teachers gauging you, and you responding back. In our course here, most of us didn't speak with each other until the third or fourth year, because I don't think anyone felt like they were really being engaged from the front. But just once, we had a very different experience, an entirely different method; teaching rather than lecturing. The professor was asking very simple questions, and he was kind of building up a general theme or building up an idea, and by asking the class the questions he was pulling them along, you know, and forcing them to reach this conclusion at the end. Because he could relate to the students, there were generally three or four people shouting out their answer, and everyone was thinking about it.
>
> (MSc student taking electronic engineering)

Lecturing is a skill in its own right, but university teaching goes beyond that; it is not just a matter of learning a few techniques or gathering tips on presentation. It is a complex art, which depends on a deep understanding, not just of the discipline or profession but also of how best to make that knowledge accessible to students in the most effective and congenial ways. As with any attempt to explain difficult ideas, it depends on a sense of audience – knowing how to pitch the explanation at the right level. And that, in turn, involves an *act of imagination*, seeing how to present ideas and set up conditions for learning in ways that will engage students' interest and encourage them to develop their own understanding of the subject area. Done well, university teaching can help students to acquire a way of thinking and learning that is indelible, and can be useful throughout their life; done badly, it can alienate them from the whole idea of learning and studying. Academics thus have a moral responsibility to teach just as well as they carry out their research, and as in every specialism, evidence and theory, as well as experience, play an important part in shaping practice.

▶ The nature of educational research

The first thing to realize about research into human behaviour is that it rarely leads to the degree of certainty that is expected in, say, the physical sciences. Humans have a good deal of freedom in determining their own behaviour, and therefore even the most precise measurement of past actions or attitudes cannot possibly lead to accurate predictions of future behaviour. Moreover, the concepts used in social science are rarely defined with the degree of precision and agreement as in the 'hard' sciences. Techniques of data collection generally lead to estimates, rather than accurate measurements, while the findings themselves are always affected by the specific context within which people operate. As a result, emerging theories remain provisional and open to challenge – as in a subject like history – but there are, nevertheless, important similarities with other forms of empirical research.

Educational researchers are trying to find explanations for the observations they make, for example, about how students learn and how teaching affects that learning. In physics, fundamental theories are by now well established and show consistent relationships between causes, situation and effects, but research in education looks at the behaviour of people who have a unique personal history and whose actions are influenced by their own attempts to make sense of the situations they meet. And these actions depend not only on past experience but also on their own intentions and goals, and on the interpretations accepted within their own cultural milieu. In everyday life, there is a strong tendency to expect a single cause for an event or action, but looking for simple solutions in education has led, all too often, to 'bandwagon' effects emerging from one or other currently popular method of teaching, and also to grossly oversimplified explanations of student failure that allocate blame solely to students, for being 'dim', lazy or lacking interest.

Research challenges sweeping generalizations by exploring the complexity of actual teaching–learning contexts to reveal more realistic patterns of explanation. In doing this, education has to draw on a wide variety of evidence, using complementary methods of collecting and interpreting that evidence. Good educational research depends on using *disciplined enquiry*, in other words collecting and interpreting evidence in systematic ways and according to agreed procedures, but not restricted to any dominant methodology.

> In discussing disciplined inquiry ... we give no narrow definition of the term. Too many writers seem to limit the term 'research' to quantitative empirical enquiry. While much has been and will be learned from social survey, measurements, and controlled experiments, the study of education requires non-quantitative as well as quantitative techniques ... [and includes] naturalistic observation. ... An inquiry generally sets out to answer a rather narrowly defined question [but] the specific findings of such enquiries are usually less important than the conceptualizations they generate.
>
> (Cronbach & Suppes, 1969: 14)

> Educational research consists in careful, systematic attempts to understand the educational process and, through understanding, to improve its efficiency.
>
> (Nisbet & Entwistle, 1972: 113)

There are thus distinctive forms of disciplined inquiry into the effectiveness of teaching and students' ways of studying, which can be used to strengthen our understanding of the processes involved. These research methods often rely on the interplay between large-scale surveys of students using questionnaires and in-depth interviews with staff and students. The qualitative analyses of interviews do not lead to measurable quantities, but they do provide important insights into influences on learning. Those insights can then be used in conjunction with the quantitative findings from surveys. For these reasons, educational researchers use evidence cumulatively to draw conclusions, just as academic historians do, judging the strengths and weaknesses of the evidence, and testing the plausibility of the arguments presented. There can be no single study or specific research approach that will reach conclusive, applicable findings.

Using interviews can lead to a form of knowing which contrasts sharply with that more commonly used in academic scholarship. Conventional scientific analysis

is the essence of academic work and thus has a comfortable feel for academic teachers, but it tends to underplay the humanness of teaching which involves making sense of contradictions and dilemmas, wrestling with ideas and methods; interacting with students and colleagues; and juggling the demands of teaching in an increasingly crowded portfolio of professional responsibilities. The complementary form of knowing, narrative or story, ... is increasingly being favoured as a way of revealing the human scale of teaching.

(Ballantyne, Bain & Packer, 1997: xix)

In research studies, a whole series of extracts from interviews is used to justify conclusions, but in this book we can only use them to illustrate the findings, and also to help bring them to life by relating the ideas more immediately to personal experience. Throughout the book such extracts have been set in a contrasting typeface to distinguish them from quotations from other sources.

Another 'complementary form of knowing' about university teaching comes from the educational researchers' own professional experience as academics. Their understanding of the nature of university teaching and its relationship to student learning is formed through continuing reflection on both research evidence and personal experience. And current teaching practice itself has been increasingly changing to take account of research findings. This two-way interplay between research and professional experience means that research-based suggestions for enhancing the quality of teaching and learning are often closely in line with what is already becoming accepted as 'good practice' in university teaching. But research helps to explain <u>why</u> particular methods work in certain circumstances, and so guides further developments in practice.

Research into teaching and learning can now offer a coherent set of concepts through which to think about ways of teaching, soundly based on cumulative evidence and also fitting in with experience. The relationships between these concepts enables researchers to create conceptual frameworks that allow staff to reflect more deeply on their practice – not just on the knowledge being taught but also on the academic understandings and distinctive ways of thinking that are the essence of university learning. These conceptual frameworks are models of the interactions between teaching and learning, but they are heuristic rather than computational, intended to guide practice rather than predict outcomes. No one framework can be claimed to be 'right', but a coherent set of concepts soundly based on research findings can be helpful, and that is what the frameworks offered in this book are designed to offer.

▶ The structure of the book

The book builds up an overview of teaching and learning by looking, first of all, at learning, then what is to be learned and finally how to support that learning through teaching and the provision of a supportive teaching–learning environment. The content has been divided into five distinct parts. The first three introduce ideas and evidence about a whole range of influences on student learning and suggest why and how teaching affects the quality of student learning. In the final two parts, this evidence is used to build up a picture of how these research findings can be used to establish guidelines for teaching for understanding and to evaluate and 'fine-tune' that teaching.

In Part 1, we look at learning initially in terms of general principles about how people learn and how differences among individuals affect what is learned; then we consider research into how students learn and study in university settings. In the process, we shall meet some of the most influential concepts used to think about how teaching influences learning. Part 2 focuses on the subject matter, how students come to understand it and the targets set by staff in deciding what they would like their students to learn. Part 3 brings us to teaching, initially by looking at its conceptual basis, and then by describing examples of research into teaching, across a range of subjects in settings, that has been designed specifically to help students reach a deeper level of understanding. In these three parts there is a deliberately light touch in the provision of references, using them in an indicative way, rather than to support every conclusion reached. The lack of detailed referencing will mean that some ideas may seem not fully justified, but hopefully the text will be more readable.

In Part 4 we shall be going into more detail of how to set up teaching and learning environments, and so a rather more formal referencing system is used. The discussion will centre on how to design teaching–learning environments that act synergistically to make learning more effective and more congenial for the students, guided by a heuristic model of influences on student learning. In the final part, we shall be looking at ways in which university teachers can monitor the effectiveness of their own teaching in ways that are conceptually robust and technically sound. It will also consider the role that professional development can play in guiding effective university teaching.

'Bridge Passages' have been used to introduce each chapter. Research into teaching and learning has been gradually evolving over the last 30 years, and these bridge passages have been used to draw attention to that historical development, illustrated through my own involvement in this research field. The 'voice' in these passages is deliberately more personal, partly to provide a 'storyline' as the overview is built up, and partly to point up some of the key ideas and issues in the chapter that follows.

Underlying this whole treatment of university teaching, as already explained, is the notion of an *inner logic of the subject and its pedagogy*, a term chosen to highlight the crucial importance of the distinctiveness of the contrasting subject areas and the need to match teaching methods to the specific requirements of learning in each subject or topic, at whatever stage of the degree or postgraduate course, and within whatever institutional context.

▷ References

Ballantyne, R., Bain, J. & Packer, J. (1997). *Reflecting on University Teaching: Academics' Stories.* Canberra: Australian Publishing Service.

Barnett, R. (2007). *A Will to Learn: Being a Student in an Age of Uncertainty.* Buckingham: Open University Press and Society for Research into Higher Education.

Bruner, J. S. (1960). *The Process of Education.* Cambridge, MA: Harvard University Press.

Cronbach, L. J. & Suppes. P. (eds) (1969). *Research for Tomorrow's Schools: Disciplined Inquiry for Education.* Macmillan: New York.

Dahllöf, U. (1991). 'Towards a New Model for the Evaluation of Teaching', in U. Dahllöf, J. Harris, M. Shattock, A. Staropoli & R. Veld (eds) *Dimensions of Evaluation*. London: Jessica Kingsley.

Laurillard, D. (2006). 'E-learning in Higher Education', in P. Ashwin (ed.) *Changing Higher Education: The Development of Learning and Teaching*. London: Routledge.

Nisbet, J. D. & Entwistle, N. J. (1972). *Educational Research in Action*. London: Hodder & Stoughton.

Ward, J. (1926). *Psychology Applied to Education*. Cambridge: Cambridge University Press.

Part 1

How Students Learn

Educational Psychology and Student Learning

First of all, I had better say something about my background and how I came to be interested in student learning, because this has inevitably affected my subsequent thinking about teaching and learning.

My initial degree was in physics and led, after teacher training, to several years' teaching in a secondary school before taking part in a major research study at Aberdeen University on the transfer of children from primary to secondary education. The initial training in physics meant that I believed in precise measurement, and consequently felt comfortable using multivariate analyses in a doctorate supervised by John Nisbet, an eminent educational psychologist. His experience led me, however, to see the value of combining quantitative with qualitative methods, and this has had a continuing influence on my subsequent approaches to research, and on my thinking about educational psychology. The research design in this study meant that we focused more closely on the learning and teaching processes within classroom settings than on the broader social influences on learning. And my experiences as a schoolteacher meant that I was well aware of the practicalities of teaching and learning, and so tended to look with a wary eye at implications suggested from research findings or psychological theory.

Towards the end of my time at Aberdeen, I became interested in research into student learning at university through the work of Desmond Furneaux, who had found that engineering students who were anxious introverts did much better in exams than other personality 'types'. That finding intrigued me, and led to research that explored similar ground. We confirmed that introversion was an advantage across different subject areas, but that effect proved to be more attributable to the students' more conscientious study habits, than to their personality *per se*. The results of our study also showed that the combination of good study habits with a motivation to succeed was even more closely related to degree class than study habits alone. That is not surprising, perhaps, but it seeded an interest that led me into the field of student learning.

The psychological research on learning in the late 1960s was still dominated by behaviourism, the ideas of which seemed totally implausible to me as a teacher. So I was strongly influenced by an article by Bill McKeachie, a past president of the American Psychological Association, entitled 'The decline and fall of the laws of learning'. McKeachie subsequently lent his authority to influential research into the motivation, cognition and learning of university students. And my thinking about learning was then taken forward by the cognitive psychology of David Ausubel and Jerome Bruner. Ausubel had drawn attention to the crucial importance of what the learner already knows, and how that knowledge had been organized, while Bruner wrote persuasively about the active thinking needed to reach a thorough understanding of complex material. And both these cognitive psychologists led the way in research into the types of thinking and learning required of students at university.

> It is an epistemological mystery why traditional education has so often emphasized extensiveness and coverage over intensiveness and depth. ... Memorizing was usually perceived by [students] as one of the high priority tasks, but rarely did [they] sense an emphasis upon ratiocination with a view toward redefining what had been encountered, reshaping it, reordering it. The cultivation of reflectiveness, or whatever you choose to call it, is one of the great problems one faces in devising curricula: how to lead [students] to discover the powers and pleasures that await the exercise of retrospection.
>
> (Bruner, 1974: 447, 449)

None of this thinking was acceptable within behaviourism, but cognitive psychology and the more recent research into educational psychology has taken our understanding of human learning much further. And these areas of research underpin much of the subsequent research into university learning and teaching, which we shall meet later on. Some of the psychological descriptions of learning are inevitably somewhat technical, and their relevance may not be immediately obvious, but ideas about memory, concept formation and motivation, and other mainstream psychological concepts, do help us to recognize how the findings on student learning fit in with the more fundamental psychological ideas.

▶ References

Ausubel, D. P., Novak, J. D. & Hanesian, H. (1978). *Educational Psychology: A Cognitive View* (2nd edn). New York: Holt, Rinehart & Winston.

Bruner, J. S. (1965). *Toward a Theory of Instruction*. Cambridge, MA: Harvard University Press.

Bruner, J. S. (1974). *Beyond the Information Given: Studies in the Psychology of Knowing*. London: George Allen & Unwin.

Furneax, W. D. (1962). 'The Psychologist and the University', *Universities Quarterly*, 17, 33–47.

McKeachie, W. J. (1974). 'The Decline and Fall of the Laws of Learning', *Educational Researcher*, 3, 3, 7–11.

McKeachie, W. J. (1994). 'Concluding Remarks', in P. R. Pintrich, D. R. Brown & C-E. Weinstein (eds) *Student Motivation, Cognition and Learning: Essays in Honor of Wilbert J. McKeachie*. Hillsdale, NJ: Lawrence Erlbaum.

Nisbet, J. D. & Broadfoot, P. (1980). *The Impact of Research on Policy and Practice in Education*. Aberdeen: Aberdeen University Press.

Nisbet, J. D. (1986). *Learning Strategies*. London: Routledge & Kegan Paul.

Nisbet, J. D (2005). 'What is Educational Research? Changing Perspectives through the 20th century', *Research Papers in Education*, 20, 25–44.

2 Learning and the Influences on It

> ### Fundamental processes of learning

In the 1950s, psychologists were pointing out that each person was, in certain respects, like everyone else, like some other people, and like nobody else. Different theorists tended to take more account of one or other of these perspectives, with some using small-scale experiments to study memory and learning processes used by everyone, and others relying on large-scale surveys to find traits distinguishing between groups of people with similar characteristics. At that time, psychotherapists seemed to be the only theorists stressing the importance of individuality, as that was the main focus of their work with clients. In this book we shall be using all these perspectives in trying to explain the effects of teaching on learning and how students react to their educational experiences. In this chapter, we shall be looking at aspects of learning that everyone shares, before considering some well-established traits describing group differences.

Practice and feedback

In psychology, there has been a tendency to discard earlier theories as newer ideas emerge, and yet some of the previous ideas remain valid and important in education. From the early behaviourist theories, we know that skills are developed through practice and that repetition of words or phrases strengthens the memory of them. But the form of practice is even more important, doing the same action repeatedly is rarely the best approach. For example, throwing a ball through a hoop set several metres away can be repeated until it can be done successfully on most occasions. Yet the real skill involves being able to do this from different distances and directions, and that depends on having <u>varied</u> practice, not just repetition. And this principle is important not only in skill learning but also in establishing concepts, as we shall see.

The other crucial finding from behaviourist psychology is the effect of reward or punishment on deciding whether an action will be repeated. The essence of conditioning is strengthening the connection between stimulus and response. We tend to repeat actions or strategies we have found rewarding, either because of the pleasure they give in themselves or from the praise, or other rewards, like grades, we receive afterwards. Behaviour is also shaped by punishment or criticism, but people react differently to praise and blame; harsh criticism rarely promotes learning, whereas most people can be encouraged to learn through praise or by gently correcting and explaining mistakes. Thus helpful, understandable comments on work carried out are essential if students are to learn from their mistakes. This may seem obvious, but such feedback is not always given at university, as we shall see later. It is true that the general notion of conditioning in education has been challenged, even discredited, as it makes the role of teacher too controlling and the approach too mechanistic, but the main principles can be applied effectively in gentler and more imaginative ways.

Attention and memory

An early theory that still holds true, describes the way sensory information is recognized by the brain and is then processed for subsequent use. The description was originally based on an analogy with a library cataloguing system, but has since been supported by evidence about neurological processes. The starting point is *attention*. Unless we focus on what is most salient in the information coming to us, and are consciously aware of it, it will barely register in our memory. Early hominids survived by being able to recognize very rapidly any important, or potentially threatening, aspect of the environment and reacting to it. In everyday life, attention is still driven in similar ways, but in university education it is generally interest or the need to pass exams, which arouses and maintains attention in lectures or while studying.

Attention is directed towards incoming sensory signals, which are initially recognized and then passed to *short-term memory* (STM), where their meaning is interpreted by comparing them to previously stored information. Short-term memory has another important function, it is where we bring together material from long-term memory to work on problems, linking together ideas or relating new knowledge with old. But short-term memory, as its name implies, does not last long – about 20 seconds on average. It is also severely restricted in size, allowing us to handle only between 5 and 9 separate pieces of information at a time. We do, however, develop strategies of grouping separate bits of information together, and this technique is crucial in building up an understanding of complex ideas. Experiences lead to concepts, and sets of concepts are brought together to create higher-level concepts or theories. But to do this, we often have to put our ideas on to paper or computer so that we can think about many more elements at the same time.

In presenting ideas to students in lectures, the restricted size of STM has important implications. It makes it impossible for students to handle more than a limited set of ideas or pieces of evidence within a short time span, so the amount of material introduced within each lecture has to be carefully weighed up. Students also need a good deal of help with techniques of handling complex information in their own studying, for example, by using concept maps or other diagrams. In this book, we shall be using diagrams to bring sets of ideas together, and we shall also be introducing a new way of using concept maps to help students develop a deeper understanding.

Conceptual development

Information that comes into STM has to be passed into *long-term memory* (LTM) and linked to relevant areas of knowledge and experience. Past events or episodes are stored in *episodic* long-term memory as visual images, often with associated sounds, smells and feelings. Knowledge and ideas are stored somewhat separately, in *semantic* long-term memory. To recall information accurately, it has to have been 'filed' correctly, making sure it is related to similar prior memories, and linking it closely with associated experiences, images or patterns (diagrams) within episodic LTM. Although episodic and semantic memories are described as being distinct, they are really closely linked, with visualization or rhymes being an important way of triggering semantic memory, through mnemonics, for example. Although long-term memory has been often likened to a library with its own categorization system, or to coding material into a computer, it is also importantly different. People not only store information, they keep it continuously under review to make connections or expand their existing knowledge. And this is done at both conscious and subconscious levels.

From an early age, grouping similar events or objects together is fundamental to cognitive development; even young babies recognize similarities and differences and group them in a process that later makes use of language to form *concepts*. The earliest concepts are of those experienced in our everyday environment: food, table, chair, horse, dog, pig, and so on. Concepts are established through meeting varied examples of them in contrasting circumstances and discriminating them from similar concepts (dog from cat, for example). The defining features of such concepts are *easy* to discern and are widely agreed upon. But with abstract concepts, like 'justice', 'freedom', 'education', 'learning' or 'understanding', consensus is much more difficult to establish, because these depend on the particular examples each person has met. So we all have rather different *conceptions* of such concepts, in which previous experience, knowledge, values and feelings become intertwined.

Indeed, the continuing search for meaningful connections among our experiences is an important driving force in human behaviour, as Gerald Edelman has argued on the basis of neuroscience. He has drawn attention to the 'correlative urges' that suffuse our thinking and have their origins in the survival demands facing early mankind. So we bring together experiences and events in creating concepts and link together concepts in developing understanding, or in creating new ideas or techniques.

> Higher-order consciousness leads to the construction of an imaginative domain, one of feeling, emotion, thought, fantasy, self, and will. It constructs artificial objects that are mental. In culture, these acts lead to studies of stable relations among things (science), ... among mental objects (mathematics) and ... between sentences that are applicable to things and to mental objects (logic). ... Thinking occurs in terms of *synthesized* patterns.
>
> (Edelman, 1992: 151–2)

Not only are these patterns or conceptions, to a certain extent, personal, we may also retain several alternative versions of a concept that we use for differing purposes. Even when we have met precisely defined technical concepts in, say, physics or economics, our earlier everyday conceptions often remain. We have to learn which conception is most appropriate for each task or situation we meet. Explaining an idea in a pub to our friends has to be geared to what they know and what they are interested in, and carried out in an appropriately colloquial manner. Giving that kind of explanation in a tutorial would not be sensible.

Rote and meaningful learning

Just as there are distinct forms of memory, there are equivalent differences in learning processes. If we want to remember essentially meaningless material, like a telephone number, we repeat it over and over until it is firmly transferred from working memory to LTM. This process of repetitive *overlearning* does not depend on links with previous knowledge; it is a matter of forcing the information directly into the memory, and is described as *rote learning*. Repetition plays an important part in learning a poem by heart or making sure you can give the technical name of a flower or a fossil when seeing it. Establishing concepts or understanding ideas, however, depends on making links with what we know already and that demands what has been called *meaningful learning* – the conscious attempt to make sense of topics for oneself. But some students come to treat academic work as being essentially meaningless, and so see rote learning as an appropriate approach to use in a routine way. Such an attitude all too easily becomes a habit, which seriously affects the ability to learn academic material, as we shall see in the next chapter.

▶ Learning processes in studying

The raw material for forming concepts comes from experiences, either first-hand or provided and organized by others. Simple concepts are formed subconsciously, but the more abstract ideas introduced in higher education generally require considerable conscious effort before the underlying meaning of a concept can be grasped. Even the term 'concept' has limited applicability; in the humanities, the looser notion of an *organizing idea* is more appropriate. But we shall use 'concept' as an encompassing idea covering both terms.

Academic concepts come at different levels. Some are the basic building blocks of a discipline – like 'current' in electronics, 'price' in economics or 'photosynthesis' in biology, while others are introduced to show important interconnections between groups of basic concepts and may be expressed as theories or laws – like 'Ohm's law' in physics, 'opportunity cost' in economics or 'optimal foraging' in zoology. In 2003, Jan Meyer and Ray Land suggested that, in many subject areas, there are *threshold concepts* that play a critical role in understanding a topic area, sometimes by integrating lower-level concepts, but always by opening up a new perspective on the landscape of knowledge to the student. Grasping such integrative concepts allows students to understand the subject more deeply, but the ideas often prove challenging. Unless they are thoroughly understood, students will find it difficult to make progress in the subject. And higher-level thresholds are even more difficult to grasp, where they involve the distinctive ways of thinking within a discipline that provide the foundation of a professional approach to the subject. Students generally only come to terms with these thresholds later in their degree.

In meeting a new topic it is crucial for students to be able to distinguish what is salient from what is incidental, and this often proves difficult in the early stages of a degree course. Without this recognition, students cannot see the important landmarks they need to guide their own explorations of an academic domain. This ability to discern what is salient has become a central part of a recent pedagogical theory of learning developed by

Ference Marton. An accurate conception depends on recognizing the defining features of the target concept, and also on discriminating it from similar ones. To be able to do this, we need to have experienced the variations that make up the characteristic features of the concept. To take a simple example, the concept of 'colour' depends on experiencing the differences between red, blue, green, and so on. This variation is something we experience every day and so we are able to build up, subconsciously, an accurate conception of 'colour'. When it comes to abstract concepts, however, the variations are rarely self-evident, and if students cannot recognize the defining features for themselves, they will inevitably develop inaccurate or incomplete conceptions.

> In order to see something in a certain way, a person must discern certain features of that thing. We should also be clear about the difference between 'discerning' and 'being told'. Medical students, for instance, might be advised by their professor to try to notice the different features of their patients, such as the colour of the lips, the moisture of the skin, the ease of breathing, and so on. This is 'being told'. But in order to follow this advice the students must experience ... how they can vary. ... By experiencing variation, people discern certain aspects of their environment; we could perhaps say that they become 'sensitized' to those aspects. This means that they are likely to see future events in terms of those aspects; ... [so learning depends] on experiencing variation.
>
> (Marton & Tsui, 2004: 10–11)

The starting point of this *variation theory* is thus *discerning* critical features, and this depends on the students' active use of prior knowledge and experience to separate out for themselves the critical features from the more incidental ones. Just being told which are the critical features will rarely suffice; they have to be experienced. The salient *dimensions of variation* within a concept or topic may be met in everyday living, or can be systematically provided by a teacher, but without the opportunity to see and reflect on the meaning of these variations, students cannot understand how they fit together. And yet a full understanding of a concept or a topic depends on being able to see the overall *pattern of variation*, the links between the various parts that create a coherent whole, so students have to keep these dimensions of variation in mind (in working memory) *simultaneously*. So understanding depends on actively exploring the interconnections that make up a concept, phenomenon or process, and comparing and ordering them until a clear overall pattern of variation is seen.

Examples of the use of variation theory in university teaching provided in Chapter 6 will help to make the idea more concrete. For now, we will use an extract from the writing of an eminent biologist, Edmund Wilson, to bring together psychological and neurological descriptions of memory and learning processes mentioned earlier.

> Mind is a stream of conscious and subconscious experience. ... It is at root the coded representation of sensory impressions and the memory and imagination of sensory impressions. ... Long-term memory recalls specific events. ... It also re-creates not just moving images and sound but meaning in the form of linked concepts simultaneously experienced. ... The conscious mind summons information from the store of long-term memory ... and holds it for a brief period in short-term memory. During this time it processes the information, ... while scenarios arising from the information

compete for dominance. ... As the scenarios of consciousness fly by, driven by stimuli and drawing upon memories of prior scenarios, they are weighted and modified by emotion ... which animates and focuses mental activity. ... What we call meaning is the linkage among neural networks created by spreading activation that enlarges imagery and engages emotion.

(Edited from Wilson, 1998: 119, 121, 122, 123, 126)

This view of how a personal web of understanding is formed is consonant with Edelman's notion of 'correlative urges' and of Marton's idea of grasping critical features and their interconnections. Creating such an integrated 'whole' is crucial to an understanding that is personally satisfying, and so has an emotional tone. It is this view of *personal understanding* that is at the heart of our thinking about university teaching and we shall look at it in more detail in Chapter 4.

▶ Influences on learning

So far we have looked at some of the processes of learning that everyone uses, but now we come to the contrasts that can be found between groups of individuals. These differences in, for example, ability, motivation and personality are no longer seen as fixed characteristics, but ones that develop through the interplay of inherited capabilities and many subsequent experiences and relationships. Their importance in thinking about university teaching lies in the effects they have on how students learn, and how they react to the teaching they experience. The concepts introduced in this chapter come from mainstream psychological research, but in the next chapter we shall meet other ideas that have been developed in trying to explain students' experiences of learning and studying.

Previous knowledge and experience

Until the 1980s, universities in Britain had a rather homogeneous intake, mainly of students coming more or less straight from school with recent experiences of studying and accredited knowledge of their chosen subject area. Now the situation is very different, with much greater diversity. The rapid expansion of higher education has provided opportunities for social groups previously unlikely to enter higher education, as well as to students coming from ethnic minorities and bringing with them different cultural beliefs and attitudes to education. There are also students at university with disabilities that might previously have excluded them. These changes have created a more varied and richer mix of experience among students, but at the same time have caused additional problems for academic staff. Syllabuses and ways of teaching that were appropriate for the top quarter of young students from homogenous backgrounds cannot offer a suitable academic diet for students who are less well prepared for university learning or have varying cultural backgrounds.

However, one of the main influences on the ease with which all students acquire new knowledge is their prior knowledge and how well it has been organized − what they already know about the subject matter and about how to handle ideas within their chosen subject area. Indeed, David Ausubel's influential book on educational psychology begins by stating:

> If I had to reduce all of educational psychology to just one principle, I would say this: The most important single factor influencing learning is what the learner knows already. Ascertain this and teach … accordingly.
>
> (Ausubel, Novak & Hanesian, 1978: iv)

This adage, while true as a logical and theoretical principle, was difficult enough to apply in the late 1970s with a large class of students. Then, individual prior knowledge was still varied, but it was possible to have a reasonable idea of what most students would know. Now it is much more difficult to know how to 'teach accordingly', given the diversity of students and the modular system, but we still need to have a good idea of the spread of subject knowledge and other differences within a class of students to prepare for teaching.

Abilities and learning styles

There continues to be considerable disagreement about the relative importance for education of what has been called *general intelligence* or '*g*', and also about how much it is likely to change over time and circumstance. Verbal and logical forms of intelligence, which are at the heart of '*g*', have clear relationships with most areas of academic attainment, and also have proved to be remarkably stable, even between childhood and old age, except where early experience has severely inhibited normal cognitive development. Nevertheless in higher education more specific abilities are also important, not just in areas such as music and art, but also in most other academic areas.

It has been suggested through studies in cognitive archaeology that separate 'modules in the mind' evolved in early humans in response to the demands of everyday life. These experiences ranged from artifacts and tool making (the physical domain) to animals and animal behaviour (the biological domain) and to other people (the social and interpersonal domain). Howard Gardner has argued that it is possible nowadays to make even finer distinctions, to recognize *multiple intelligences*, including logical thinking, and also the specialized abilities involved in, for example, mathematics and music, as well as the interpersonal intelligence needed in human relationships and the intrapersonal ability to understand oneself. Students' academic progress is quite strongly related to general ability, and also depends on having a profile of other abilities compatible with their chosen subject area. But people also learn to use their intelligence and abilities more effectively over time, making better use of their whole profile of abilities and other qualities by using stronger elements to compensate for weaker ones.

A different line of research has drawn attention to the distinctive preferences that people have for learning in particular ways, for example, by a specific mode of sensory input (e.g. visual, auditory, kinaesthetic) or through contrasting forms of mental representation. These so-called *learning styles* are often described in terms of polar opposites, thought by some researchers to be rooted in contrasting hemispheric brain functions, with the right brain involved more in imagery and the left brain dealing with analytic processes. And distinctive learning styles have been found in how students tackle their academic work.

For example, Gordon Pask contrasted *serialists* with *holists* through the ways in which they went about studying. When starting a new piece of work, serialists prefer to go about it step-by-step, thriving on the logical development of topics, and building gradually towards an overall understanding. In contrast, holists look straightaway for the whole picture and depend on lively illustrations and anecdotes to help them fit the details and the evidence into it. Pask also identified stylistic differences in students' explanations of what they had understood, with serialists presenting more formal, well-structured scientific descriptions and holists developing a more personal narrative account. In other research, in which students were asked to mark and comment on short essays written in deliberately contrasting styles, higher marks were given to the essays in the learning style closest to their own. But a thorough academic understanding generally involves a *versatile* interplay between overview and detail, as we shall see in Chapter 4.

What implications can be drawn from this research for university teaching? Lecturers have to aware not just of the range of abilities to be found in any class, but also of the existence of distinct stylistic preferences. This means that presentations have to start at a level that all the students can understand and build gradually in complexity, and also that they should contain both the strong logical development favoured by serialists and broad overview and more personal approach preferred by holists. This idea will be revisited in Chapter 5 to suggest a more general – 'multipli-inclusive' – approach to teaching.

Personality and motivation

As we saw in the Bridge Passage, introverts are likely to be more successful at university than stable extroverts, whose need for social interaction distracts them from studying. But it was subsequently found that the more direct influences on academic success came from a combination of motivation and well-organized study methods. Although, like intelligence, the term motivation is often used to denote a single entity, it again has importantly different forms. A basic distinction can be made between *intrinsic* and *extrinsic* motivation. Intrinsic motivation comes from interest in what is being learned and the feelings of pleasure derived from it, while extrinsic motivation depends on external rewards, such as grades or praise. The early research on conditioning saw reward solely in extrinsic forms, but in higher education it is intrinsic motivation that engages learning processes leading to personal understanding.

Other important forms of motivation are vocational motivation, achievement motivation and fear of failure. Students from non-western cultures are more likely, in addition, to describe motives relating to *social responsibility* – acquiring knowledge for the benefit of other people in their country. Where students have a clear vocational goal, it forms an important driving force in studying, leading them to look for immediate relevance in their courses. If they do not find that link, however, they may rapidly become demotivated. Some courses, of course, have no obvious vocational target, and so depend on interest in the subject matter or the need to obtain a degree.

When it was introduced into the psychological literature, *achievement motivation* was described as a stable personality characteristic, fed by 'hope for success' and the rewards that came from high grades. In higher education, it was often found to fuel strong competition with other students, being found more frequently among men than women, and in applied areas such as business studies and engineering. *Fear of failure* can also drive attainment through feelings of anxiety, but it is likely to lead to the 'safer' approach of rote learning, rather than the more 'risky' attempts to reach an independent understanding. In some of the early research into student learning, the distinction between achievement motivation and fear of failure was seen as creating marked differences in how students perceived both themselves and their whole university experience.

> Some students are stable, confident and highly motivated by hope for success, while others are anxious, uncertain of themselves and haunted by fear of failure, and yet both groups are capable of high levels of academic performance. The interview data take the differences even further. Students of differing personality and motivational types not only tackle their academic work in different ways but, from their descriptions of their university experience, they evidently perceive themselves to be in differing environments.
>
> (Entwistle, Thompson & Wilson, 1974: 393)

Although, at the time of this research, motivation was seen as a relatively fixed characteristic, subsequent studies have shown that it is much more malleable, being strongly affected by experience. Intrinsic motivation and interest in the subject, in particular, are affected by the nature of the teaching experienced. Nevertheless students have a responsibility to develop their own motivation and interest, it is not a one-way process.

Thinking dispositions

So far we have concentrated on separate concepts describing aspects of learning, but recent research has been looking at groups of concepts that act together in affecting how people think. David Perkins and his colleagues at Harvard have been using the term *thinking disposition* to indicate the ways in which several relatively stable characteristics of individuals seem to work together synergistically to affect academic learning.

> The three aspects of thinking are called sensitivity, inclination, and ability. *Sensitivity* concerns whether a person notices occasions in the ongoing flow of events that might call for thinking, as in noticing a possibly hasty causal inference, a sweeping generalization, a limiting assumption to be challenged, or a provocative problem to be solved. *Inclination* concerns whether a person is inclined to invest effort in thinking the matter through, because of curiosity, personal relevance, ... habits of mind, and so on. *Ability* concerns the capability to think effectively about the matter in a sustained way, for instance, to generate alternative explanations for the supposed causal relationship.
>
> (Perkins & Ritchhart, 2004: 358–9)

Perkins has subsequently argued that we should be encouraging students to go 'beyond understanding'. Academic understanding, in itself, may be of little value unless it is used actively, looking out for and recognizing opportunities to make use of it in everyday life;

in problem finding as well as problem solving, and in designing specifications as well as designing to specifications. And in education, we need to invite students to discover, not just perform, leading to a culture of opportunity, rather than a culture of compliance. In Chapter 4 we shall be extending the notion of a thinking disposition more directly into the sphere of student learning by introducing the idea of a *disposition to understand for oneself*.

▶ An alternative research paradigm

This chapter has been mainly following the evolutionary path in educational psychology from behaviourism, through descriptions of the memory and information processing, and the identification of individual differences in ability and personality, towards the more integrative conception of dispositions. All this research is essentially positivist, seeking the *causes* of differences in learning outcomes, but educational psychology has also followed an importantly different line of development, originating in the work of Vygotsky. He saw learning in terms of the interactions between young people and adults in social contexts. Out of this seminal work, an alternative view of human learning has developed, seeing human actions as dependent on their intentions, on their interpretations of their experiences in the everyday social world and on the language through which those experiences are discussed. Bruner has argued that the most important intellectual activity is 'meaning-making', which is inevitably social, depending on culturally acquired ways of thinking and on social conventions about the aspects of phenomena or events that are seen to be salient. He argued that psychology

> must venture beyond the conventional aims of positivistic science with its ideals of *reductionism, causal explanation* and *prediction*. ... To reduce meaning or culture to a material base, to say that they 'depend', say, on the left hemisphere, is to trivialize both in the service of misplaced concreteness. ... To insist upon explanation in terms of 'causes' simply bars us from trying to understand how human beings interpret their worlds and how *we* interpret *their* acts of interpretation. ... The study of human mind is so difficult, so caught in the dilemma of being both the object and the agent of its own study, that it cannot limit its inquiries to ways of thinking that grew out of yesterday's physics.
>
> (Bruner, 1990: xii–xiii)

As we shall see in the next chapter, much of the research into student learning and university teaching has followed a research approach that is both cognitive and social, focusing on learning within specific academic contexts, as it has tried to understand the differences in how students tackle their academic work and the reasons for those differences. Seeing human action within this perspective, however, does not mean that we have to abandon the findings of positivist research. The cognitive processes and individual differences discussed earlier are still important to bear in mind, underpinning, as they do, the more directly relevant research into student learning.

In his 1990 book, Bruner stressed that meaning has to be constructed by the individual in relating new experiences both to previous knowledge and to earlier experiences within a social setting. But in academic study, students' understandings have to be sufficiently in line with the requirements of the teachers to satisfy assessment criteria. In some subject areas students will be encouraged to arrive at their own interpretations, but in all subject areas understandings have to be expressed within an accepted academic discourse, using the concepts and ways of treating evidence that are characteristic of the discipline being studied. And each discourse amounts to a contrasting culture into which students have to be gradually inducted. In the traditional university disciplines, the ways of thinking are derived, historically, from the underlying philosophy of the Western world, involving causal explanations and critical reasoning, which can be alien to students coming from very different cultural backgrounds. With the substantial influx of overseas students into universities in Europe, North America and Australia, there needs to be a greater awareness of the ways of thinking and acting that are found in other cultures, and the implications these have for university teaching.

▶ Concluding summary

The simplest forms of learning depend on attention, practice and feedback, and these are also important in more complex forms of learning. The two main learning processes established from psychological research are rote learning and meaningful learning. Rote learning transfers information in an unchanged form into long-term memory, whereas meaningful learning creates connections with knowledge already held there, often across quite varied topics. Meaningful learning thus not only takes in information, it can integrate it into a personal understanding.

There are definite limits in how many pieces of information we can process together within the short-term working memory and these constraints also affect the number of interrelationships we can handle in thinking about concepts. Concepts have agreed defining features, and for simple concepts these are readily recognized through repeated experiences in varying contexts. But abstract and complex concepts are often understood in quite different ways – people develop individual *conceptions* that depend on their own prior knowledge and experience.

Some students have considerable difficulty in developing conceptions that match the 'target understandings' expected by university teachers. Certain abstract concepts may prove difficult for a substantial proportion of students, and yet these often have a crucial part to play in understanding the subject, acting as *threshold concepts* that open up the subject in important ways. Students can be helped with such concepts or other difficult topics by focusing on their *critical features* and how those aspects relate to each other.

There are many influences on the effectiveness of learning. Here we have surveyed some of the more basic ones – previous knowledge and experience, abilities and learning styles, personality and motivation – while the idea of thinking dispositions suggests how several of them can work together to bring about learning and understanding. The final section introduced an alternative approach to educational psychology that describes learning as being social in origin, with meaning-making being a major activity, and this underpins much of the research into student learning we shall be coming to next.

▶ **Further reading**

Fundamental processes of learning and influences on learning

Bruner, J. S. (1996). *The Culture of Education*. Cambridge, MA: Harvard University Press.

Deary, I. J. (2000). *Looking Down on Human Intelligence: From Psychometrics to the Brain*. Oxford: Oxford University Press.

Entwistle, N. J. (1988). *Styles of Learning and Teaching: An Integrated Outline of Educational Psychology*. London: David Fulton.

Gardner, H. (1999). *Intelligence Reframed: Multiple Intelligences for the 21st Century*. New York: Basic Books.

Renfrew, C., & Zubrow, E. B. W. (1994). *The Ancient Mind: Elements of Cognitive Archaeology*. Cambridge: Cambridge University Press.

Vygotsky, L. S. (1986). *Thought and Language*. Cambridge, MA: MIT Press.

Learning processes in studying

Marton, F. & Pang, M. F. (2006). 'On Some Necessary Conditions of Learning', *The Journal of the Learning Sciences*, 15, 193–220.

Meyer, J. H. F. & Land, R. (2006). *Overcoming Barriers to Student Understanding: Threshold Concepts and Troublesome Knowledge*. London: Routledge.

Pask, G. (1988). 'Learning Strategies, Teaching Strategies and Conceptual or Learning Style', in R. R. Schmeck (ed.) *Learning Strategies and Learning Styles*. New York: Plenum Press.

Vosniadou, S., Baltas, A. & Vamvakoussi, X. (eds) (2007). *Reframing the Conceptual Change Approach in Learning and Instruction*. Oxford: Pergamon.

▶ **References relating to the quotations (not already shown above)**

Ausubel, D. P., Novak, J. D. & Hanesian, H. (1978). *Educational Psychology: A Cognitive View* (2nd edn). New York: Holt, Rinehart & Winston.

Bruner, J. S. (1990). *Acts of Meaning*. Cambridge, MA: Harvard University Press.

Edelman, G. (1992). *Bright Air, Brilliant Fire: On the Matter of the Mind*. London: Penguin Books.

Entwistle, N. J., Thompson, J. B. & Wilson, J. D. (1974). 'Motivation and Study Habits', *Higher Education*, 3, 379–96.

Marton, F. & Tsui, A. B. M. (2004). *Classroom Discourse and the Space of Learning*. Mahwah, NJ: Lawrence Erlbaum.

Perkins, D. N. & Ritchhart, R. (2004). 'When is Good Thinking?', in D. Yun Dai and R. J. Sternberg (eds) *Motivation, Emotion, and Cognition: Integrative Perspectives on Intellectual Functioning and Development* (pp. 351–84). Mahwah, NJ: Erlbaum.

Wilson, E. O. (1998). *Consilience*. London: Little, Brown & Co.

Bridge into Chapter 3
The Impact of Approaches to Learning

In the early 1970s, psychological research into learning was gradually abandoning the straightjacket of behaviourism, with a recognition that what happened inside the head was worth treating seriously. So instead of learning and memory being investigated through lists of nonsense syllables to avoid 'contaminating' the experiment with effects of prior knowledge, cognitive psychologists began to investigate the comprehension of short passages of text. But, still, they sought the safe ground of precise measurement by measuring comprehension in terms of the accuracy of verbatim recall of the text itself.

In the early 1970s I was using this psychological research on learning, along with the work on individual differences, when asked to talk to lecturers about teaching and learning. These sessions proved to be extremely uncomfortable, with many of my colleagues failing to see any relevance in the research findings to their own experience of teaching, no matter how clearly I thought I had pointed out the implications. Out of this discomfort, however, came a realization that it really was impossible to extrapolate the psychological findings directly into the realm of everyday teaching and learning. And as university teachers are trained to detect and attack implausibility, my sense of disillusionment was justified. The basic ideas on learning outlined in the previous chapter, while valuable, need to be seen in the light of research into student learning within university contexts. That was where the research led next.

I was fortunate enough to be invited to take part in planning a Council of Europe symposium designed to bring together researchers and administrators to discuss university teaching and learning. At the first meeting, I met Ference Marton from Gothenburg University who told me about his latest research, which 'would change the whole way we thought about learning'. His discovery, as he explained, was that students approached their learning in importantly different ways. When reading a short academic text some students tried to understand the author's message for themselves, while others concentrated on remembering the facts and details they expected to be tested on. And those who had not looked for meaning, not surprisingly, did not find it. These contrasting ways of reading were described as 'deep' and 'surface', and Marton was able to demonstrate that deep approaches led not only to a good understanding of the author's message but also, when used consistently in everyday studying, to much better examination results than those who had adopted a surface approach.

My initial feeling was that this simple dichotomy was implausible, but I was intrigued enough to ask my undergraduate students to read an article for the next tutorial. When I met them next, I went round the group asking them how they had tackled the reading, and all their descriptions could be seen as either 'deep' or 'surface'. Although this distinction between approaches to learning now seems obvious, at the time it was groundbreaking, because the research had looked at the text in terms of the students' intentions, their understanding of it and how they had gone about their learning.

One of Marton's research team, Lars-Owe Dalgren, looked at what students said they had learned from the text. He classified these answers into qualitatively different categories representing steps from complete misunderstanding to an understanding of one or other aspect of the author's argument and then to a full understanding often linked to the student's own ideas. This idea of a hierarchical set of categories reoccurred in later research, leading to the notion of *phenomenography*, which described qualitative differences in students' conceptions of specific topics or concepts.

Another researcher working with Marton, Anders Fransson, carried out an experimental study into the effects of the context. Students read different academic texts under contrasting situations. One text they read was directly relevant to one group, but only indirectly relevant to the other; the groups were also subdivided to give different experiences of learning. In one, the students learned under relaxed, supportive conditions while, in the other, students were told that one of them would have to explain out loud to the rest of the group what they had learned. The hypothesis was that reading a relevant, and so more interesting, article under relaxed conditions would lead to a deep approach, while the less interesting article under more anxiety-provoking conditions would produce a surface approach. Surprisingly, no such effects were found. But the students had also been asked to report how interesting they had found the article, and how anxious they had felt about the situation. Then, significant findings emerged; it was not so much the way the experiment had been set up, as how the individual student had <u>perceived</u> the situation, that affected the approach to learning. Some students had found the less relevant article interesting, while the stressful condition had not aroused anxiety in everyone who had experienced it.

The ideas and findings from Marton and his research group altered the way in which student learning was investigated in Britain and Australia. Now it was possible for us to investigate the outcomes of learning in terms of the meanings that students found in what they were studying. We could see the crucial importance of the student's intention in bringing about qualitatively different learning processes, and how perceptions of the context affected the approach to learning. Interest is not just a characteristic of an article (or a lecture); some students can see interest, or make themselves interested, in material which other students find boring.

These ideas about approaches to learning were taken forward at Lancaster, along with Paul Ramsden and Dai Hounsell, by interviewing students about their experiences of everyday studying and producing a questionnaire that indicated the relative strengths of the various approaches. As the implications of this line of research were established more clearly, our ideas about teaching and learning in higher education became fundamentally transformed. By looking at the students' experiences of learning realistically complex academic material within university contexts, an altogether different set of concepts and research findings emerged, ones that we could then present to our colleagues and to students with much more confidence. And these descriptions of learning and studying have generally been found to be not just plausible but also convincing.

▶ **References**

Dahlgren, L-O. & Marton, F. (1978). 'Students' Conceptions of Subject Matter: An Aspect of Learning and Teaching in Higher Education', *Studies in Higher Education*, 3, 25–35.

Entwistle, N. J. (ed.) (1976). *Strategies for Research and Development in Higher Education*. Amsterdam: Swets & Zeitlinger.

Entwistle, N. J. & Ramsden, P. (1983). *Understanding Student Learning*. London: Croom Helm.

Fransson, A. (1977). 'On Qualitative Differences in Learning: IV – Effects of Motivation and Test Anxiety on Process and Outcome', *British Journal of Educational Psychology*, 47, 244–57.

Marton, F. & Booth, S. (1997). *Learning and Awareness*. Mahwah, NJ: Lawrence Erlbaum Associates. (Describes phenomenography.)

Marton, F. & Säljö, R. (1984). 'Approaches to Learning', in F. Marton, D. J. Hounsell & N. J. Entwistle (eds) *The Experience of Learning* (pp. 36–55). Edinburgh: Scottish Academic Press, available in an electronic edition at http://www.tla.ed.ac.uk/resources/EoL.html.

3 How Students Learn and Study

As we have just seen, the nature of research into student learning changed in the mid-1970s, and now we will see how the field has moved on since then. This different approach introduced a broader perspective on learning, one that saw individuals as having their own intentions and seeking to make sense of the world for themselves within a social setting. This approach relied much less on the concepts and categories developed by theorists from other disciplines and, instead, sought explanations based on the experiences of students. Marked differences were found in how students studied and in the reasons students gave for studying in those ways, which then provoked questions about how existing teaching methods affect student learning, as we shall see in Chapter 5.

▶ Concepts describing student learning

The concepts come with different explanatory breadths, with broader constructs describing *identity, orientations to learning, conceptions of knowledge* and *conceptions of learning*, and the more narrowly defined concepts, covering *approaches to learning and studying*, which focus on the specific subject matter being learned and the study tasks that students undertake. The great advantage of these concepts is that they relate to aspects that are immediately recognizable by both staff and students, and that they are all open to change, being influenced by students' experiences at university as well as by the teaching they meet. Although inevitably oversimplifying a more complex reality, the concepts have not only proved powerful in describing and explaining salient differences in how students learn and study, they have led to a clearer understanding of how different types of teaching and assessment affect the quality of learning being achieved.

Identity and self-confidence

One of the most important influences on how students go about learning is their previous experience, not just of education, but also in the family and with their peers. Social and cultural attitudes are formed early and have a continuing influence on how students adjust to higher education. Interviews with students have shown the importance of their feelings about themselves – their self-confidence in the role of student and in social interchange – and their allegiances to their individual social and cultural backgrounds. The term 'identity' has been used widely in sociology to describe our sense of self within the varying social situations we find ourselves in and the differing roles we have to play. This sense of self develops through comparing ourselves with other people and is strongly dependent on how we are seen and described by parents, partners and friends – our *significant others*. In schooling, and higher education, teachers can also affect the development of identity quite strongly, and in particular the sense of identity as a student and feelings of self-confidence or the lack of it.

Although the term 'identity' sounds as if it were a single characteristic, we actually see ourselves in several quite distinct ways, depending on the situation we are in and the role we are expected to play. Sociological descriptions often relate identity primarily to group membership (such as social class or ethnicity) or to power relationships, and that is certainly an important aspect of the sense of self, but it is only one aspect. There is also a tendency to stress changes in identity over time, and yet people also have a strong feeling of continuity about who they are, sustained by internal or shared narratives about their life history.

Identities do not change easily or quickly, and so the adaptations students have to make as they enter higher education often prove difficult and take time. If they have come straight from school, young people are still in the process of establishing their social and sexual identities, while at the same time trying to discover how the demands of teaching and learning at university differ from those experienced at school: they may also be living away from home for the first time. Overseas students are also having to learn how to live in a different society, as well as possibly meeting very different expectations and forms of teaching than those in their own country. And mature students, whatever their origins, often have to juggle multiple demands on their time, with work and family commitments. How students settle into their new role as students, and the self-confidence or otherwise they have in that role, markedly affects their academic progress, particularly in the early stages of a degree course.

The composite narrative in Table 3.1 has been built up from interview comments by mature students to illustrate how personal circumstances may affect students' perceptions

Table 3.1   Mature students' comments about their experiences of studying at university

---

The whole set-up of the thing, the buildings, trying to find out who people were, where you should be, [was difficult]. I know everybody's an adult when they come to university but I just felt, 'Oh, God!'. When you walk in you haven't a clue what building or where to go for them. ... I realized before I came that everything would be unfamiliar and that I would need to get used to how things worked. Coming up to the essays, I just felt that I wasted a whole lot of time, getting the wrong kinds of information, getting readings that I didn't really need. ... You [have to] do a lot more yourself and there's nobody to spoon-feed you, as such. It's a bit of a shock to the system, but you just have to adapt quick! ... That's the big difference; ... you're expected to do it yourself, and the help you get is minimum ...

It's a constant struggle between looking after the kids, work and study. I sometimes have to do my university work from eleven at night till four in the morning. Then I have a quick sleep, then breakfast, get the kids to school, and then off to work: that's what a day's like for me. ... Because you don't have a lot of time, you've got to work out if it is worth going to that, or is it something I'm never going to use: you really have to be quite selective ...

Dipping in confidence [early on] seems to be a very common thing, but I came back in term two with a renewed determination that ultimately this is what I want to do, and some bits you just have to work through and you might not particularly like, but you've got to achieve it and that's it. ... This term I'm quite happy to join in tutorials; last term it made me nervous, but I just had a word with myself and now I feel better.

Source: Composite of selected quotes from interviews analysed by Viviene Cree, Hazel Christie, Jenny Hounsell, Velda McCune and Lyn Tett, at the University of Edinburgh.

of their university experience, as well as their attitudes and their self-confidence about themselves as learners. Although these were all mature students who have additional difficulties in adjusting, other students also struggle to make sense of their initial experiences of university, often with much less help than they feel they need in those early stages.

Personal and vocational aspirations

The sense of self in university or college becomes bound up with the reasons for continuing one's education and often with a vocational goal that can strongly affect the emerging sense of adult identity. It is hardly surprising to find that students' aspirations have a major influence on how well they do, but it is important to be clear what reasons are typically given. Liz Beaty introduced the idea of a *learning orientation* which described not just reasons students gave for attending university, but also the continuing, and changing, attitudes and feelings they expressed towards their studying. The contrasting orientations she identified represent the four main social functions of higher education – academic, vocational, personal and social. She suggested that each of these could be separated into two distinctive kinds of interest in the courses being taken – extrinsic and intrinsic.

> The idea of an orientation assumes that students have an active relationship with their studying, [with] ... success and failure judged in terms of the extent to which students fulfil their own aims ... [and which] may change over time. The analysis of learning orientation ... sets out to ... show the implications of different types of orientation for the approach a student takes to learning. ... It is important to recognize that the categories and sub-categories used to describe learning orientations are simply an analytic framework and not descriptions of the types of student found in the study. In fact, any particular student's orientation [at any one time] will usually be a complex mix of two or more of these [categories].
>
> (Beaty, Gibbs & Morgan, 1997: 76–7)

The warning about not using categories to label students applies to all the qualitative research described in this chapter, as students have mixed motives, and ways of studying alter according to circumstances. The analytic framework shown in Table 3.2 can be used to make sense of the aspirations and attitudes of individual students, and also to map the general pattern shown in a particular class or intake. Beaty went on to suggest that students establish an implicit *learning contract* with themselves – what they want to achieve while at university – and this changes over time as students adjust their expectations to the level of grades they are obtaining and how interested they are in their academic work.

Conceptions of knowledge and learning

William Perry in Harvard carried out some of the earliest interview research with university students. He was interested in how they developed intellectually while at university or college, his analyses revealing an important trend in how they were thinking about the

Table 3.2   Categories describing differing learning orientations

Orientation	Interest	Aim	Concern
Vocational	Intrinsic	Training	Relevance of course to future career
	Extrinsic	Qualification	Recognition of qualification's worth
Academic	Intrinsic	Intellectual interest	Choosing stimulating lectures
	Extrinsic	Educational progression	Grades and academic progress
Personal	Intrinsic	Broadening or self-improvement	Challenging, interesting material
	Extrinsic	Compensation or proof of capability	Feedback and passing the course
Social	Intrinsic	Making a contribution to society	Courses focusing on improving social or personal conditions
	Extrinsic	Having a good time	Facilities for sport and social activities

Note: The social intrinsic category was not in the original study but was found in subsequent research.
Source: Beaty, Gibbs & Morgan, 1997: 77.

nature of knowledge – their *conception of knowledge*. Students entering university tended to see knowledge as firmly established and conveyed to them by teachers or in books. Only gradually did they begin to understand how knowledge changes over time, and so recognize its provisional nature. The starting point of Perry's developmental scheme involved seeing knowledge as either 'right' or 'wrong' (dualistic) and then moved, first, towards a recognition of how evidence is used to reach conclusions, and beyond that to an acceptance that knowledge is still developing and open to challenge, and thus ultimately uncertain and socially constructed (relativism). The initial recognition of relativism takes students

over a watershed, a critical traverse in our Pilgrim's Progress. ... In crossing the ridge of the divide, ... [students] see before [them] a perspective in which the relation of learner to knowledge is radically transformed. In this new context, Authority, formerly a source and dispenser of all knowing, is suddenly authority, ideally a resource, a mentor, a model, and potentially a colleague in consensual estimation of interpretations of reality. ... [Students] are no longer receptacles, but the primary agents responsible for their own learning.

(Perry, 1988: 156)

Subsequent research has largely supported Perry's developmental scheme, but has suggested gender differences in the extent to which the learning is seen in more personal or impersonal terms and has also led to debates about whether his scheme should be seen as applying generally, or as differing across subject areas. Nevertheless some of the learning 'blocks' that students come up against while studying are caused by their struggles in coming to terms with the nature of disciplinary knowledge. And it is only towards the end of a degree course that students begin to discern, in a conscious and reflective way, how evidence and reasoning are being used to create new knowledge. The slowness in this 'pilgrim's progress' is often not sufficiently appreciated by academics who are already comfortable with the knowledge in their specialism, but the finding reminds us how important it is not to overestimate students' grasp of the subject in the early stages of a degree.

Subsequent interviews by Roger Säljö in Gothenburg also showed important differences in how students think about the nature of learning. He asked adults to explain what they meant by 'learning' and found that these *conceptions of learning* also showed a developmental trend from simpler to more complex views. At the simplest level, learning was seen as taking in bits of knowledge that could then be given back later on, in the same form. This meant that learning was being equated with memorizing or rote learning. A slightly more advanced view recognized that learning involved acquiring knowledge for future use. This conception seemed to be carried over from experiences in school and seemed to be quite resistant to change as students entered higher education. However, a significant change came about when learning was seen to depend on understanding the material for oneself, and so coming to see aspects of the world in importantly different ways. Subsequent research suggested an even greater sense of personal involvement, with learning involving a change in oneself as a person.

In the later stages of this intellectual and ethical development an important additional change takes place, with students realizing that, for some purposes, rote learning is still necessary, even though conceptual understanding is the main goal at university. In other words, memorizing often plays a supportive role in building up initial understanding, but also later on, ensuring that understanding is firmly lodged in the memory. In general, the more sophisticated views of academic knowledge and learning tend to be broader, more inclusive and more coherent than the less sophisticated ones, and this also applies to the ways students approach their studying, and even to how academics see their role as university teachers, as we shall see in Chapter 5.

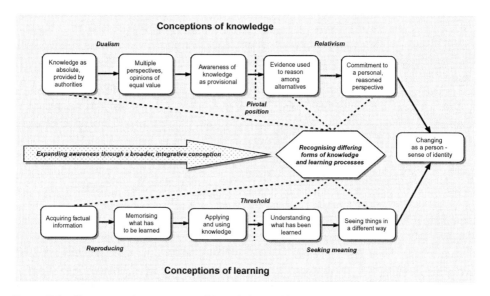

Figure 3.1 Categories of conceptions of knowledge and learning

There is a clear parallel in the developmental trend shown in the work of Perry and Säljö, and this is illustrated in Figure 3.1. Both sets of categories show an increasing sophistication in the conceptualizations of knowledge and learning and also identify critical points at which students' conceptions appear to change radically – the pivotal position of acknowledging relativism in knowledge and the threshold through which learning at university level comes to be seen as seeking meaning for oneself. The sets of categories are essentially hierarchies in which the more sophisticated conceptions incorporate aspects of the earlier conceptions, add others and also show a growing awareness of the implications of the different ways of seeing knowledge and learning. This recognition then shows itself in a greater awareness of the students' own ways of studying.

▶ Approaches to learning

While conceptions of knowledge and learning are rather abstract notions, approaches to learning and studying relate very directly to students' experiences at university. The idea originated with Ference Marton and his research team, as we have already seen. Students had been asked to read an academic article and were then asked questions about it. First of all, they were asked to describe the author's main message, with responses varying from a complete misunderstanding of the argument to a good grasp of it, with some cogent additional comments. They were then asked how they had gone about the task, with the interview transcripts then being analysed to discover possible reasons for different levels of understanding. What emerged was the dichotomy in *approaches to learning*, distinguishing a *deep* from a *surface* approach. In the words of the researchers:

> All our readings and re-readings, our iterations and reiterations, our comparisons and groupings, finally turned into an astonishingly simple picture. We had been looking for the answer to the question of why the students had arrived at those qualitatively different ways of understanding the text as a whole. What we found was that the students who did not get 'the point', failed to do so simply because they were not looking for it. The main difference we found in the process of learning concerned whether the students *focused on the text itself or on what the text was about*: the authors intention, the main point, the conclusion to be drawn.
>
> (Marton & Säljö, 1997: 43)

The approach essentially depends on the student's intention. Students adopting a surface approach see the task as no more than second-guessing the examiner, they decide what type of questions they expect and then trawl through the article looking for likely questions. They then memorize just those pieces of information and are totally floored by any question that demands an understanding of what they have read. Students adopting a deep approach set about the task with the intention of understanding it for themselves which, of course, makes it much more likely that they will grasp the author's meaning. Other research showed that both the deep and the surface approach varied in terms of how much effort the students had put into that approach, making four categories in all (see Table 3.3).

Table 3.3 Students' descriptions of their approaches to learning

---

Approaches to learning adopted in reading an academic article

Surface passive – Level of understanding = mentioning
In the beginning I read very carefully, but after that I hurried through it. I lost interest (and) I didn't think about what I was reading.

Surface active – describing
In reading the article I was looking out mainly for facts and examples. ... I thought the questions would be about the facts in the article (and) ... this did influence the way I read: I tried to memorize names and figures quoted ... I tried hard to concentrate – too hard – therefore my attention seemed to be on 'concentration' rather than on reading, thinking, interpreting and remembering.

Deep passive – relating
I read it in a casual, interested manner, not being influenced by the fact that I was to be questioned, mainly because I didn't expect (to be asked) any details of the article. Consequently, I read with impartial interest – extracting the underlying meaning, but letting facts and examples go unheeded.

Deep active – explaining
Whilst reading the article, I took great care to understand what the author was getting at, looking out for arguments, and facts which backed up the arguments. ... I found myself continually relating the article to personal experience, and this (helped me to understand it). The fact of being asked questions on it afterwards made my attention more intense. (*From Entwistle, 1988: 78*)

Approaches to learning in electronic engineering

Surface approach
I suppose I'm mainly concerned about being able to remember all the important facts and theories that we've been given in the lectures. We are given an awful lot of stuff to learn, so I just plough through it as best I can. I try to take it all down in the lectures, and then go over it until I'm sure they won't catch me out in the exams. ... (With the problem sheets) the first step is to decide which part of the lecture course the problem comes from. Then I look through my notes until I find an example that looks similar, and I try it out. Basically, I just apply the formula and see if it works. If it doesn't, I look for another example, and try a different formula. Usually it's fairly obvious which formula fits the problem, but sometimes it doesn't seem to work out, and then I'm really stuck.

Deep approach
It is not easy, you know. There is a great deal to cover, and I am not satisfied unless I really understand what we're given. I take quite full notes, but afterwards I go through them and check on things which I'm not clear about. I find that working through the problem sheets we're given is a good way to test whether I know how to apply the theory covered in lectures, and I do that regularly. Once you realise what lies behind the problems – that's the physics of it and what makes it a problem – then you can do them. You get a kick out of it too, when it all begins to make sense. Applying the right formula is not difficult, once you know you are on the right lines. (*Adapted from Entwistle et al., 1989*)

Seeing what students themselves actually said in interviews may help to clarify the meaning of these important categories. The first set of extracts in Table 3.3 illustrates the four categories of approach and effort shown in the original research reports, along with the levels of understanding that students showed after reading the article. The second set illustrates how deep and surface approaches are seen in everyday studying, when students are asked how they go about tackling their work – in electronic engineering in this instance.

The distinctive intentions associated with approaches stem from different motives and lead to contrasting processes of learning – essentially rote/reproductive or meaningful learning. Intrinsic motivation and interest in the subject are more likely to lead to a deep approach, particularly if these intentions are supported by a sophisticated conception of learning. With this combination, students will generally try to understand for themselves, leading them to look for relationships between ideas and also to check the logic of the argument and the evidence supporting it. But to be effective, a deep approach does depend on having adequate prior knowledge to link the new ideas to, and also the necessary reasoning ability to make sense of those links.

In contrast, seeing learning in terms of building up bits and pieces of knowledge to give back to the teacher almost inevitably leads to an intention to memorize or reproduce material. And if this develops into a habitual way of learning, without considering its consequences for understanding the subject matter, the effect on studying is damaging. A surface approach often stems from, but also creates, a lack of interest in the subject, no matter how much time and effort the students may put into studying. The effort is almost always misplaced because the requirements of the task are not fully appreciated. Moreover, a surface approach is often associated with higher levels of anxiety and fear of failure as the students begin to realize that their attempts at studying are not meeting academic requirements. There can then be a downward spiral of demoralization that leads to less effort being put into the work, as interest and self-confidence drain away.

Although the terms 'deep' and 'surface' were chosen to describe the specific instance of reading an academic article, subsequent research showed that they can be applied equally well to the way students take notes in lectures, write essays and prepare for examinations: indeed, to whatever task the students meet. But that does not mean that any individual student will use the same approach for every assignment, or in every course they take. Marton emphasized that approaches should be seen as essentially 'relational', in other words they necessarily depend on how the student interprets a particular task: does it seem interesting, important and worth doing, or not. It is thus quite wrong to characterize students as 'deep learners' or 'surface learners'; approaches certainly change as students meet different types of teaching, as we shall see later on. And yet there remains an element of consistency in the approach, which may reflect personality differences or vocational aspirations, and that leads some students to adopt surface approaches habitually, while others generally seek personal understanding. Most students, however, lie between these extremes, so that even where an approach proves to be relatively consistent, students will still show different reactions to individual teachers and to specific courses, so approaches are essentially variable.

Table 3.4 sets out the defining features of approaches to learning as they have emerged from the research, but the danger in looking through these lists of characteristics is that they may come to be seen as polar opposites. In earlier descriptions, that tendency was marked, but the current meaning introduces an important qualification.

Table 3.4   Defining features on approaches to learning

Deep Approach   *Seeking meaning*

Intention – to understand ideas for yourself   by

Relating ideas to previous knowledge and experience
Looking for patterns and underlying principles

Checking evidence and relating it to conclusions
Examining logic and argument cautiously and critically
Using rote learning where necessary

                                                                          And as a result
Being aware of one's own understanding as it develops
Becoming more actively interested in the course content

Surface Approach   *Reproducing*

Intention – to cope with course requirements   by

Treating the course as unrelated bits of knowledge
Routinely memorizing facts or carrying out set procedures
Studying without reflecting on either purpose or strategy

                                                                          And as a result
Finding difficulty in making sense of new ideas
Seeing little value or meaning in either the courses or the tasks set
Feeling undue pressure and worry about work

Source: Adapted from Entwistle 1997, Table 1.1:19

Students with an intention to understand, and who have a sophisticated conception of learning, will realize that memorizing is an appropriate learning process for some tasks – like remembering the names of fossils or plants, or historical dates – and that this rote-learned material can then be used, in subsequent learning, to develop conceptual understanding. Some students consistently adopting a deep approach may also feel undue pressure and worry about work, as they try to understand complex abstract material for themselves.

In a forthcoming publication, Carol Bond is arguing that we should see progressions from surface to deep approach as representing not separate categories, but rather an improving awareness by students of which learning processes are most appropriate for specific purposes, with a gradual development taking place paralleling those shown in conceptions of learning (see Figure 3.1). She has identified experiences of learning that describe, initially, a preponderant use of reproductive learning, merging later with an emphasis on acquiring knowledge, before gradually incorporating the processes involved in developing, first, a passive form of understanding to satisfy a lecturer and, finally, an active form of understanding that involves transforming previous ways of seeing the world, and oneself in relation to it. We shall meet this final form again in Chapter 4 in looking at the *disposition to understand for oneself*.

The main difference between deep and surface is in the *intention* – either to reproduce the material presented or to understand it for oneself, and that is a dichotomy. It is also important to realize that the generalized description of the processes of learning involved

Table 3.5   Deep approaches shown in contrasting subject areas

Physics	I suppose I'm trying to imagine what the experiment is about, in a physical sense, sort of get the picture. ... I was looking for pattern [in the results] which I could relate to the theory. I knew what was supposed to be happening and I was looking out for it happening in the graph – fortunately it did.
Engineering	You have to go through quite a few different designs to get the right one. I'm always thinking about what I can put into the conclusion when I'm writing about a project and I'll try to show what I have understood from the project.
Psychology	I started to realize that the English I'm doing as an option is very closely connected to psychology – the novelist is just more artistic – and when I realized they were so close, then I saw how interrelated all the topics in psychology were and that putting your own pattern on an essay would probably make it better – and it did – it's just a better way of learning.
History	There are always underlying themes in any period of history, and if you can sort of pick out those themes and really understand what was going on and what it was all about, then you've got a good chance of discovering it on an equal basis to the tutor or in an exam.
English	The work demands, in a way, a completely different sort of intelligence. For us, it's more interpretation, analysis, penetration into the material – you have to see implicit meaning. ... For example, seeing whether Tennyson compromised his art to the age or whether he wrote what he really wanted to write. That's what I'm thinking about all the time as I'm reading it.

Source: From Entwistle & Ramsden, 1983: 142–5.

in a deep approach cannot apply in the same form to each subject area. The way understanding is developed in contrasting disciplines is so different that what is involved in a deep approach is bound to vary (as illustrated in Table 3.5). In thinking about how best to support a deep approach by students, it is important to clarify, for each subject area, and even for each topic, the processes of learning that are necessary to develop deep conceptual understanding. That will then be the most useful definition of a deep approach in that context.

Even though there are these major differences in the <u>specific</u> processes of learning involved in contrasting disciplines, the common features shown in Table 3.4 can still generally be seen in the approaches adopted by students across subject areas. Besides the contrasting intention, students adopting a deep approach will be looking for patterns and connections, and viewing the subject as a whole; they will also be alert to exceptions, looking for alternative interpretations and be aware of the types of learning the subject requires of them.

Organized effort

The terms 'deep' and 'surface' apply to learning and were observed originally within a naturalistic experimental setting, as we saw earlier. Although the task was one commonly met by students, it lacked one crucial ingredient – formal assessment. In the work done subsequently with Paul Ramsden, we asked students how they went about their everyday

Table 3.6 Items used to identify the 'organized effort' put into studying

---

Organized studying
- I organize my study time carefully to make the best use of it.
- I carefully prioritize my time to make sure I can fit everything in.
- I work steadily during the course, rather than just leaving things until the last minute.
- I'm quite good at preparing for classes in advance.

Effort
- I try really hard to do just as well as I possibly can.
- I generally put a lot of effort into my studying.
- I generally keep working hard even when things aren't going all that well.
- Whatever I'm working on, I generally push myself to make a good job of it.

Source: From the ETL project website – http://www.etl.tla.ed.ac.uk/publications.html.

studying, which extended the notions of deep and surface approaches to a range of other academic tasks besides reading, such as learning from lectures, writing essays and revising for examinations. And the effect of assessment then became very clear, and required an additional category to describe it – a *strategic approach to studying* that involved the intention to achieve high grades, driven by either achievement motivation or a sense of responsibility.

Recent work with Velda McCune, however, has suggested that use of the term 'approach' is not really appropriate. The questionnaires used to measure strategic behaviour defined it in terms of systematic organization of studying, time management, effort and concentration. The determination to do well is still a characteristic of organized effort, but the competitive element no longer appears to be consistently strong. Typical items used in the questionnaires to cover this aspect of studying are shown in Table 3.6 to clarify its specific meaning.

Organized effort can be applied to either a deep or a surface approach to learning. Combined with a surface approach it has often served students well prior to entering university and may well still lead to satisfactory levels of performance early in a degree course. But later on it will become increasingly ineffective, as tasks and assessment criteria change. When understanding becomes a more important criterion in assessment, only a deep approach combined with organized effort will be consistently rewarded.

Recently, there has been growing concern in British universities about an imbalance in the reasons given for student failure, with poor teaching or inadequate supervision often being seen as the culprits. Of course that may be true in some instances, and a contributory cause in others, but the legal proceedings, brought by some students against universities or colleges they accuse of being responsible for their failure, have led to attempts to redress the balance. Some universities have been considering formal contracts with students that require attendance at classes and satisfactory completion of course work. Other institutions have been introducing students to the idea of *responsible learning* right from the beginning of the course, with a moral imperative to put sufficient time and effort into their independent learning. Students are then regularly reminded why study organization, time management, effort and sustained concentration are their own responsibility. Of course, lecturers, too, have a moral and contractual responsibility for helping students to learn, but in the end it is the students who have to do the learning.

We shall come to the role of assessment in affecting approaches to learning and studying in Chapter 8, but it is important to note here just how strongly assessment works as a 'driver', affecting how much effort students put into their studying and what direction that effort takes – towards reproducing or understanding. Some forms of assessment are likely to increase a deep approach in most students, while others are more likely to evoke a surface approach, in ways we shall explore later.

▶ Cultural differences in learning and studying

The differences described so far come from research into the relatively homogeneous student intakes found in British higher education until comparatively recently. Now, not only are there many more mature students entering higher education, but also increasing numbers of students from other countries. Such students bring with them not only experiences of a different educational system and ways of teaching, but may also have quite different cultural expectations about the nature of academic learning. It is, of course, impossible to generalize about overseas students, but it is clear that there are marked variations in previous educational experience, even within Europe. For example, students coming from the southern countries are likely to have experienced more didactic approaches to teaching than those from Northern Europe. Students from the Middle East and Far East may rely more on rote learning than in Western countries, and may also be used to an authoritarian climate in educational institutions. As a result such students are more likely to see what university teachers and academic textbooks present to them as 'the truth', which has to be learned uncritically, but they also will show more respect for their teachers and see learning as depending mainly on their own efforts.

There are cultural differences in the way that memorizing is used, with it being an integral part of the process of developing understanding within many Eastern cultures. An example comes from the extensive research on student learning carried out in Hong Kong.

Although Hong Kong is a modern society substantially affected by Western views, it is still influenced by traditional Chinese values. There is no formal Confucian teaching in schools, and yet traditional beliefs still prevail in child-rearing practices. The Confucian heritage emphasises the virtue of effort and 'filial piety', which includes respect for teachers as purveyors of authoritative knowledge. The belief that academic success comes from effort, and that knowledge is presented for students to learn, puts a premium on memorization in learning, even when personal understanding is sought. From a very young age, students in Hong Kong are expected to adopt rote memorization as a routine way of learning. ... By the end of secondary school, memorization and understanding seem to have become part of a single process of learning; ... students tend to see memorization and understanding as often taking place at the same time; they believe that if they really understand the material, ... [that] will help them to memorize without much effort. ... This form of combined understanding and remembering has been labelled *deep memorising*.

(Adapted from Au & Entwistle, 1999)

This description should not be taken to suggest that Chinese students do not develop critical thinking, but rather that their respect for teachers and academic authority means that they are more cautious in challenging interpretations until they have sufficient well-established knowledge.

▶ Students with disabilities

Whereas, in the past, students with disabilities were effectively excluded from entering higher education, government legislation in Britain has meant that universities and colleges have had to adjust their facilities and teaching approaches to cater for at least some forms of disability. And these policies mean that university teachers have to be equally inclusive in their attitudes and methods of teaching.

In a recent study of the experiences of disabled students within the ESRC Teaching and Learning Research Programme (TLRP), staff were found to differ markedly in their readiness to make special arrangements to allow these students to learn effectively. Usually, the university has to put in place procedures to allow, for example, Braille translations of lecture notes, provision of special laptops, and allowing extra time for students with dyslexia. But these arrangements are not flexible enough to take into account differing degrees of disability, and so university teachers have to be willing to make additional adjustments to their teaching, and to discuss individual requirements where necessary. The researchers were, however, concerned that special provisions draw attention to disability, whereas flexible arrangements in teaching and learning introduced more generally would benefit all students, and so avoid singling out individuals. However, the level of flexibility necessary for this may be impossible to achieve, leaving a mixed approach as all that can be achieved. The types of adjustments made in the universities taking part in this study included:

> *Individual assimilations* ... – special arrangements made for [various categories of] disabled students to help them cope with existing learning, teaching and assessment practices, [such as] being given extra time or a separate room in exams, or being provided with a note-taker. ...

> *Alternative arrangements* ... are provided for particular disabled students. Examples include a virtual field course for a student with a mobility impairment, and a viva ... as an alternative [to a written] assessment.

> *Inclusive arrangements* ... are provided for all students. One example ... is to make alternative assessments designed to test the same learning outcomes available to all students, [and] the provision of handouts before lectures.

> (Healy et al., 2008)

▶ Concluding summary

This chapter drew on research carried out in universities and colleges to present a series of concepts that describe students' experiences of learning and studying in higher education. The broadest concepts are 'identity' and 'aspiration', along with conceptions of both knowledge and learning. Students entering university have to adjust to the social situation, as well as to different ways of learning, which can affect their sense of identity and self-confidence. They also have differing reasons for studying, and varied conceptions about the nature of academic knowledge and how it should be learned. These conceptions develop along recognizable paths during the degree course, beginning with the uncritical acceptance of the new ideas and gradually coming to an appreciation that knowledge has to be judged in terms of the strength of the evidence and ultimately in relativistic terms. In the early stages of a degree course, however, students' ideas about knowledge and learning may be far removed from what university teachers would hope them to be, and limited conceptions make it difficult, if not impossible, to learn and study in effective ways.

One of the most influential concepts describing student learning distinguishes between deep and surface approaches, showing how students' intentions affect how they learn, and thus the levels of understanding they reach. Surface approaches involve an intention to reproduce the learning material, with only limited engagement, and are found in much the same form across subject areas. Deep approaches depend on the intention to understand for oneself, involving relating ideas and using evidence, but the specific learning processes needed depend on the discipline. Each of these approaches can be carried out with differing levels of self-confidence and with varying amounts of organized effort. These other aspects interact with the approach to affect what is learned.

Although some students can reasonably be called 'deep learners' or 'surface learners' because of their relatively consistent use of one approach or the other, approaches more often vary, depending on reactions to both the subject matter – whether it is perceived to be relevant and interesting – and the context – whether that is supportive or anxiety provoking. And later on we shall find that experiences of teaching and assessment have important effects on how students go about their learning.

The burgeoning numbers of overseas students in British universities has increased the importance of recognizing the effects of differing educational systems and contrasting cultural experiences on students' learning. Universities are also making it easier for disabled students to take degree courses, which depends not just on 'reasonable adjustments' to general procedures, but also on university teachers being more sensitive to any special arrangements that may be needed for individual students.

Underlying much of this chapter has been a stress on making sense for oneself of the academic content of a course, and that emphasis will continue in the next chapter. Starting with students' experiences of developing their own personal understanding, we shall go on to explore 'target understandings' – what university teachers expect students to acquire in terms of knowledge, skills and understanding.

▶ Further reading

Belenky, M. F., Clinchy, B. M., Goldberger, N. R., & Tarule, J. M. (1986). *Women's Ways of Knowing*. New York: Harper Collins.

Biggs, J. B. (2007). *Teaching for Quality Learning at University* (3rd edn). Buckingham: SRHE & Open University Press.

Bond, C. H., Bain, J. D., & Thomas, P. R. (2009). The development of university students' experiences of learning (Journal article, in preparation).

Entwistle, N. J., & Tomlinson, P. D. (eds) (2007). 'Student Learning and University Teaching', *British Journal of Educational Psychology Monograph Series* II, 4. Leicester: British Psychological Society.

Haggis, T. (2004). 'Meaning, Identity and "Motivation": Expanding what Matters in Understanding Learning in Higher Education', *Studies in Higher Education*, 29, 335–52.

Marton, F., Hounsell, D. J., & Entwistle, N. J. (eds)(1997). *The Experience of Learning: Implications for Teaching and Studying in Higher Education* (2nd edn). Edinburgh: Scottish Academic Press, now available in an electronic version at http://www.tla.ed.ac.uk/resources/EoL.html.

Ramsden, P. (2003). *Learning to Teach in Higher Education.* (2nd edn). London: Routledge.

TLRP (2008). *Disabled Students in Higher Education: Experiences and Outcomes.* Teaching and Learning Research Briefing, No. 46, available at http://www.tlrp.org/.

▷ **References relating to the quotations**

Au, C., & Entwistle, N. J. (1999). '"Memorisation with understanding" in Approaches to Studying: Cultural Variant or Response to Assessment Demands?', paper presented at the European Association for Research on Learning and Instruction Conference, Gothenburg, August 1999 available at http://www.leeds.ac.uk/educol/documents/156501.htm.

Beaty, L., Gibbs, G., & Morgan, A. (1997). 'Learning Orientations and Study Contracts', in F. Marton, D. J. Hounsell, & N. J. Entwistle (eds) *The Experience of Learning* (2nd edn) (pp.72–88). Edinburgh: Scottish Academic Press.

Biggs, J. B. (1996). 'Western Misperceptions of the Confucian-Heritage Learning Culture', in D. A. Watkins & J. B. Biggs (eds) *The Chinese Learner: Cultural, Psychological and Contextual Influences* (pp. 46–67). Melbourne: The Australian Council for Educational Research.

Entwistle, N. J. (1988). *Styles of Learning and Teaching: An Integrated Outline of Educational Psychology for Students, Teachers and Lecturers.* London: David Fulton.

Entwistle, N. J. (1997). 'Contrasting Perspectives on Learning', in F. Marton, D. J. Hounsell & N. J. Entwistle (eds) *The Experience of Learning* (2nd edn) (pp. 39–58). Edinburgh: Scottish Academic Press, available at http://www.tla.ed.ac.uk/resources/EoL.html.

Entwistle, N. J. (2007). 'Conceptions of Learning and the Experience of Understanding: Thresholds, Contextual Influences, and Knowledge Objects', in S. Vosniadou, A. Baltas & X. Vamvakoussi (eds) *Reframing the Conceptual Change Approach in Learning and Instruction* (pp. 123–44). Oxford: Pergamon.

Entwistle, N. J., Hounsell, D. J., Macaulay, C., Situnayake, G., and Tait, H. (1989). *The Performance of Electrical Engineering Students in Scottish Higher Education.* Edinburgh: Scottish Education Department.

Entwistle. N. J., & Ramsden, P. (1983). *Understanding Student Learning.* London: Croom Helm.

Healy, M., Roberts, H., Fuller, M., Georgeson, J., Hurst, A., Kelly, K., Riddell, S., & Weedon, E. (2008). 'Reasonable Adjustments and Disabled Students' Experiences of Learning, Teaching and Assessment', *Interchange*, Spring 2008, available at http://www.tla.ed.ac.uk/interchange.

Marton, F., & Säljö, R. (1997). 'Approaches to Learning', in F. Marton, D. J. Hounsell & N. J. Entwistle (eds) *The Experience of Learning* (2nd edn) (pp. 39–58). Edinburgh: Scottish Academic Press, available at http://www.tla.ed.ac.uk/resources/EoL.html.

Perry, W. G. (1988). 'Different Worlds in the Same Classroom', in P. Ramsden (ed.) *Improving Learning: New Perspectives* (pp. 145–61). London: Kogan Page.

Part 2

What is Learned

Understanding Understanding – or Do We?

The work on approaches to learning had made it clear how important the deep approach was, with its intention actively to understand the meaning of whatever was being learned. When I was explaining this, a student once asked, 'But what do you mean by under-standing'? That stopped me in my tracks, and I stumbled towards an answer that convinced nobody. So I trawled through books on cognitive psychology to find a better answer, and yet all I found was a conclusion that it was 'too broad a concept to be investigated'. The nearest I could come was an article by Raymond Nickerson on 'Understanding under-standing' using research into problem solving, but that led only to an admission that it was not understood at all clearly.

> Understanding is an active process. It requires the connecting of facts, the relating of newly acquired information to what is already known, the weaving of bits of knowledge into an integral and cohesive whole. In short, it requires not only having knowledge but also doing something with it. ... [Nevertheless], all understanding is tenuous and, in a sense, transitory. We are obliged to understand the world in terms of the concepts and theories of our time. ... At root, understanding is a true paradox: the more one learns ... the more one ... [becomes] aware of the depth of one's ignorance. [And yet] if understanding is a primary goal of education, an effort to understand understanding would seem to be an obligation, even if ... [it is] only a partially successful effort.
>
> (Nickerson, 1985: 217, 234,236)

I felt that obligation too, and started by organizing two symposia in Edinburgh that brought together several members of the Gothenburg group, John Nisbet from Aberdeen, Hazel Francis from the London Institute of Education and several colleagues at Edinburgh. I also invited David Perkins who, with his colleagues in the Harvard Graduate School of Education, was conducting a large-scale project into 'Teaching for Understanding' at school level that will be described in Chapter 6.

From these discussions, we were able to see several lines of development for the work at Edinburgh. Colin Smith carried out a major cross-disciplinary review of the meaning of 'understanding', focusing on the school level, which led him to distinguish between the *target understanding* set by the examiners and the teachers and the *personal under-standing* reached by the students.

> 'Target understanding' derives in part from the formal requirements of the syllabus but is interpreted from the teacher's own perspective. 'Personal understanding' reflects how the student comes to see the topic presented by the teacher, influenced by the teacher's view, but also by the student's prior educational and personal history.
>
> (Entwistle & Smith, 2002: 332)

At the top end of the Scottish secondary school system, a published syllabus outlines what students are expected to know and understand, supplemented by 'syllabus notes' for the teachers, which help them, and the students, to interpret the targets being set.

> Teachers adjust their teaching to the syllabus notes, the type of questions set, and the pattern of marks their students are obtaining. In this way, the syllabus becomes interpreted and the *target understanding* more precisely fixed. However, the target experienced by the students is filtered still further through the individual teacher's understanding of the subject and expectations about attainable levels of understanding. This perceived target is an 'object of study', built up from teachers' comments and explanations over many occasions. This process of transmission inevitably leaves the target somewhat hazy in the students' minds, affecting their ability to achieve the understandings expected by the teacher or examiner. ...
>
> Young people's behaviour and thinking in school is, as we know, substantially influenced by their experiences at home, by 'significant others', and by their peer group. Students bring to any situation in the classroom, not just varying levels and mixes of abilities, prior knowledge and understanding, and approaches to studying, but also differing sets of motives, expectations and beliefs about educational learning and its relevance. All of these affect their intentions and their readiness to engage with the tasks set by the teachers, and also their understanding of what is required in the classroom. ... *Personal understanding* thus becomes the product of all these experiences and may involve overlapping, even potentially contradictory and fuzzy conceptions. Even when the feeling of understanding is strong, it may remain idiosyncratic or incorrect in comparison to target understanding.
>
> (Entwistle & Smith, 2002: 333–4)

This distinction between target and personal understanding proved valuable in later work, in which we investigated understanding separately, from the students' point of view and that of the teachers. Having asked students in the earlier research to describe how they went about studying in general, we decided to focus on their experiences of developing and achieving their own understanding in advance of final examinations, which were intended to test their conceptual understanding. Our first analyses identified very different *forms of understanding*, while later collaborative work with Ference Marton suggested the existence of *knowledge objects* – closely integrated forms of understanding that students reported experiencing as they revised for their final examinations. These ideas were taken further after discussions with David Perkins, and became linked with new ideas about concept maps being developed by David Hay at King's College, London.

In other recent research, it was possible to explore target understanding by analysing what university teachers across several different subject areas expected their students to learn. The ETL project, directed with Dai Hounsell and involving researchers in Edinburgh, Durham and Coventry Universities, has had an important influence on this book. This project looked at ways of 'Enhancing Teaching-Learning Environments in Undergraduate Courses', as part of the UK-wide ESRC Teaching and Learning Research Programme. Several new concepts were developed in this research that added to the network of ideas describing how teaching influences learning. Two of these concepts will help us to understand target understanding, drawing on the comments of university teachers in contrasting subject areas, while other ideas from the ETL project will be introduced later, when describing the research on teaching in Chapter 6 and Part 4.

▶ References

Entwistle, N. J. & Marton, F. (1994). 'Knowledge Objects: Understandings Constituted through Intensive Academic Study', *British Journal of Educational Psychology*, 64, 161–78.

Entwistle, N. J. & Smith, C. A. (2002). 'Personal Understanding and Target Understanding: Mapping Influences on the Outcomes of Learning', *British Journal of Educational Psychology*, 71, 321–42.

Hay, D. B. (2007). 'Using Concepts Maps to Measure Deep, Surface and Non-Learning Outcomes', *Studies in Higher Education*, 32, 39–57.

Nickerson, R. S. (1985). 'Understanding Understanding', *American Journal of Education*, 93, 201–39.

Perkins, D. N. (1998). 'What is Understanding?', in M. S. Wiske (ed.) *Teaching for Understanding: Linking Research with Practice* (pp. 39–57). San Francisco: Jossey-Bass.

Smith, C. A. (1998). 'Personal Understanding and Target Understanding: Their Relationships through Individual Variations and Curricular Influences', unpublished Ph.D. thesis, University of Edinburgh.

Teaching and Learning Research Programme (2007). 'Learning and Teaching at University: The Influence of Subjects and Settings', *Research Briefing No. 31*, available at www.tlrp.org. (Summary of the ETL project.)

4 The Nature of Academic Understanding

So far we have looked at human learning in general and student learning in particular. Now we need to consider the subject matter of learning, and we shall do this by contrasting the target understanding set by the teachers and the personal understanding reached by the students. In thinking about the subject matter, the main focus is on academic understanding, which is a commonly agreed target for teaching at university level. We shall also have to keep firmly in mind the idea that there is an *inner logic of the subject and its pedagogy*, shown through both the distinctiveness of a discipline's organizing ideas and theories and the ways of thinking and practising used to explain phenomena or to guide practice. In the next chapter, we begin to link that inner logic to its pedagogy, but here we start by focusing on students' experiences of reaching their own understanding as they prepare for their final examinations, before considering the types of learning that the staff said they were trying to encourage.

The student's individual understanding has a validity of its own for many purposes, but at university level that understanding must be explained within the agreed parameters of academic discourse and with the appropriate use and interpretation of evidence. While university teachers decide what they believe students should learn, in the end what is actually learned depends on the student's own aspirations, interests and self-confidence, as well as the amount of organized effort they are prepared to put into their studying. This personal understanding is what students take away with them when they leave university, so the different forms this can take should be considered in some detail.

▶ Personal understanding

In the previous chapter, the distinction between a deep and a surface approach was seen in terms of contrasting intentions, which led to differing ways of going about learning. There is, however, another way of looking at this distinction. Lennart Svensson, another member of the Gothenburg group, reinterpreted the deep/surface distinction using terms that echo Pask's contrast in learning styles, the serialist and holist distinction, described in Chapter 2. A surface approach involves not only a reliance on memorization but also being *atomistic*, concentrating almost exclusively on the parts, in other words the specific facts or details, which are mainly incidental features rather than important ones. A deep approach depends on looking at the evidence and also the relationships between ideas, and this can be seen as a *holistic* approach, using organizing principles of various kinds, including narrative, logic and theory, in order to explore links between the critical features of the concept or topic. Using a deep, holistic approach, the student is making sense of the topic as whole, through its linkages with the parts, that is the constituent concepts and evidence, and this way of learning is more important for effective studying than just having the technical skills of studying, such as note-taking or essay-writing techniques.

> Learning for understanding does involve learning facts. However, the learning of facts may involve only very limited understanding. This is why it is so important to consider the learning of larger wholes and the role of organisation in learning for understanding. ... The concept of holistic approach ... suggests that, in learning for understanding within a deep approach, the student forms wholes corresponding to complex phenomena of the world, including facts and their interrelations. It is the skill of forming integrated wholes that constitutes the most central aspect of the skill in learning through understanding. ... [And this] is dependent upon sensitivity to the material and the exploration both of the content ... and of the relevance of the organising principles to the content.
>
> (Svensson, 1997: 60, 68)

Experiences of developing and reaching an understanding

In Edinburgh, we decided to explore how students experienced understanding as they prepared for their final exams, which generally involved writing three one-hour answers to questions that required them to show their grasp of the subject. From analysing transcripts of the interviews, we found several common features in these experiences, but also important differences among students in the form of the understanding they had sought.

What students told us reinforced the idea that understanding depends on integrating parts into wholes in personally meaningful ways. Understanding was experienced as a *feeling of satisfaction*, although it varied in its expression from the sudden 'aha', as confusion on a particular topic was replaced by insight, to the less dramatic feeling stemming from the *meaning and significance* they were beginning to see in their notes. It also involved a perception of *coherence and connectedness*, and *provisional wholeness*. As the students explained:

> [It's] the interconnection of lots of disparate things – I think that's probably the best way to describe it – the way it all hangs together, the feeling that you understand how the whole thing is connected up – you can make sense of it internally. ... It's as though one's mind has finally 'locked in' to a pattern. ... When I understand, it is when each step is something I can intuitively think is right, and it's based on a lot of things I have already [learned,] ... building up from what you already have. ... You're making lots of connections which then make sense and it's logical ... – like natural selection; once you accept that concept, it's like a million things fit together and you can say 'I understand'. Almost everything I look at I can understand within this framework. ... I think when you can do that, you can say you understand something. ... If you really understand something, why it works, and what the idea is behind it, you can't not understand it afterwards – you cannot 'de-understand' it!

The students' personal understandings were seen as complete for the purposes of the exam, but some of the students realized that was not the end of the story; their understandings might well expand later on. Nevertheless, once firmly established, these provisional understandings were believed to be *irreversible*. Initial understanding can develop, but not disappear. The sense of coherence and connectedness also led students to feel *confidence about explaining*; they believed they could explain to others what they now understood. And that understanding allowed them to be *flexible in adapting and applying* ideas and information to new situations. It was this confidence, both in being able to provide a convincing explanation and to adapt ideas flexibly for use in varying and in novel contexts, which distinguished 'understanding' from 'knowledge'.

It was mainly students who had actively sought to understand the topics for themselves, adopting a deep, holistic approach to revision, who experienced this sense of tight interconnection. Reading through the transcripts of the interviews we saw differences in how the students were carrying out their revision and in what they were aiming to understand. Some students were so concerned about the exams that they paid little attention to understanding the topics for themselves, while others showed the opposite pattern, with a failure to prepare strategically for the exam. The differences in these *forms of understanding* could also be described in terms of their breadth, depth and structure. *Breadth* described the amount of material students were including in their revision activities, while *depth* related to the amount of effort they were putting into integrating these aspects into a meaningful whole. *Structure* referred to the extent to which the understanding was a personal construction, rather than a passive reliance on the lecturer's understanding or what had been found in a book or elsewhere. Effective academic understanding depends on the progressive incorporation of more and more of the supportive evidence and critical features of the topics and an increasing ability to explain the interrelationships existing among concepts and evidence. Relying too much on the teacher's understanding may leave the student without a fully functional personal understanding, being able to pass exams by mimicking the lecturer's understanding, but not able to use it in other situations.

The disposition to understand for oneself

Most of the students interviewed were, not surprisingly, focusing closely on the exam itself, but some of them had also enjoyed the process of developing their own understanding. Sometimes this reaction could be attributed to a strong feeling that they <u>had</u> to understand the subject for themselves and also show in the exam how much they had understood. This urge to 'tell it all' might well create problems for such students, and for the examiner, making potentially excellent essays incomplete or unbalanced, and thus be difficult to mark. A student's experience is described in the following interchange.

I: *How well did you manage to demonstrate your understanding in the exams?*

S: Well, there were cases where I knew too much ... and I would spend half the essay giving the background and showing what I understood ... I <u>had</u> to go through all the stages of working through (the topic) and showing that I had understood it. I couldn't gloss over the surface. And once I started writing, it all just 'welled up'. I felt that I couldn't interrupt the argument half-way as it was developing.

I: *Why did you feel you had to do that?*

S: Basically, the way it ties together as a whole – it's very difficult to pick something like that apart, when you understand the theory like that. ... I have to explain it in that way – you can't cut it up and avoid bits. Half an understanding doesn't make sense!

I: *Are you saying that you have to explain it in the way you understand it for yourself?*

S: Yes ... It's <u>essential</u> to demonstrate your understanding of the whole, and its implications and limitations and you also need to demonstrate a critical approach to any evidence.

I: *Might that insistence affect your exam marks?*

S: You could say I shouldn't be (doing) that in an exam, but basically I <u>have</u> to do it that way, because that's me.

I: *Is that what you want to get out of it?*

S: ... Among many of my friends it's more [fundamental] than that; it's not even the will to succeed, it's almost an <u>obsession</u>.

The underlined words accurately reflect the strength of feeling within these responses, and this intense commitment to understanding puts it at the top end of the developmental progression in conceptions of knowledge and learning summarized earlier in Chapter 3 (Figure 3.1), and so it becomes part of this student's sense of identity as a learner.

This strong sense of 'deep' can also be found in a recent study of medical students, almost all of whom were actively seeking understanding. But again the form of understanding differed, with some students feeling threatened by ideas that challenged their hard-won initial understanding. As a result, their understanding remained 'fixed', as they thought it was 'right'. These students could explain their understanding perfectly well in the exams, but were much less comfortable in adapting it to new situations. In contrast, other students who were more flexible, were ready to expand and refine their initial understanding, welcoming new insights and were also more confident about applying their understanding to their work with patients. These students also differed in the way they used evidence in building up their understanding. With the 'fixed' form of understanding, evidence was used simply to build up a fixed path of logical reasoning, whereas the 'flexible' form involved

a continuous restructuring and reframing of facts and knowledge. ... It seems that [these] students continuously shift between details and wholes, and are simultaneously aware of the overall picture and details, even though their focus is on one of the two ... [From this perspective], understanding cannot be lost as a result of challenges and alternative explanations. Rather, the student continuously moves between different perspectives and learning modalities in order to reshape and refine his or her understanding. ... Interestingly, it is not only the number of different activities that is of importance, but the way the students construct meaning out of the activities. Consequently, variation is not solely something that can be created by course planners, but has to be conceived as such by the student.

(Fyrenious, Wirell & Silén, 2007:160–1)

In earlier research, Roy Heath had found that students across disciplines varied in their willingness to adapt their ways of learning flexibly and in their ability to spot opportunities in the teaching and learning activities that would help them to develop their understanding further. He called these students, who were both flexible and alert, *reasonable adventurers*.

> The principal characteristic of Reasonable Adventurers is the ability to create their own opportunities for satisfaction. They seem to have their psychological house in sufficient order to release them to attack the problems of everyday life with zest and originality. And they seem to do so with an air of playfulness. ... In pursuit of a problem [they] appear to experience an alternation of involvement and detachment, ... the combination of two mental attitudes, the curious and the critical. These do not occur simultaneously but in alternation.
>
> (Heath, 1964: 30–3)

This notion of 'alternation' between differing mental attitudes or learning processes, along with the combination of 'zest and originality', were associated with academic success; the alternation seems to be equivalent to the versatile use of both holist and serialist thinking processes found by Gordon Pask (Chapter 2).

Recently Velda McCune and I have been thinking about deep approaches to learning in relation to David Perkins' work on 'thinking dispositions' (Chapter 2), which involved the combination of ability, willingness to engage and alertness to context. We have begun to see the intensely deep engagement with learning found in some students as more than just an approach, more like an underlying *disposition to understand for oneself*, involving a similar interplay of characteristics. 'Ability', in our own research, can be seen in the appropriate use of prior knowledge and in thinking strategies directed towards personal understanding. 'Willingness' is seen in the effort put into integrating critical features into a meaningful and coherent whole, while 'alertness' involves being ready to seek out opportunities for developing understanding and also for using that understanding tellingly in the future. This combination of ability, willingness and alertness is more than a set of empirical relationships; it acts as an organic whole, with the student engaging in the continuing process of seeking and using personal understanding.

The construction and use of knowledge objects

The original interviews on experiences of understanding also produced another way of seeing the interrelatedness of understanding. Looking at them again, Ference Marton and I found repeated indications that students often felt they could visualize their understanding as an integrated whole. This led us to call such occurrences *knowledge objects*, although this term implies a fixed structure, whereas flexibility and interrelatedness were their main features; these understandings were malleable to specific requirements. Typical comments from several different students are shown in Table 4.1.

Some students had drawn diagrams to make the structure of their understanding more visible. The main aspects were then used rather like Internet 'buttons' to pull in details that had been rote learned, but these mind maps were not just for remembering details, they also offered a logical pathway through which to develop the explanation.

Table 4.1   Students' comments about their experiences of knowledge objects

---

I can see that [part of my revision notes] virtually as a picture, and I can review it and bring in more facts about each part. Looking at a particular part of the diagram sort of triggers off other thoughts. I find schematics, in flow-diagrams and the like, very useful because a schematic acts a bit like a syllabus; it tells you what you should know, without actually telling you what it is. The basic diagram is on paper, but details about the diagram are added on later by myself in my head. The facts are stored separately, and the schematic is like an index, I suppose.

[With my mind-map] it's almost like a jigsaw puzzle of knowledge. You have all these disparate bits of information and, because you are thinking about it, the pieces start to click into place, so you begin to see the overall picture. The mind map keeps me going with the structure, in the sense that the mind map is basically visual – a pictorial representation of what I want the whole essay to have in it, and so it stops me wandering off track. It's a way of grasping on to all the details without being bogged down in them, and without losing sight of the relevance these details may have.

[As I wrote], it was almost as though I could see it all fitting into an overall picture. I think you're developing what you know, and are playing it in a slightly different way to fit the question set. Following the logic through, it pulls in pictures and facts as it needs them, but each time I describe [a particular topic], it's likely to be different. Well, you start with evolution, say, and suddenly you know where you're going next. Then, you might have a choice – to go in that direction or that direction – and follow it through various options it's offering. Hopefully, you'll make the right choice, and so this goes to this, goes to this – and you've explained it to the level you've got to. Then, it says 'Okay, you can go on to talk about further criticisms in the time you've got left'.

The more I have done exams, the more I'd liken them to a performance – like being on a stage; ... having not so much to present the fact that you know a vast amount, but having to perform well with what you do know ... – sort of, playing to the gallery. ... I was very conscious of being outside what I was writing. ... In an exam, you have to have background knowledge of the subject, and an ability to interpret the information in your own way. ... You don't sit down and think 'How much can I remember about this particular subject'; you try and explain your ideas, using examples which come to mind. ... You can't use all the information for a particular line of argument, and you don't need to; you only need to use what you think is going to convince the examiner.

Source: Entwistle, A. & Entwistle, 1992; Entwistle & Entwistle, 2003

'Following the logic through, <u>it</u> pulls in pictures and facts as <u>it</u> needs them.' This comment illustrates just how aware this student had been of her 'understanding' as an entity. Of course, different details might be pulled in on another occasion to make the same point, and so take the explanation in a rather different direction, although along similar lines. Students also mentioned the audience of examiners they had in mind as they shaped their answer to fit whatever they believed to be required. In writing essays, then, students need to be alert to several aspects: the form of the question, the logical structure of their under-standing, the expectations of their audience and also how their emerging answer matches the perceived requirements of the question. This is indeed a daunting task.

The knowledge objects described so far were, of course, produced for a particular purpose – preparing for an exam – and they might be expected to survive only for a short time afterwards. There is anecdotal evidence, however, that strong visual imagery associated with a knowledge object can reactivate the structure of a knowledge object even five years later. And it is not just students who report an awareness of a knowledge object. David Perkins described preparing a talk on facilitating group discussions. In spite of his wide experience of this activity, he had never given a presentation on this topic where it was treated as a whole. His starting point was making a 'dump' of potentially relevant ideas and experiences, which gradually came together in a loose assembly, seen as a *knowledge ensemble*. This material was then organized into a more tightly integrated and coherent structure, which became recognizably a knowledge object that then guided the presentation (described more fully in my 1998 article). This experience is by no means an isolated instance; lecturers, and authors for that matter, commonly use knowledge objects to structure their presentations or their writing.

Making understanding visible through concept maps

Mind maps are generally just rough and ready diagrams, but *concept maps* have some basic rules, including explicit labelling of the links drawn between concepts. David Hay and his colleagues at King's College London have shown how, by using concept maps repeatedly, students develop their maps from simple 'chains', with single links between concepts or 'spokes' from a superordinate concept, into integrated webs, signalling more structured understandings, rather like knowledge objects (see Figure 6.1). Within these webs, the level of understanding can be seen, to some extent, in terms of the number of concepts and the complexity of their interconnections. In traditional concept mapping, the links between concepts are described in just a few words (see Figure 4.1), but these, on their own, cannot do justice to complex understandings. For this reason, a new approach is being developed, called *dialogic concept mapping*, in which students are encouraged to explain the connections not only within the maps they draw, but in relation to the various activities that have been influencing their understanding.

To develop his emerging idea of dialogic concept maps, David Hay recently asked me to explore my own understanding of 'learning' in this way. He suggested that we produce a series of maps and consider what lay behind their development. The interactions between us as I was deciding on the concepts and arranging them were recorded and transcribed. A series of different 'takes' on my understanding resulted as maps and explanations. The starting point was a rather formal and limited description of 'learning', as I tried to answer the question set. My focus gradually shifted into 'understanding', and then explained it as 'ideas made personal', before exploring it from different perspectives. At that time, the shift from 'learning' to 'understanding' appeared incidental, but it took on much more significance on further reflection. The word 'understanding' seemed to have attracted sets of related ideas, which could then be organized into a series of further concept maps, each with a different focal concept. Changing the target thus can bring in importantly different sets of ideas, each of which then attracted other concepts. Such a target may then emerge as a *leitmotif* running through subsequent concept maps.

The process of producing a sequence of maps and explaining them shows understanding in a rather different light, again challenging the apparent fixity of a 'knowledge object'. Understanding represents a feeling of confidence about creating a coherent explanation relating to a topic, but not just a single explanation, rather the potential for a series of explanations that move towards a more satisfying representation. What then guides the introduction of concepts and related information seems to be the logic through which they had been organized into memory at some time, or several times, in the past, driven by the attempt to communicate an understanding to a particular audience. And that is what the students were describing about their ways of revising for finals.

Looking over the whole set of different 'takes' on my understanding, and realizing there were still aspects missing, led me to produce a more complete concept map, but still keeping it within bounds. Any explanation has to balance competing emphases on structure and detail; increasing the amount of information within a map can interfere with its main purpose, which is to make sense of a landscape. Figure 4.1 is used here to illustrate the form of a concept map, and also to summarize links between some of the main ideas introduced in this chapter and in the previous one. Its dialogic element came initially from the discussion of the emerging concept maps, and reflection on what they implied, which was later reflected in the commentary used to explain the final one, shown below the diagram.

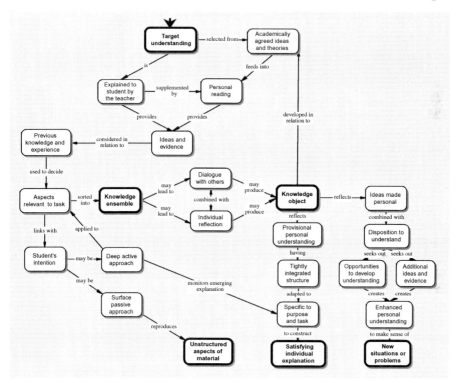

Figure 4.1   Dialogic concept map leading from target understanding to learning outcomes

EXPLANATION OF THE CONCEPT MAP

This particular concept map takes the form of a flow diagram to demonstrate a series of logical pathways. It starts at the top from the target understanding, which is selected by the teacher from academically agreed ideas and theories. The target is then explained to the student, who draws on personal reading to make the understanding more secure. This provides the ideas and evidence necessary for subsequent learning which, considered in relation to previous knowledge and experience, will be used to decide what aspects are relevant to the task.

How the task is carried out depends on the student's intention. A passive surface approach leads only to the reproduction of unstructured aspects of what is being learned, but a deep active approach enables the selected aspects to be sorted, at first, into a loose 'knowledge ensemble'. After subsequent reflection and dialogue, this may result in a tightly organized 'knowledge object' that constitutes a satisfying, if still provisional, understanding constructed with the specific purpose of preparing for an assignment or an exam. The content of that knowledge object can then be adapted to the target understanding set by a teacher so as to construct a satisfying, well-targeted explanation.

The knowledge object can also be expanded and be altered from its original form. 'Ideas made personal', linked with a disposition to understand, may lead to an active search for opportunities to develop the provisional knowledge object, created for a specific purpose, by seeking out new ideas and evidence. The resulting enhanced understanding can then be used to interpret, and make sense of, new situations or problems.

Since this exploratory work was carried out, David Hay has been extending the horizon conveyed by the term 'dialogic concept mapping' to reflect what lies behind the explanations students are giving. This brings into play the many dialogic interactions that take place in higher education, as students read, write, listen and think, and maps the complex juxtaposition of arguments held in tension, rather than being wholly resolved.

Integrative personal understandings

At university level, the importance of students understanding the main ideas they meet can hardly be overemphasized, and we have argued that it needs to take a particular form. When students reach a deep personal understanding, it has a holistic quality for them, and brings together related ideas along with the supportive detail that also makes it academically acceptable. This type of understanding is not just integrated, it becomes actively integrative, as it pulls in additional related ideas to create an enlarged understanding. The disposition to understand for oneself engenders an attitude towards knowledge and evidence that can become habitual when encountering problems and issues later on. And this disposition has a lasting quality that will serve students well in later life. But at university the understanding cannot just be 'personal' in the sense of idiosyncratic. As we have already stressed, it has to be constructed within the conventions and conceptual frameworks agreed within a discipline or group of disciplines. These conventions bring together concepts that have proved to have powerful explanatory value and the ways of thinking with them that control the use of evidence in reaching conclusions. As a result an acceptable integrative academic understanding is only personal in the sense that the student has recognized the critical features within the concept or topic and has actively worked out, independently, a set of interconnections between them that is personally satisfying, but also in accord with the specific academic conventions of the discipline or professional area.

The research we have seen so far in this chapter, although from relatively small-scale studies, builds up into a strong argument for the importance of helping students to reach an integrative understanding for themselves, a process that can then be generalized more widely to other subject areas and different academic tasks. Sometimes, such an understanding will be limited to making sense of the ideas and information presented by the teacher but, given the opportunity for dialogic reflection on a wider set of ideas through written work, discussion or concept maps, a more powerful individualistic understanding may well emerge. The level reached will obviously vary between students and across year groups, but its value comes from the attempt to bring ideas together and to think about the interplay between them.

As we shall see in the next section, university teachers are also looking for this form of understanding. And this idea of a holistic view of subject matter will be taken up again in the next chapter, where we find that teachers, who themselves see their subject in broad integrative ways, are likely to reflect that perspective in their teaching. And in Chapter 6, we shall be looking at a series of examples of teaching designed to encourage such understanding.

▶ Target understanding across the disciplines

The novelist C. P. Snow drew attention to the implications of major differences in not just the content of university disciplines but also in the ways of thinking and in the underlying values of the teachers of those disciplines. He suggested that there was 'a gulf of mutual incomprehension' between physicists and literary intellectuals (at extreme poles) to the extent that they represented two separate cultures.

> Constantly I felt that I was moving among two groups – comparable in intelligence, … not grossly different in social origins, earning about the same incomes, who had almost ceased to communicate at all, who in intellectual, moral and psychological climate had … little in common. … Literary intellectuals at one pole, at the other scientists, and the most representative, physical scientists. Between the two, [there was] a gulf of mutual incomprehension – sometimes … hostility and dislike, but most of all lack of understanding. They have a curiously distorted view of each other. Their attitudes are so different that, even on the level of emotion, they can't find much common ground.
> (Snow, 1964: 2–4)

Recently, Becher and Trowler in their book *Academic Tribes and Territories* described similar differences between academic staff, although they found the 'gulf' no longer as clear as Snow had suggested. Disciplinary specialists from differing fields have been collaborating more, particularly in applied research areas, so that the boundaries between disciplines are increasingly being broken down. Nevertheless interdisciplinary contrasts still remain, both in the ways of thinking exhibited by teaching staff and in the academic communities. These differences, indeed, define the very nature of the disciplines, as Bruner has argued:

> The great disciplines like physics or mathematics, or history, or dramatic forms in literature, were … less repositories of knowledge than of methods for the use of mind.

They provided the structure that gave meaning to the particulars. ... The object of education was to get as swiftly as possible to that structure – to penetrate the subject, not to cover it. ... [And] mastery of the fundamental ideas of a field involves not only the grasping of general principles, but also the development of an attitude toward learning and inquiry, toward guessing and hunches, toward the possibility of solving problems on one's own. ... To instil such attitudes by teaching requires ... a sense of excitement about discovery – discovery of regularities of previously unrecognised relations and similarities between ideas, with a resulting sense of self-confidence in one's abilities. ... For if we do nothing else we should somehow give [students] a respect for their own powers of thinking, for their ability to generate good questions, to come up with interesting informed guesses ... to make ... study more rational, more amenable to the use of mind in the large rather than mere memorizing.

(Bruner, 1960: 20; 1966: 96)

Currently, staff are required to produce detailed lists of 'intended learning outcomes', which specify what students are expected to learn. In the interviews with academics in our ETL project, however, these lists were hardly ever mentioned, except to criticize their effects. Staff complained that students often used these lists as 'tick boxes' to show what they had covered, and so could subsequently forget. The academics were looking beyond the specifics of knowledge and skills towards an understanding of the discipline itself and of the values of the profession. The interviews in our project suggested that this broad aim could best be described as *ways of thinking and practising in the subject*, abbreviated for convenience to 'WTPs', a term which was used

to describe the richness, depth and breadth of what students might learn through engagement with a given subject area in a specific context. This might include, for example, coming to terms with particular understandings, forms of discourse, values or ways of acting, which are regarded as central to graduate-level mastery of a discipline or subject area.

(McCune & Hounsell, 2005: 257)

And seeing university aims in this broader way

brings into central focus the ways in which individual disciplines represent (or at least debate) the *nature* of knowledge in their domains, what counts as 'evidence' and the processes of creating, judging and validating knowledge. It also brings into view expectations concerning how a discipline's practitioners should orient themselves towards, and interact with, its theories, accounts of subject matter and evidence. ... A common concern among [staff] was to wean first-year students away from a relatively unproblematized view of [academic] knowledge. They sought to move students towards a more complex, differentiated understanding of knowledge and its relationship to evidence, ... associated with the encouragement of a questioning approach and flexibility of mind.

(Anderson & Hounsell, 2007: 469)

Although WTPs were described in relation to graduate level mastery, the term was also used to reflect the distinctive aims that apply within an area of a discipline, or even in a specific course unit. And, in most areas of study, a range of rather different WTPs will be found, with their own 'inner logic' and distinctive pedagogy. The link between aims and teaching will be discussed more fully in Chapter 6, but here the nature of the differing WTPs will be illustrated within the five subject areas covered in the ETL project, electronic engineering, biological sciences, economics, history and media studies. The next sections describe briefly some of the main ways of thinking staff expect students to acquire in their subject area. More details can be found in the Subject Area Reports to be found on the project website (see Chapter References).

Electronic engineering

In electronic engineering generally one of the main problems facing students is that they have to move back and forth between contrasting representations of electrical devices. Taking circuits as an example, there are several rather different ways of thinking that students have to come to terms with. First, there is the actual circuit, but that has to be reduced to a circuit diagram to show the electrical components and how they are connected. To decide how the circuit alters the characteristics of the input into that circuit, simplifying assumptions have to be made involving transformations using abstract concepts from which the necessary calculations can be carried out by solving algebraic equations. Computer simulations of circuits are now widely used, which adds yet another form of representation.

In solving problems or designing circuits, students also need to understand the function of a circuit in both practical and theoretical ways, including the engineering applications and the physics that explains how the components within a circuit interact. The link between the real world and theory can be difficult to make, as one student explained:

> The amount of maths we're all able to do is quite high level. So, we can do the maths, and we can do the general circuit design that everybody's proved in the labs, but it's somehow relating the two. It's finding a middle ground where you've got enough of a practical real world application being proved using, say, feedback. ... I mean, you can prove pretty simply a feedback system, which maybe would then have clicked through people's brains a bit more, connected things. Because I think for me [a main difficulty] early on was probably trying to make a connection between what was up on the board or in the notes, and something that I actually experienced in real life.

In analogue electronics, an additional difficulty seems to be that understanding involves both analytic skills and the 'intuitive' grasp of circuit characteristics – intuitive in the sense that the characteristics of analogue circuits are less transparent and predictable than digital ones. Students thus have to build up substantial experience of the properties of many different kinds of circuit before they can 'see' what lies behind any new circuit diagram they meet, or can decide what type of circuit will be required in a design problem.

As in other disciplines, the ways of thinking differ to some extent across branches of the subject, as one of the lecturers explained about the difficulties posed by analogue electronics.

> Digital gives you exact answers [and] there are certain fixed ways of doing things, [whereas] analogue decisions are often very hard to make [and] to justify. ... It's intuitive and frequently

two or three solutions that are radically different will actually be just as good as each other. ... In analogue, there's more imagination involved and then, when you've set up the models, you've got to analyze them. In comes the heavy maths ... [and you] end up with an expression. It might be relatively accurate, but you have lost all intuitive feeling for what's going on. ... Analogue just doesn't come naturally to most people. ... Many of the concepts are ... quite abstract ... [and involve] a lot of lateral thought. ... You've got to understand how [a] circuit works and you've got to understand the model that is behind that transistor and small signal model, and how that behaves. ... That doesn't stick out in a circuit diagram and hit you in the face. You've got to know what's beyond that. And that's tricky. You've got to understand things like how a transistor is biased, what points they operate at, how you can use the characteristics of the transistor path and the linear region that you get. ... There are all sorts of issues. It's just a lot more airy than digital.

Here we see a good example of the differences that exist in ways of thinking between areas within the same discipline – digital and analogue – and yet the lecturers in each of these areas were seeking to present a broad integrative overview of their subject, which went beyond specific knowledge and individual skills. Knowledge and skills had to become part of the broader context within which a professional engineer would think and act.

Biological sciences

In biology, the central WTPs involve being able to appreciate how evidence is collected and interpreted. Students are required to develop a critical understanding of the collection and use of information and data, and the relationship between findings and theoretical frameworks, while recognizing that much of what they are taught is provisional, due to continuing scientific advances. This process involves recognizing patterns of relationships and taking a broad holistic view of the subject, as well as coming to understand the nature and origins of knowledge in the biosciences. Above all, the staff wanted students to become cautious and critical about evidence and interpretations of it.

I think the concept that nobody knows what's right in everything is definitely what we're trying to put across. ... The idea that we don't have all the solutions yet; to challenge things, to question things, [to ask], 'Can both these people be right?' I think that's very important at an early stage. A good healthy dose of cynicism, I think, will make you a better scientist. ... In then end of the day, it's you and your data, and you make up your mind what you think, keep your mind very open in case new data comes in. [It's] not that we're training them all to be research scientists, but I think that it's good training for being a human being.

By their final year, the students had recognized the importance of scientific method and the types of reasoning used to interpret evidence and develop a synoptic view, although they still found the primary literature difficult to follow.

[To do well, you have to] give your own opinion and find evidence, and base your opinions on evidence – give reasons for your opinion. That seems to be the main thing this year, giving your own opinions, correctly evaluating the stuff you're getting as opposed to just 'This is good because it says so'. ... We read the original papers, and you have to understand exactly what they did, what experiments did they do and exactly what they get. ... It's so difficult, ... scientific reading from such a level, way above our heads. It's people who've been doing this for years and years and they forget that students read these as well! So, when we are reading them we don't have to say, 'Oh yeah, OK, these are the conclusions, yeah, cool'. But we have to say, 'Why did they do these experiments, why not others? OK, why is this working this way, why these conclusions?' So we always have to ask why things are happening and I think that if we are able then to answer, [then] this is our understanding. ...

I think probably the most important thing that I've learned over the past years is the ability not just to remember stuff, but to actually think about it. It's not enough to memorize a big bunch of lecture notes, you've actually got to think about what the point of learning this is. ... I always find it easier to think of biology in a context. I always find it so difficult to think of it in a molecular context, but when I think about it in context related to, like, people or animals, then I find it so much easier and more interesting.

In this final paragraph we have again seen evidence of a shift from surface to deep approaches to learning, and also of students developing understanding by linking the unfamiliar and abstract to the familiar and concrete. And once more, staff were emphasizing broad aims for their students, rather than narrow ones.

Economics

In Economics, lecturers recognized, quite explicitly, that they were instilling a way of thinking.

More recently I've come round to the view that economists have acquired a way of looking at the world which is indelible, and even though [students] may not find themselves in a position where they can use their analytical techniques very consciously, in fact their whole way of treating questions is affected by this kind of training.

Looking at more specific ways of thinking in economics, students were expected to understand how abstract concepts were being used to model real-world economic systems, and yet also to realize the ultimate inadequacy of the match between theory and actuality.

We have to instill in students a kind of acceptance of modelling which is quite fundamental to the way in which we approach most of our analysis. ... We want our students to start to think about problems, issues. You get them to formulate, if not explicitly at least implicitly, some kind of formal analytical structure or model that simplifies things, but then allows someone to think through a problem in a very structured way. That's something fundamental I think. ... I sense that, sometimes, students see abstract models as [just] abstract models, and don't see the link between them and the real world. ... The idea that models which look abstract ... actually talk about the real world, perhaps that is a crucial factor, ... [students] tend to put models into one box and then the discussion about the policy issues in another box. They don't necessarily see that the two must be linked.

What happens when you're confronted with the data, theory is never tight. Theory is never sufficient to specify an actual model for estimation. The data will never conform fully to it, there's absolutely no question about that. And so ... as you're actually doing the work ...

[you're] having to account for things that the theory hasn't accounted for. But that's in the nature of economics.

There were other important aspects of economics that students often found difficult, some at a general level and others relating to the threshold concepts that opened up a future understanding of the subject, as was mentioned in Chapter 2 and will be discussed again later.

> I think that the hardest thing for the students is the relationship between all the different variables like unemployment, inflation, economic growth, balance payments and the instruments that we have available to deal with problems and I think they find that extremely difficult.
>
> Yes, there are a couple [of threshold concepts] ... I think one of them is 'opportunity cost' and the other 'scarcity' – that time and resources have alternative uses, and that they are limited. But I think the key concept, that I always look towards to check to see if students are understanding, is this notion of 'elasticity'. Price elasticity of demand is a notion, which we borrowed from physics. ... That how responsive demand is to price changes, and how responsive to price changes is supply. ... They can come to grips with 'scarcity' and 'opportunity cost' and others in a fairly abstract way, but I think if they fundamentally understand elasticity, ... they have passed the threshold in that sense.

Students saw their courses as requiring them to learn how to think for themselves about economic issues and to handle uncertainty, in predictions from theory to practice and in the contested nature of theories.

> I think the module's quite logical. It teaches you how to think. ... There's an awful lot of diagrams involved, so it is all quite ... conceptual. You have to be able to understand and interpret diagrams, so I think that's an important skill.
>
> I think it's a module that's full of debate. For example, for every topic we have, one part ... says this and we have another part that says a different thing, ... and you have got to sort of weigh them up against each other. It's basically you come to a conclusion about what you think of it at the end of the day, which is nice because it is your opinion. ... We weigh different situations and find a middle road. ... You must be very critical in that particular course because there are so many different points of view that you must choose your own, that one that you think is the right, but that makes 'macro' so interesting because you can never know what is wrong, what is right, you must really study about it and you must make your own decision.

History

In this discipline, the staff explained the importance of helping students to appreciate that historical descriptions have been socially constructed, often within a different period from the one when the original events took place. Students had to be helped to avoid 'presentism', the cardinal error of trying to interpret historical events within the perspective of the current era, with its contemporary assumptions and values, and to become comfortable with the 'strangeness of the past'. Students also have to develop the skills involved in obtaining, handling and interpreting historical evidence, as well as being able to set their interpretations within broader contexts and see important links among the data collected. In the ETL project, the researchers looking at this subject area concluded that

> [o]ver the course of their undergraduate studies it was expected that students would acquire sensitivity to the 'strangeness of the past' and develop what can be described as their perspective-taking skill, ... [which] entails a readiness to separate out one's own preconceptions ... [and] to view matters from the perspective of the original actors whom they are studying, ... [being] vigilant about how accounts of an episode may be recast as events unfold. Students at the same time [have] to gain expertise in communicating their increasingly differentiated representations of particular subject matter in a coherent manner and in disciplinarily appropriate forms of expression and argument.
>
> (Anderson & Day, 2005: 14)

Final-year students were well aware of the importance of using evidence in convincing ways to build up their own interpretations of historical events, and of the need to be cautious in reading others' interpretations.

> People, other people, can make mistakes when they look at evidence. ... It's not just, you know, what have they looked at; it's what questions have they asked of that source, and whether that source is appropriate to back up what questions there are, or if they've got ... the wrong source – asked the right questions, looked at the wrong sources: and therefore brought up the wrong answers. ... You do find everyone's got an agenda for what they're writing ... [so] you don't take things at face value. You look behind and see the motivation of the person writing [and ask], 'Can I rely on this person?'
>
> You've got to be prepared yourself to change your own views, considerably. Because you read one thing and you were going along with them, and they'll say. 'Have you totally agreed with this thing, you totally oppose them?'. You've got to assess it yourself. ... As soon as you get to third year, you realize there's all these different schools of historians, ... with all these different ideas behind them too, and it's actually really interesting because it's controversial. In first year you just can't hear the whole story.

Media and communication studies

Many of the ways of thinking ascribed to historians are also found in the cultural studies component of this subject area, but there is an additional dimension. Students are expected to acquire a set of values that media studies endorses, to become more aware, for example, of ethnic and social differences, and of the part these play in portraying attitudes and behaviour. Staff explained how they tried to challenge prior assumptions about, for example, media images.

> [This] training video from broadcasting organizations ... deals with how TV editors deal with images of violence. ... It shows what the editors leave out, on grounds of taste and decency. This is an intellectual shock to students ... because they think 'seeing is believing'. Seeing that news 'protects' them – half of them become angry and half of them are grateful to the broadcasters. This is the first time they question the role of the media. ... The first fundamental understanding is to grasp that all is not what it seems to be.

Tutors stressed that the content of the subject made students very aware of issues such as 'power' and 'racial stereotyping', and yet that awareness could also create difficulties in tutorials where such issues became real, through the social relationships between staff and students, and among the students themselves. This feeling affected both staff and students.

> The tutor has the power because you have the knowledge. But when the personal [aspect] is brought in … [then if] they know you respect [them], then the power thing doesn't have to be so off-putting. … Its usually about pointing out that no matter how democratic the classroom is, and the sharing of points of view, at the end of the day, this is a class, I am the teacher and I will be assessing their work. … We try and think about what that means with our relationships. *(Tutor)*

> Some of the time obviously it's quite difficult. … It must be difficult for [the tutor] because we've got a lot of people from, like, different religions and different races, and you have to make sure that, … especially when you're talking about race and stuff, you're not obviously upsetting people. … And so I think, … you've got to try and make sure that what you say is being fair to everyone who is in the room. *(Student)*

****

This section has illustrated some of the major differences that exist among the disciplines in the 'ways of thinking and practising' students are expected to acquire. This included making sense of analogue circuits, interpreting biological data, modelling economic systems, appreciating the strangeness of the past and handling human relationships sensitively. And yet common features remain, such as adopting a critical stance to evidence and argument and the use of an appropriate academic perspective and discourse in discussing conclusions. We have also seen that staff want students to develop a broad understanding of the nature and purpose of the discipline or professional area being studied, one which goes well beyond a grasp of the technical details. Perry's work on conceptions of knowledge, discussed in Chapter 3, showed that such ways of thinking develop only slowly during a degree course, more slowly, and often more painfully, than staff appear to realize. The difficulty students have is that these broad target understandings are not communicated sufficiently clearly by staff, often being taken for granted and therefore not made explicit in the teaching. Even within specific topic areas, it will still be possible to draw attention, in an integrative way, both to the overall theme being presented, and also to how that relates to the wider WTPs of the discipline or professional area.

We shall look at general ideas about teaching in the next chapter, before returning to teaching within specific subject areas, but first we look again at one of the other ideas that emerged within our ETL project.

▷ Threshold concepts

Besides the difficulties created through students not being able to grasp the necessary ways of thinking, most subjects involve concepts or topics which are intrinsically difficult. David Perkins has developed a theory of difficulty that can be used to guide thinking about 'trouble spots' in devising a syllabus, and argues that it is not sufficient just to recognize these areas of difficulty, we have to find good ways of helping students through them. He points out a range of potential causes of trouble for students, such as the conflation of similar concepts (mass and weight), the strangeness of technical language, mathematical expressions (for the non-mathematician) or foreign cultures, the dangers of persisting with knowledge frameworks that no longer work (such as 'presentism' in history) and inert knowledge that is easy to reproduce without coming to terms with the ideas, and so on.

As mentioned earlier, Erik Meyer and Ray Land, working with economics teachers within the ETL project, came to the conclusion that there were certain concepts that were crucial for students' future understanding of the subject, and yet had often proved extremely difficult for students to understand – *threshold concepts* that open up the subject for students in important ways.

> In certain disciplines there are 'conceptual gateways' or 'portals' that lead to a previously inaccessible, and initially perhaps 'troublesome', way of thinking about something. A new way of understanding, interpreting, or viewing something may thus emerge – a transformed internal view of subject matter, subject landscape, or even world view. ... [These 'threshold concepts'] may be *transformative* (occasioning significant shift in the perception of a subject), *irreversible* (unlikely to be forgotten, or unlearned only through considerable effort), and *integrative* (exposing the previously hidden interrelatedness of something). ... In conversation with professional colleagues 'threshold concepts' have found an immediate appeal as being a 'pedagogically fertile' and energising topic to consider.
>
> (Meyer and Land, 2005: 374–5)

Examples of such concepts come from various subject areas. In the humanities and social sciences, typical threshold concepts are 'signification', 'deconstruction', 'modularity, 'otherness', 'precedent' and 'parliamentary sovereignty', while in mathematics and the sciences, we find 'limits', 'particle-wave duality', 'spin', 'reactive power' and, more generally, 'proof'. In a recent paper, Meyer suggests that the identification of threshold concepts provides us with a lens through which to identify and examine the acquisition of *discipline-specific* ways of transformative thinking and shifts in ontological position.

In other work, Peter Davies and Jean Mangan have suggested that there are different kinds of thresholds. In the early stages of a degree course, some of the basic concepts within a discipline may open up the subject for students, by enabling them to make better sense of aspects they had previously thought about only in everyday terms. Later on, threshold concepts may open up the subject by connecting groups of related concepts into an integrated whole, either as a higher-level concept or a theory. This notion has been found valuable in a wide range of subject areas, although sometimes in the form of broader thresholds that are more like ways of thinking. History is a good example, where, as we have seen, 'thinking like a historian' involves an essential change in perspective to interpret events within the values and social setting of the time, rather than in current terms. Threshold concepts act as organizing ideas that enable researchers and students alike to make sense of the broad aspects of the subject they are studying.

As we shall argue in Chapter 9, inviting staff to identify threshold concepts in their own specialism, and to consider why students seem to find them difficult, raises important issues that can lead to a reconceptualisation of their teaching. And it is the contrasting ways in which academic staff currently think about their teaching that we shall explore in the next chapter.

▷ Concluding summary

To make the nature of academic understanding clearer, we first made the broad distinction between the target understanding set by the university teachers and personal understanding reached by the students. In interviews, students described their understanding in terms of meaning and significance, provisional wholeness (complete at that time for their current purpose) and irreversibility, all of which gave them confidence in explaining what they had understood and flexibility in adapting and applying their ideas. Students nevertheless differed markedly in the forms of understanding they had sought, whether they were focusing mainly on preparing for the exam or on trying to understand the meanings for themselves. And some students had developed an intense personal need or *disposition* to understand for themselves, which brought together the ability to adopt appropriate learning strategies, a willingness to put in the necessary effort, and an alertness to opportunities provided in the teaching and learning environment for developing personal understanding.

Students who had such a disposition were likely to experience their understanding as a tightly structured whole that they could 'almost see' – a *knowledge object* – and that they used in the exam to provide a logical path for their evolving explanations. Knowledge objects are also experienced by academic staff as they prepare presentations, organising what are initially loosely structured 'knowledge ensembles' into tightly integrated wholes. Recent research into *dialogic concept-mapping* has suggested how students' understandings can be made visible, and discussed, as they develop from simple concept chains into the integrated webs of meaning that represent an academic understanding that is personally satisfying and yet is expressed in terms of established concepts and accepted ways of thinking and reasoning within a specific discipline or professional area.

The second half of the chapter looked at subject matter from perspective of the university teachers. Interviews made it clear that they focused not so much on the 'intended learning outcomes' that they had to provide for their students but on the much broader *ways of thinking and practising* (WTPs) that were characteristic of the discipline or professional area. These WTPs were illustrated through the five subject areas involved in a recent major study into enhancing teaching and learning environments – the ETL project – which also led to the idea of there being *threshold concepts* in some subject areas. Such concepts open up the subject for the students in important ways that can have lasting effects. This focus on the specific types of learning required in the different disciplines and professional areas, and the specific teaching and learning activities needed to support them, the *inner logic of the subject and its pedagogy*, will become a recurring theme in later chapters.

▷ Further reading

Entwistle, N. J. (1998). 'Approaches to Learning and Forms of Understanding', in B. Dart & G. Boulton-Lewis (eds) *Teaching and Learning in Higher Education*. Melbourne: Australian Council for Educational Research.

Entwistle, N. J. & McCune, V. (2009). 'The Disposition to Understand for Oneself at University and Beyond: Learning Processes, the Will to Learn, and Sensitivity to Context', in L-F. Zhang & R. J. Sternberg (eds) *Perspectives on the Nature of Intellectual Styles*. New York: Springer.

ETL Project (2006, 2009). *Subject Area Reports* at www.etl.tla.ed.ac.uk/publications. html.

Hay, D. B. (2007). 'Using Concepts Maps to Measure Deep, Surface and Non-Learning outcomes', *Studies in Higher Education*, 32, 39–57.

Hay, D. B. (in press). 'Facilitating Personal Understanding in Higher Education: The Role of Dialogic Concept-Mapping', Psychology Journal (of Greece).

Hay, D. B. & Entwistle, N. J. (in press). '"Ideas Made Personal": Visualising and Explaining Understanding through Dialogic Concept-Mapping', *British Journal of Educational Psychology*.

Meyer, J. H. F. (2008). 'Helping Our Students: Learning, Meta-Learning and Threshold Concepts', paper presented at 'Taking Stock: Symposium on Teaching and Learning Research in Higher Education', organized by the Higher education Quality Council of Ontario, April 25–6, 2008, Guelph, Ontario, Canada.

Perkins, D. N. & Tishman, S. (2001). 'Dispositional aspects of intelligence', in J. M. Collis & S. Messick (eds) *Intelligence and Personality: Bridging the Gap in Theory and Measurement* (pp. 233–58). Mahwah, NJ: Lawrence Erlbaum.

Perkins, D. N. (2007). 'Theories of Difficulty', in N. J. Entwistle & P. Tomlinson (eds) *Student Learning and University Teaching*. British Journal of Educational Psychology Monograph Series II, Number 4 – *Student Learning and University Teaching* (pp. 31–48). Leicester: British Psychological Society.

▶ References relating to quotations

Anderson, C. & Hounsell, D. J. (2007). 'Knowledge Practices: "Doing the Subject" in Undergraduate Courses', *The Curriculum Journal*, 18, 463–78.

Anderson, C. & Day, K. (2005). *ETL Subject Area Report – History*, available at http://www.etl.tla.ed.ac.uk/publications.html.

Bruner, J. S. (1960). *The Process of Education*. Cambridge, MA: Harvard University Press.

Bruner, J. S. (1966). *Towards a Theory of Instruction*. Cambridge, MA: Harvard University Press.

Entwistle, A. C. & Entwistle, N. J. (1992). 'Experiences of Understanding in Revising for Degree Examinations', *Learning and Instruction*, 2, 1–22.

Entwistle, N. J. & Entwistle, D. M. (2003). 'Preparing for Examinations: The Interplay of Memorising and Understanding, and the Development of Knowledge Objects', *Higher Education Research and Development*, 22, 19–42.

Fyrenious, A., Wirell, S. & Silén, C. (2007). 'Student Approaches to Achieving Understanding – Approaches to Learning Revisited', *Studies in Higher Education*, 32, 149–65.

Heath, R. (1964). *The Reasonable Adventurer*. Pittsburgh: University of Pittsburgh Press.

McCune, V. & Hounsell, D. J. (2005). 'The Development of Students' Ways of Thinking and Practising in Three Final-Year Biology Courses', *Higher Education*, 49, 255–89.

Meyer, J. H. F. & Land, R. (2005). 'Threshold Concepts and Troublesome Knowledge (2); Epistemological Considerations and a Conceptual Framework for Teaching and Learning', *Higher Education*, 49, 373–88.

Snow, C. P. (1964). *The Two Cultures and a Second Look*. Cambridge: Cambridge University Press.

Svensson, L. (1997). 'Skill in Learning and Organizing Knowledge', in F. Marton, D. J. Hounsell & N. J. Entwistle (eds) *The Experience of Learning* (2nd edn) (pp. 59–71). Edinburgh: Scottish Academic Press, available at http://www.tla.ed.ac.uk/resources/EoL.html.

Part 3

How Academics Teach

Evolving Approaches to Teaching

In Lancaster, Paul Ramsden and I had begun to investigate what aspects of teaching students saw as influencing their approaches to learning and studying. From interviews with students, we developed a *Course Perceptions Questionnaire* and so identified aspects of teaching and assessment linked to either deep or surface approaches. Perceptions of 'good teaching' were related to deep approaches to learning, while a 'heavy work-load' was linked to surface approaches. And students said that 'good teaching' depended, above all, on whether staff had prepared their lectures thoroughly, were pitching the material at the right level, appreciated students' difficulties and were ready to provide advice and support. But this questionnaire only described students' perceptions of teaching, without looking at how the teachers themselves saw their teaching. As a result of the success of the research into student learning, a similar strategy was subsequently used with university teachers, asking them to explain how they went about their teaching.

In Australia, Mike Prosser and Keith Trigwell found striking differences in the way science lecturers described their ideas about teaching and how they carried it out. Most of the lecturers looked at the subject matter only from their own perspective and saw their role as helping students to acquire the knowledge they needed to pass examinations. In other words, they thought about their teaching pragmatically, only in terms of specific techniques and assessment procedures. But some lecturers were more reflective about their teaching, either drawing on staff development seminars or, in one striking example, by considering the nature of knowledge in his discipline – physics.

Some years later I happened to meet this lecturer, Paul Walker, at a conference. Together we talked about his experiences of teaching, and came to realize that his approaches were the result of a long, gradual period of evolution. At first, he taught in the way most of his colleagues did, but the more he thought about the uncertainty of knowledge, even in physics, the less satisfied he became about formulaic methods of teaching that passed on information, while avoiding the big questions at the frontiers of the subject. And that led to a fundamental shift in his approaches to teaching, as the following extract from his retrospective account illustrates:

> At first, the learning outcome I sought, as a matter of traditional expectation, was students' knowledge of the curriculum material as demonstrated by their answers to questions in both informal and formal settings. The approach to teaching was primarily a matter of presenting the curriculum material in a factually correct (and hopefully interesting) way, with ancillary activity designed to reinforce the intake of knowledge and its retention.
>
> As I prepared my teaching and tried to make it more interesting and memorable, I found that my own understanding of the concepts increased markedly. ... This development in

my own relationship with the material led me to focus on the understanding of the content as a major outcome of learning. ... Over time, I became increasingly intrigued by the discrepancy between my greater command of the concepts, with their wider connections, and the apparent inaccessibility of those concepts and connections to most of my students. ... I began, increasingly, to question the way I had been teaching, and to try to focus more on encouraging students to reflect on their own learning. ...

As this shift of focus created apparent unease and concern about the examination papers, I had to develop a more strategic approach, in which this new agenda ran through my teaching like a thread, rather than featuring somehow as part of the course. ... Over time, I have developed a teaching approach which begins to satisfy simultaneously a tacit demand for content, for understanding of content, for relevance and applicability of that content, and yet still challenges and attempts to undermine those expectations by only partially fulfilling them. This is a 'multipli-inclusive' strategy, wherein different students may have different expectations. ...

I wanted to share with students my realisation that knowledge, even in something as mundane as physics, could be seen as a collection of models of the world, invented by individuals, rather than as solid facts which had to be swallowed like so much castor oil. Thus learning was much more than gaining knowledge, even understanding how things worked; it was <u>being a learner</u> that was important, and for intrinsic rather than merely instrumental reasons.

This outlook seemed to me ... to be a potentially powerful catalyst for stimulating interest and inquiry among my students. ... It did not imply the need for radical changes in the curriculum, but simply sought to engender a spirit of inquiry in the broad majority of students, rather than in the small minority who may have already have happened upon it. The point was to enable students to relate to the edifice of disciplinary knowledge and the business of learning differently than most of them normally seemed to. ... And examinations could then be regarded as one of the outcomes of meaningful learning, a by-product rather than the primary goal.

(Entwistle & Walker, 2002: 24–8)

This collaborative study, along with the earlier research into staff perceptions of their teaching, convinced me that approaches to teaching depended on an interplay between understandings of the subject and of the students. It also became clear that, over time, these could change in fundamental ways. Moreover, there was a solution to the dilemma facing many lecturers, namely, 'How can I pitch material at the right level for a class with very different knowledge and intentions? Should I focus on the brightest students or on those who are struggling?' Paul Walker's solution involved designing the teaching to be *multipli-inclusive*. He taught in ways that allowed all the students to draw something worthwhile from it, either instrumentally, just to get through the course, or by engaging to varying degrees with the fundamental ideas of physics. Putting this principle into practice remains a daunting challenge, but it is now even more important to use it in course design, given the increasing diversity of student intakes.

▶ **References**

Entwistle, N. J. & Ramsden, P. (1983). *Understanding Student Learning.* London: Croom Helm.

Entwistle, N. J. & Walker, P. (2002). 'Strategic Alertness and Expanded Awareness within Sophisticated Conceptions of Teaching', in N. Hativa & P. Goodyear (eds) *Teacher Thinking, Beliefs and Knowledge in Higher Education* (pp. 15–40). Dordrecht: Kluwer Academic Publishers.

Prosser, M., Trigwell, K. & Taylor, P. (1994). 'A Phenomenographic Study of Academics' Conceptions of Science Learning and Teaching', *Learning and Instruction*, 4, 217–31.

5 Ideas about Teaching and Learning

▶ ## Understanding pedagogy

Discussions about university teaching in the educational literature, as well as in staff rooms, generally focus on deciding the most appropriate methods, such as lectures, tutorials, practicals, e-learning, problem-based learning or work-based learning, and on how to use them more effectively. But good teaching also depends on understanding why a particular method works better for a specific purpose or in a specific context, and how it can be used to support student learning. And that requires some careful thought about the nature of teaching and learning.

> It is only when we have a fair understanding of what learners are expected to learn, what they actually learn in those situations, and *why* they learn something in one situation but not in another, that pedagogy becomes a reasonably rational set of human activities. ... Pedagogical discussions are often about how learning is organized. What is the best way of going about lectures, group work, individual studies and so on? ... [But one] way of organizing learning cannot be the best for all forms of learning – the best regardless of the purpose. ... It should be obvious that it is important <u>how</u> the content is taught. In problem-based learning, [for example,] even with the same learning objectives, the quality of the problems, and thereby the student's learning, may vary a great deal. That is true also of other forms of teaching, such as the lecture, where the same content may be dealt with in entirely different ways, with consequent differences in the students' learning.
>
> (Marton, 2007: 22–3)

Responding to such challenges, a series of studies has been looking at differences in how university teachers go about their teaching, and then comparing these approaches with how they describe their understandings of the subject. And underlying the emerging differences were contrasts in how university teachers perceive their role and the nature of teaching and learning in their subject.

Contrasting beliefs and approaches

As we saw in the Bridge Passage, Michael Prosser and Keith Trigwell, among others, have found a useful distinction between staff who look at their teaching broadly and think deeply about its effects on students, and those who have a more limited view, concentrating mainly on how to organize and present the subject matter logically and involve students in worthwhile study activity. Some academics seem to take the role of the teacher rather for granted, seeing it in terms of conveying information and ideas to students in the ways conventionally accepted within their subject area. But 'good teaching' also depends on explaining ideas in ways that are accessible to most of the students and monitoring how much has been understood.

The essential difference between contrasting approaches to teaching is in the relative attention given to the subject matter, seen from the teacher's perspective, and to the activities that best support learning, as experienced by the students. Seen from teacher's perspective alone, the intention is to convey information as efficiently as possible but, if we introduce the student's perspective, this shifts the focus towards encouraging both active learning and conceptual change. The distinction can be seen, in its simplest terms, as a contrast between *teacher-focused* and *student-focused* approaches to teaching, rooted in contrasting ways of thinking about teaching and learning. Table 5.1 illustrates these differences from comments made by two of the lecturers interviewed.

Table 5.1   Contrasting ways of thinking about university teaching and learning

Teacher-focused	It is my duty and responsibility to help students develop the specific knowledge and skills which are needed to pass the examinations, although I'm fully aware that this might narrow the kind of education I'm giving the students. ... I put great emphasis on objectives and making sure that I cover the syllabus thoroughly. In preparing a lecture, ... I know exactly what notes I want the students to get. Students don't have to decide when to take notes: I dictate them.
Student-focused	I'm aware of how much I used to assume. I now try to take nothing for granted and to question my assumptions about how students learn things. ... What I want to achieve is confronting students with their preconceived ideas about the subject. ... [Conceptual understanding is developed] by arguing about things and trying to apply ideas. ... What we're trying to do is ... to shift (students) from the layperson's view, to what we would call a scientific ... (or academic) view.

Source: From interviews by Trigwell, Prosser & Taylor, 1994.

These comments have been chosen to illustrate polar opposites and so inevitably exaggerate the differences found. Figure 5.1 shows a progression from one extreme to the other, moving from imparting information to structuring it more carefully, and then ensuring that students learn more actively. But the activity has to be designed to support the development of understanding, leading to a recognition of the importance of conceptual change. This final conception still retains a strong focus on the content being taught, but introduces the crucial step of <u>imagining</u> how best to help students to understand it. Teaching is no longer seen as a set of techniques, but as an act of imagination that translates 'dead' information into the more engaging ways of thinking that bring it to life, creating an expanded awareness of the effects of teaching on learning. It encourages students to think for themselves and to be critical about both evidence and theory. Of course, radical differences in theory are met more frequently in the humanities and social sciences than in the sciences, where evidence depends much less on individual interpretation. But, in all subject areas, a rigorous appreciation of the internal structure of the subject has to be balanced by a conviction that it should directly encourage and support the development of integrative understanding in students.

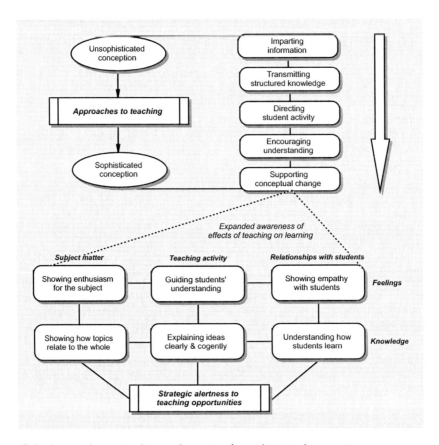

Figure 5.1 Approaches to teaching and aspects of a sophisticated conception

Figure 5.1 shows how such a sophisticated conception of teaching and learning brings together knowledge and feelings, and links them together in thinking about the subject matter, teaching activities and relationships with students. Some of the academic staff interviewed expressed what amounted to a passion for conveying their understanding of the subject to their students. This description of 'good teaching', although valid, provides just a first 'take' on its nature and so must be treated with caution. The reality is both subtler and more complex; lecturers will have different ways of teaching first-year and final-year students, and also of teaching different topics, while the specific methods used will depend crucially on the nature of the discipline. Moreover, preferred ways of teaching can be constrained by unfavourable circumstances (unsuitable rooms or a crowded syllabus), or by competing demands on time. Nevertheless important differences remain in the relative attention lecturers give to explaining the discipline from their own perspective and within their own technical language, and in considering the difficulties students may have in grasping the new ideas being introduced.

Jerome Bruner pointed out many years ago the importance of providing organizing principles that help students to make sense of details in relation to a broader picture.

Teaching specific topics or skills without making clear their context in the broader fundamental structure of the field is uneconomical in several deep senses. In the first place, such teaching makes it exceedingly difficult for the student to generalize from what has been learned to what will be encountered later. In the second place, learning that has fallen short of a grasp of general principles has little reward in terms of intellectual excitement. The best way to create interest in a subject is to render it worth knowing. ... Third, knowledge one has acquired without sufficient structure to tie it together is knowledge that is likely to be forgotten. An unconnected set of facts has a pitiably short half-life in memory. Organizing facts in terms of principles and ideas from which they may be inferred is the only known way of reducing the quick rate of loss of human memory ... [But] designing curricula in a way that reflects the basic structure of the field requires the most fundamental understanding of that field.

(Bruner, 1960: 31–2)

This focus on seeing parts in terms of a whole and the need for a teacher to have a fundamental understanding of the field can be seen clearly in Prosser and Trigwell's recent work. In the deep approach to learning, the focus of a student's attention, as we have seen, is on the meaning of a topic as a whole, coming to see its critical features and recognize the interrelationships between them. Interviews with university teachers suggest that a similarly holistic view of teaching and learning is important, making clear how aspects of the subject fit into an overall picture. But it also seems, perhaps surprisingly, that there is a close correspondence between how lecturers describe their understanding of their subject specialism and how they go about teaching that subject. In both they appear to focus consistently on either the whole picture or on its parts, on overview or on details.

At one extreme, the subject is seen as a series of topics or issues with little or no attention being paid to the whole discipline. When the subject is seen in this way, lecturers tend to talk about 'delivering' discrete 'packages' of information to students. ... In such a scenario, there is little opportunity for students to see how they might integrate what they learn into a larger field of knowledge; what they know is likely to remain a series of isolated facts. At the other extreme, when the subject matter is seen ... as a coherent whole, students are more likely to be helped into a relationship with the field as a whole and to experience, and develop, a personal understanding of that whole. The focus on cohesive wholes, as opposed to unrelated parts, has been shown by our previous work to be associated with higher quality learning outcomes. ... So, simply put, we argue that how university teachers understand their subject will affect the ways in which they will represent that subject to their students and, ultimately, how effectively their students will learn that subject.

(Prosser, Martin & Trigwell, 2007: 56–7)

A similar distinction can also be found within lecturers' explanations of their own research, seeing it either in the context of the field as a whole or describing the sequence and the details of specific studies. And this again corresponds with their ways of understanding the subject they are teaching.

These consistent ways of thinking about different aspects of their work suggest a common mindset through which staff plan and carry out their activities and explain them to the interviewer. Focusing on the meaning of the subject as a whole, and explaining how the different facets of the subject fit together, provides a much more effective explanation than a detailed description of the various topics. And that is also true for students trying to follow explanations, whether in lectures, during tutorials or through e-learning.

This description may, however, give the impression that lecturers have rather consistent and even fixed ways of thinking about the subject and how to teach it. While that may be true of some staff, others will be changing their ideas as they reflect more deeply on the nature of knowledge in their discipline and on how it can cause difficulties for students, as the recollections of Paul Walker in the Bridge Passage illustrated. And that broader, more sympathetic, view of student learning enables academics to convey a better sense of the discipline to the students through explanations that make important connections between the component parts, and by exemplifying the forms of reasoning used in the discipline.

These more sophisticated conceptions of teaching and learning also help lecturers to realize the importance of making their teaching 'multipli-inclusive', and so allowing students at different levels, and with differing interests and goals, to take something valuable from the experience. While it may seem obvious that such inclusive forms of teaching would be welcomed, in reality students' reactions to them are by no means uniform, depending, as they do, on individual expectations and aspirations. Nevertheless looking at the response of a class as a whole does provide one of the best indicators for a lecturer of how well the teaching is going, as we shall find later on in this chapter.

▶ The role of the university teacher

What makes a good university teacher?

This is the question that many academics ask themselves as they begin their teaching careers. There are many collections of reports bringing together teachers' views about the essence of good practice in university teaching, but a particularly valuable source is a collection of 44 'academics' stories' brought together by Roy Ballantyne and his colleagues in Australia. Not only did they make summaries of individual interviews across a whole range of subjects, they also identified important recurring themes (see Table 5.2).

Table 5.2   Themes from university teachers' views of 'good teaching'

Conveying feelings and arousing interest	Conveying enthusiasm for the subject Creating and maintaining student interest
Recognizing the student perspective	Combining humanistic qualities with academic rigour Pitching material at the right level in accessible language Showing the relevance to the students' everyday experience Using professional experience to provide concrete examples
Creating a learning ethos	Teaching for learning and discussing what is involved Managing discomfort by accepting that learning can be difficult Talking to students about their emerging understanding Fostering generic and lifelong skills

Source: Ballantyne, Bain and Packer, 1997: xx–xxvii.

The underlying message was that the essence of good teaching depends on the relationship that exists between staff and students, balancing a rigorous approach to the subject with a caring attitude towards the students. The teacher's role involves acting as a conduit between knowledge and understanding, to show how the various facets of the subject, specific forms of evidence, can come together to enable the subject to be seen in more personally meaningful ways. As Stanford Ericksen put it:

> Students learn what they care about and remember what they understand. … Each student comes to a class with a repertoire of information, ideas, facts, beliefs, and skills (manipulative and conceptual) that serve as the frame of reference, the context, within which new information and events are perceived. … Meaning is never exactly the same from one person to the next. … For the student, the process of studying is the process of reorganising an internal, personal language in response to probes from the teachers, … the need to solve a problem or write a sensible paper, or simply to satisfy curiosity. …
>
> The isolated presentation of facts is done well by books, computers, and other media, while the special emphasis by the human teacher is to develop and illustrate those ideas, methods, and values that give meaning to the particulars. … Good teaching bears down on concepts as the means by which factual information takes on meaning, procedures are understood, theories are evaluated, values and points of view are judged, and applications are tested. Even so, most of the enduring ideas in a course are open-ended; they allow some degree of distinctive interpretation.
>
> (Ericksen, 1984: 20, 51, 55–6, 76)

In more recent thinking, the role is seen as dependent on being 'authentic', through openly expressing personal ideas and values, and feelings about the subject, while also showing a warm regard for the students.

> The subject matter is not just a 'prescribed curriculum' that needs to be conveyed to students, but it matters crucially to us [as teachers] and, by sharing it with our students, we also bring parts of ourselves into our teaching. … [University teachers] create the vital connection between themselves and the 'subject', themselves and students, and students and the 'subject'. This includes developing an informed sense of why particular content areas *matter*, an understanding why students may not yet see why these *matter*, and sensibilities around and skill in helping them understand why they *matter*.
>
> (Kreber, 2007: 2–3)

Of course, there are major differences between the sciences and the humanities in the extent to which the expression of feelings and authenticity in teaching play a part in good practice. Indeed, Ericksen, himself a scientist, warned against making feelings too explicit, speaking out strongly against what he believed to be an unfortunate trend.

> Some teachers get carried away by the lures of the affective interchange, and move outside the subject matter track as they strain to be liked by students. They become educationally permissive, engage in intellectual wanderings, and distribute emotional palliatives designed to keep students happy – but uninformed. This fixation on affective tangentials short-changes the cognitive goals of instruction and related motivation.
>
> (Ericksen, 1984: 23)

This rather extreme reaction is in danger of denying the important part emotion plays in learning, but there remain strong, contrasting views about the role of the teacher. All too often, extreme stereotypes are used to mount 'straw-man' arguments in favour of 'traditional', didactic approaches or 'progressive', student-centred ones. A teacher <u>does</u> have the authority that comes from expert knowledge and experience, and students are generally ready to accept and learn from that expertise. What they do not accept is being made to feel inferior through inappropriately authoritarian or patronizing behaviour by teachers. So a middle way needs to be found which allows staff to maintain the authority that stems from their knowledge and experience, without seeming to appear distant and uncaring to the students. But that 'middle way' is not easy to find. Figure 5.2 shows a mind map produced by a teacher that illustrates one way of dealing with this balancing act. She was trying to make sense of contrasting views about 'What makes good teaching' in a primary school. Disturbed by the oppositional polemics she had encountered, she tried to work out how to avoid a 'false dichotomy' between education as 'putting in', and as 'drawing out'. Identifying

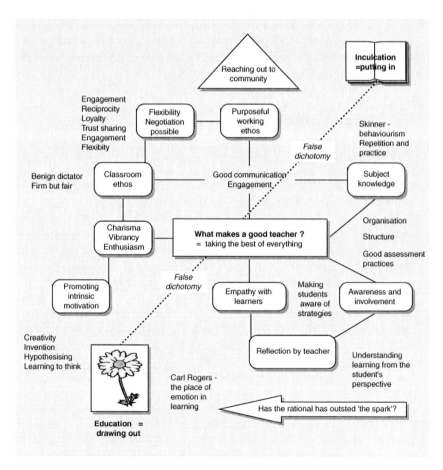

Figure 5.2 An integration of contrasting ideas about the role of a teacher
Source: Entwistle et al., 2000.

all the positive aspects from the differing perspectives, she put the more didactic elements mainly to the right of her diagonal line and the more student-centred ones to the left.

At university level, an engineering student wrote an award-winning essay, 'What makes a good lecturer?', showing what he felt had helped him in his learning.

Good lecturers trigger enthusiasm and are often passionate themselves about their subject, even if that subject happens to be the design of operational amplifiers. ... Indubitably, humour is an important factor in grabbing student's interest, but I would say that a good lecturer goes beyond that stage. They are the ones that realize the power of visual demonstrations that are so frequently overlooked ... [but] made my lectures entertaining, and memorable. ... Pictures and even short videos illustrating real-life applications and perspectives are always welcome. Not just once at the start of the course, but throughout all lectures!

Lecturers are often engaged in fascinating research, which can form the basis of interesting examples. Some go to great lengths to prepare learning tools that complement teaching, like short software simulations ... [or] even set up online workspaces for their courses, and use Tablet PC technology allowing them to record and broadcast online additional worked examples, fully narrated by the lecturer. These tremendous resources really make a difference, and it's even better when lecturers make these available for students outside lectures. Equally engaging are lecturers that discuss real-world case studies. ... One I found particularly stunning was when a lecturer described the structural failure of a pipe in a cyclohexane plant, and demonstrated that any first year engineer could have spotted the initial pipe's design flaw. What is that famous saying, again? A *case study* is worth a thousand words?

Exceptional educators implement a variety of these techniques in their lectures. Good lecturers are also the most approachable and understand the learning perspective of students. They are the ones that generously give of their time after lectures to answer the questions of the hoards of students who have no idea where equation 5 on page 6 of the notes came from, or of that odd student in the back row that thinks he has invented a perpetual motion machine. Open-minded lecturers contribute so much to our learning experience and gain remarkable respect with students.

(Rieutort-Louis, 2008: 1–2)

Coping with contrasting roles and working within constraints

So far the role of the teacher has been kept separate from the role of the academic, and yet the work of a university teacher in practice involves several quite different roles, which can interfere with each other. Besides teaching in a classroom, there is a research role that involves carrying out investigations, giving papers, reviewing articles for publication and joining in academic debate. Delivering an academic paper to an audience of fellow researchers involves a formal approach and technical language, and this can become the dominant voice of an academic. It can be difficult then to keep the undergraduate audience firmly in mind, and adjust stance and language to the level of the students. And joining in academic debate with colleagues often depends on sharp critique, while encouraging discussion in tutorials requires an altogether gentler voice. Finally, staff may also be involved in advising and guiding individual students that can call for great sensitivity and understanding. Managing these very different aspects of the role of a university teacher is, to say the least, extremely challenging.

These days, academics are also working under a range of constraints and pressures that add to these difficulties. Balancing the time and effort involved in keeping up to date in scholarship and contributing to it, perhaps with a Research Assessment Exercise looming, while planning new courses in course teams, preparing one's own teaching along with the supportive learning materials increasingly expected, taking part in committees and coping with administrative demands, all add up to a complex and daunting set of tasks. Beyond all that, staff may also be involved in external professional work, or in developing companies. So finding time to think about better ways of teaching and encouraging students to learn is far from easy, but deriving satisfaction from teaching does depend on keeping the content up to date and the presentation fresh and appreciated by the students. And students are quick to recognize teaching that has not been well prepared and staff who would rather be somewhere else!

▶ Students' experiences of teaching

The first part of this chapter has relied on the analysis of interviews and some anecdotal accounts, and may seem too impressionistic. But in all the research on teaching and learning, it is the combination of evidence and ideas from various sources that builds up more convincing impressions. We shift now from the staff perspective to that of the students, while bringing together questionnaire data with interviews. As approaches to learning are affected by students' <u>perceptions</u> of teaching, those perceptions provide important evidence about the effectiveness of teaching. The questionnaire developed with Paul Ramsden, mentioned in the Bridge Passage, is one such example. Results from its use, combined with interview comments, help to provide a view of teaching from the students' perspective.

Perceptions of lecturing

Students had been asked to explain in interviews what aspects of teaching had most affected their ability to learn, with certain recurring themes emerging (see Table 5.3). Students' comments from the interviews were then used to produce items within the *Course Perceptions Questionnaire*. Large samples of students across several universities completed this questionnaire and so provided a more complete coverage of students' experiences of lecturing. Combining these results with findings from another large-scale study by Herbert Marsh, confirmed the importance of the five aspects highlighted in interviews, but added two other aspects, namely 'clarity' and 'structure'. The meaning of the whole set of seven features of lecturing is indicated briefly below.

- *Clarity* indicates that the teacher can be heard clearly even at the back of the class and also implies that audio-visual supporting material can be heard or seen easily.
- *Level* describes whether the material has been pitched at an appropriate level for the range of students taking the course.
- *Pace* applies to the speed of delivery in a lecture, but also, critically, to the rate at which new ideas are introduced within the course.
- *Structure* indicates how well the components of the course seem to fit together and whether the steps in any argument presented are seen as logical.

- *Explanation* indicates that the meaning of concepts is made clear, including links between the ideas and with prior knowledge, in language that is easy to follow.
- *Enthusiasm* refers to presentations which are lively and evoke interest, and demonstrate the teachers' own engagement with the topic.
- *Empathy* relates to the relationship with students and how aware staff seem to be of possible difficulties for students and, more generally, of how well the teaching is going.

The first four of these categories describe the basic requirements that make the material accessible and intelligible, and without which students find it difficult to make sense of the

Table 5.3 Comments from students about aspects of teaching affecting their learning

Level	Some staff seem unaware that the concrete knowledge we have is virtually nil about some of the topics that we're talked at, at a very high level, so you can't attach anything that you've been told to something you know already, which, of course, is very important in learning. I think it's the problem of experts coming in and they have such a wealth of knowledge in that area that they start at too high a level.
Pace	In very few of the lectures was I picking [the principles] up as we did them; the pace is too fast. You don't follow what is going on. I put this down to this very keen desire [of staff] to cover that much work. ... The concepts are really difficult anyway, but the lecturers assume we know it and they just keep going, and once you get behind it, you know you can't really get back on terms.
Explanation	Recently we were doing Fourier analysis, and the lecturer mentioned in passing that they used it when they transmit moon pictures back to earth. ... That makes a lot of difference – you can see it being used. Another example was an explanation he gave that it was like when you banged a drum and got lots of different sounds. He said, 'If you look at it this way, you can see why', and he was right, you could see why.
Enthusiasm	Some lectures have been very good, partly they've been delivered humorously and with an entertaining streak. ... If the tutors have enthusiasm, then they really fire their own students with the subject, and the students' really pick it up. ... I'm really good at and enjoy this subject, but that's only because the tutor has been so enthusiastic that he has given me an enthusiasm for it and now I really love the subject.
Empathy	I do most work on courses where I get on with the tutors best. A tutor can put you off the subject. ... Some of them don't seem to like students. They're not interested in what the students have to say unless it's relevant to their approach. ... There are some lecturers who will think about anything you say, and say, 'Oh, I hadn't thought of that, let's see where that leads to', and there are others who will just go on talking almost to themselves.

Source: Entwistle & Ramsden, 1983.

material. In some courses, new ideas are introduced at a pace that creates problems for many students, as we shall see in Chapter 9. But it is the last three aspects, explanation, enthusiasm and empathy – the '3-Es' – that seem most directly to encourage a deep approach in students. These comments fit in quite well with university teachers' views on 'good teaching' (Table 5.2), but there are additional aspects that need to be considered in the next chapter and in Part 4.

Perceptions of discussion classes

Small-group tutorials are used widely in Britain, especially in the humanities and social sciences, as discussion classes to supplement lectures, with one of their main functions being to encourage students to recognize the contested nature of academic knowledge in these fields. This teaching, done well, becomes another example of encouraging deep approaches and integrative understanding. In a wide-ranging qualitative study, Charles Anderson at Edinburgh University looked at the ways in which tutors worked with students in such discussion groups. He talked to tutors, observed tutorials, tape-recorded them, and interviewed students to explore what made successful tutorials. Drawing on the views of both staff and students, Table 5.4 shows what they believed to be the main characteristics of successful tutorials.

Successful tutorials were seen to depend crucially on the intellectual and social climate created by the tutors – a form of *moral order* expected by both staff and students within which students felt ready to express opinions and challenge each others' views, and in which there was a recognition that success depended on the active participation of the whole group. Too much control by the tutor would constrain understanding, while too little might prevent it from developing at all. The tutor's role thus becomes of

Table 5.4 Features promoting active participation and listening

Preparation and other work	Not too much pressure from other coursework
	Appropriate topic to encourage active discussion
	Clear focus for preparation provided by the tutor
	Appropriate preparation by the students
Tutor skills	Creating a good atmosphere while focusing discussion
	Modelling academic debate in the discipline
	Scaffolding students' attempts to think for themselves
	Challenging evidence and logic without hurtful criticism
Student characteristics	Knowledge of the topic and the discipline as a whole
	Interest in the subject matter
	Confidence and self-esteem
Social climate	Informal group atmosphere
	Mutual respect among students and with tutor
	Students themselves investing effort in discussion

Source: Based on descriptions by Anderson, 1997.

crucial importance in encouraging open discussion and deep approaches, as students explained:

> I find that tutorials are at their best when there is a very informal nature about the class, … because then you can feel as if you can open up, and ask questions without fears of being thought stupid. … But I don't like them to be just unfocused: they are a waste of time if you just sit there and everyone just talks about whatever they feel like talking about. … Having an encouraging tutor helps, rather than someone who is … so clever that they can't see your problem, because they understand the topic too well. It's nice having someone that can see why you've got a problem … and can help you and the other students, and help you yourself sort out what you mean.
>
> (Edited composite from Anderson, 1997)

Perceptions of set work and assessment

In interviews, students also mentioned the effects of set work and assessment procedures in influencing how they go about learning. We met the influence of assessment earlier when considering organized effort in studying (Chapter 3), but other aspects were also mentioned, as Table 5.5 shows. Students believe that their studying is directly affected by their experiences of teaching and set work, with assessment procedures being the strongest influence of all.

It is important, therefore, that students see the purposes of assessment in the ways intended by staff, and yet this may often not happen. And, as we saw in Anders Fransson's work (Bridge into Chapter 3), it is the students' perceptions, rather than the staff's beliefs about the assessment, which affect the quality of the learning that takes place.

The immediate impression from the students' comments is that assessment made most of them act strategically, and that is hardly surprising; passing exams and getting good marks are the main ways in which students are rewarded, and rewards strongly affect subsequent behaviour. But assessment can also interfere with deep approaches to learning. The nature and form of the questions set as assessment tasks, and the type of feedback provided to students about their performance, all influence the approaches students adopt and so the likelihood of reaching a satisfying level of personal understanding. Essentially, the assessment procedure shapes the learning and studying process, which is why so much emphasis is placed on *formative assessment* – ongoing assessment designed specifically to encourage learning, as we shall see in Chapter 8. If students are to be encouraged to adopt deep approaches, then the form of the questions that are set, and the emphasis shown in the tutor's comments in feedback, have both to focus on understanding. But, as students have their eye mainly on the assessments that have the greatest weighting, those coming at the end of a module often have the strongest influence. And students often see such assessments as inviting the reproduction of earlier learning.

Comments made by tutors on set work are intended to play an important part in supporting learning, but sometimes students find the feedback less than helpful. In the early stages of university education, students may not be able to make sense of what staff believe are clear comments, because their meaning depends on a much broader knowledge of the subject and of terms like 'descriptive' or 'analytical'. And the tone of the comments can also be off-putting to inexperienced students,

Table 5.5 Comments from students about aspects of assessment affecting their learning

Perceptions of essay marking	With that essay … I wrote with an image of the marker in mind. … An essay is an expression of thought, really, but that's not what they're after; they're after a search through the library, I think, and cribbing of other people's ideas.
Effects of mark schemes	The lecturer told us his marking scheme: most of the marks were about the design, building and performance of the bridge and very few were available for the report. So obviously I didn't spend three weeks writing it up!
Delayed feedback	You give an essay in – I gave in two at the beginning of the second term and didn't get them back until this term. … It's a bit difficult when you're writing the next essay, because you want to know where you've gone wrong and the points that have been alright. … After waiting a whole term, you've forgotten what it's all about and it doesn't really mean much then.
Workload	Basically its all a bit of a struggle, just to hand things in, as opposed to being interested; you're working against a time deadline instead of for your own benefit. … I know even the staff admit the workload is high – tough on us.
Criticisms of course work	I was pretty satisfied with [my essay], but I was really put off when I saw the tutor's comments on it. What I did I thought was very relevant; I just answered the question, which the tutor didn't think was right, 'cause the tutor wanted 'how' and 'why' factors.
Perceptions of exam demands	[With short-answer questions], I hate to say it, but what you have to do is have a list of the 'facts'; you write down ten important points and memorize those, then you'll do alright in the test. … If you can give a bit of factual information – so and so did that and concluded that … – then you'll get a good mark.

Source: Adapted from Entwistle & Ramsden, 1983; Hounsell, 1987.

who have yet to acclimatize to the cut and thrust of academic critique. So, what is intended to be helpful guidance may be perceived as being hurtful and demoralizing criticism.

> Tutors' comments often amount to summary judgements rather than specific diagnoses, alluding to an academic form of discourse, which is largely tacit, and thus invisible to students who have not already perceived its distinctive features. … At the core of the problem is what Bruner has described … as *telling* out of context rather than *showing* in context. Yet even where well-documented comments have made the diagnosis readily comprehensible, the gulf which lies between diagnosis and remedy may remain unbridged and, for some students, unbridgeable without sustained support.
>
> (Hounsell, 1987: 251–2)

The nature of assessment, and of the feedback on it, is thus as important as the initial presentation of the content in affecting the approaches to learning and studying adopted by students, as we shall see in Chapter 8.

National reviews of teaching quality

The *Course Perceptions Questionnaire* was subsequently revised by Paul Ramsden to create the *Course Experience Questionnaire (CEQ)*, which was then used extensively in Australia to evaluate and compare the quality of the teaching provided by institutions. Recently, this instrument was adapted to form the basis of the British *National Student Survey Questionnaire*, which is being circulated to all students as they graduate. There is now a growing database providing evidence of the ratings of students on specific degree courses, which can be accessed at the Teaching Quality Information website at http://www1.tqi.ac.uk/.

This national questionnaire looks at six areas of students' experiences – teaching, assessment and feedback, academic support, organization and management, learning resources and personal development – with a final question asking about overall satisfaction. John Richardson from the Open University analysed over 140,000 responses from the 2005 survey, and found that over 80 per cent of students had been satisfied with the overall quality of the course, while under 10 per cent were clearly dissatisfied. There were similarly high ratings for the teaching, with students being well satisfied with lecturers' explanations and enthusiasm and also with the degree of interest and intellectual stimulation provided. But what degree of dissatisfaction is acceptable? Where less than two-thirds of students feel satisfied there must surely be a problem, while even three-quarters agreement still leaves a quarter of the students dissatisfied. And in some areas there was substantial dissatisfaction, particularly with a lack of promptness in receiving feedback (only 53 per cent agreeing it was prompt), and with feedback that had not clarified their misunderstandings (again 53 per cent), perhaps due to the lack of detail in the tutors' comments (only 60 per cent agreeing that they had received detailed comments).

The results of these surveys, as they accumulate more data from successive years, will provide a valuable indicator of the overall satisfaction with degree courses across institutions, and are already providing the kind of leverage for improvement in teaching that the Research Assessment Exercise has done for research. The questionnaire for the National Survey has proved effective in identifying areas where improvement is needed, such as prompt and useful feedback on assessed work, but the items are at too general a level to indicate any specific weaknesses clearly. In Chapter 9 we shall describe a questionnaire that has been used for this purpose and explain how it can be used in practice.

▶ Concluding summary

Lecturers describe their teaching in ways that suggest a major division between *teacher-focused* and *student-focused* approaches. With a teacher-focus, the main concern is with the subject matter, seen from the lecturer's own perspective while, with a student-focus, ways of encouraging students to develop their own integrative conceptual understanding are more central. Of course, experienced staff do not use a single approach;

their teaching varies with the level of the class and the nature of the topic. And yet consistent differences among lecturers are still found, reflecting both their focus (teacher or student) and whether they see their subject as an integrated whole or as a series of discrete parts. The way they understand their subject affects how they explain it to their students. This link was illustrated in the Bridge Passage through the experiences of a physics lecturer, who described how his own teaching approaches had evolved over time. Like many academics, he started with a teacher-focus, but this evolved gradually into a student-focus, which eventually led him to teach in a 'multi-inclusive' way that allowed students at different levels and with different intentions to draw what they wanted from the lectures.

Students have clear ideas about which characteristics of lectures are most effective in helping them to learn; they mention clarity, level, pace and structure. These four aspects described the basics of effective lecturing, but it is three other aspects that encourage a deep approach to learning – explanation, enthusiasm and empathy. Discussion groups encourage deep approaches if they provide a supportive climate within which students feel ready to make mistakes and where staff can make challenges that clarify understanding without damaging students' self-confidence.

Approaches to learning are also affected by students' experiences of assessment, with the quality of feedback on the work submitted being of paramount importance. Although teaching and assessment affect the overall approaches to learning, it is the students' <u>perceptions</u> of these, rather than the staff's intentions, which affect how any individual student learns. So far we have been treating teaching and assessment as separate influences on the quality of learning, but they are, of course, closely related. And as we move on, we shall meet a broader range of influences from the whole learning environment that includes assignments and feedback on them, individual and group support offered to students, library provision and access to databases, as well as opportunities for e-learning. Some of these aspects will emerge in the next chapter, but they will be developed further in Part 4.

▶ Further reading

Forest, J. J. F. (1998). *University Teaching: International Perspectives*. New York: Garland Publishing.

Hativa, N., & Goodyear, P. (eds). *Teacher Thinking, Beliefs and Knowledge in Higher Education*. Dordrecht: Kluwer Academic Publishers.

Marsh, H. (1987). 'Students' Evaluations of University Teaching: Research Findings, Methodological Issues, Directions for Future Research', *International Journal of Educational Research*, 11 (3) (whole issue).

Prosser, M. & Trigwell, K. (1999). *Understanding Learning and Teaching: The Experience of Higher Education*. Buckingham: SRHE and Open University Press.

Ramsden, P. (1991). 'A Performance Indicator of Teaching Quality in Higher Education', *Studies in Higher Education*, 16, 129–50.

Ramsden, P. (2003). *Learning to Teach in Higher Education* (2nd edn). London: Routledge Falmer.

Richardson, J. T. E. (2005). 'National Study Survey: Interim Assessment of the 2005 Questionnaire', report to HEFC, accessed at www.hefc.ac.uk/rdreports/2005/rd20_05/ on 27 June 2007.

Trigwell, K., Prosser, M. & Waterhouse, F. (1999). 'Relations Between Teachers' Approaches to Teaching and Students' Approaches to Learning', *Higher Education*, 37, 57–70.

▶ References relating to quotations

Anderson, C. (1997). 'Enabling and Shaping Understanding through Tutorials', in F. Marton, D. J. Hounsell & N. J. Entwistle (eds) *The Experience of Learning* (2nd edn) (pp. 184–97). Edinburgh: Scottish Academic Press – available at www.tla.ed.ac.uk/resources/EoL.html.

Ballantyne, R., Bain, J. & Packer, J. (1997). *Reflecting on University Teaching: Academics Stories*. Canberra: Australian Publishing Service.

Bruner, J. S. (1960). *The Process of Education*. Cambridge, MA: Harvard University Press.

Entwistle, N. J. & Ramsden, P. (1983). *Understanding Student Learning*. London: Croom Helm.

Entwistle, N. J., Skinner, D., Entwistle, D. & Orr, S. (2000). 'Conceptions and Beliefs about Good Teaching: An Integration of Contrasting Research Areas', *Higher Education Research and Development*, 19, 5–26.

Ericksen, S. C. (1984). *The Essence of Good Teaching*. San Francisco: Jossey-Bass.

Hounsell, D. J. (1987). 'Essay-Writing and the Quality of Feedback', in J. T. E. Richardson, M. W. Eysenck & D. Warren-Piper (eds) *Student Learning: Research into Education and Cognitive Psychology* (pp. 109–19). Buckingham: SRHE and Open University Press.

Kreber, C. (2007). 'The Scholarship of Teaching and Learning as an Authentic Practice', *International Journal for the Scholarship of Teaching and Learning*, 1, 1–4.

Marton, F. (2007). 'Towards a Pedagogical Theory of Learning', in N. J. Entwistle & P. D. Tomlinson (eds) *Student Learning and University Teaching*. British Journal of Educational Psychology, Monograph Series II: Psychological Aspects of Education – Current Trends (pp. 19–30). Leicester: British Psychological Society.

Prosser, M., Martin, E. & Trigwell, K. (2007). 'Academics' Experiences of Teaching and their Subject-Matter Understanding', in N. J. Entwistle & P. D. Tomlinson (eds) *Student Learning and University Teaching*. British Journal of Educational Psychology, Monograph Series II: Psychological Aspects of Education – Current Trends (pp. 49–59). Leicester: British Psychological Society.

Rieutort-Louis, W. (2008). 'What Makes a Good Lecturer?', winning essay for the Engineering Subject Centre Student Award, 2008, viewed on 12 February 2009 at http://www.engsc.ac.uk/an/student_awards/archive/winner2008.asp.

Trigwell, K., Prosser, M. & Taylor, P. (1994). 'Qualitative Differences in Approaches to Teaching First-Year University Science', *Higher Education*, 27, 75–84.

Teaching for Personal Understanding

We have already seen that students develop integrative personal understandings when encouraged to bring together ideas for themselves, and that university teachers believe such understanding is crucial, based on the distinctive ways of thinking and practising in the discipline or professional area. In the last chapter, we were looking at general ideas about what 'good teaching' at university seems to involve, but that can only take us so far. Although we shall be looking out for general principles that can guide thinking about teaching and learning, there will always remain the proviso that these guidelines will need to be reassessed within specific subject areas, according to what we have called 'the inner logic of the subject and its pedagogy'. Looking at examples of teaching that encourage understanding within contrasting subject areas should help us to see what they have in common and also how they have been developed for particular purposes.

Returning to the 'Understanding understanding' seminar in Edinburgh, mentioned earlier, David Perkins told us about a project in Harvard designed to encourage school-teachers to plan their teaching with an explicit focus on understanding. Through discussions with teachers, he and his colleagues had begun to see understanding, not just as an end point of learning, but in terms of ongoing sets of thinking processes that led students towards understanding, what he called a 'performance perspective'.

> Understanding is a matter of being able to do a variety of thought-demanding things with a topic – like explaining, finding evidence and examples, generalizing, analogizing, and representing a topic in a new way. ... [It is] being able to carry out a variety of actions or 'performances' that show one's grasp of a topic and at the same time advance it. ... Even though teachers are trying, typical classroom practice does not give a sufficient presence to thoughtful engagement in performances that show understanding. To get the understanding we want, we need to put understanding up front. And that means putting thoughtful engagement in understanding performances up front; ... explaining, solving problems, building an argument, constructing a product. ... [And] what learners do in response not only shows their level of current understanding, but very likely advances it. By working through their understanding in response to a particular challenge, they come to understand better. ... Understanding shows its face when people can think and act flexibly around what they know. In contrast, when a learner cannot go beyond rote and routine thought and action, this signals a lack of understanding.
>
> (Perkins & Blythe, 1994: 5–6; Perkins, 1998: 41–2)

Thinking about understanding in this way suggested how to encourage it within the classroom. Direct teaching is not powerful enough on its own to develop students' understanding; the curriculum as a whole has to support it. And so the researchers at Harvard produced a *Teaching for Understanding* framework to guide teachers' planning of their teaching. The design of our ETL project was influenced by these ideas about an overall curriculum framework and also by the notion of *constructive alignment*, developed by John Biggs in Australia. He had drawn on Perkins' ideas about understanding to stress the importance of ensuring that all elements of a curriculum should act together to encourage the construction of individual understanding, and so produce a 'constructivist' perspective on teaching and learning.

> In aligned teaching, there is maximum consistency throughout the system. The curriculum is stated in the form of ... the level of understanding required rather than simply a list of topics to be covered. Teaching methods are chosen that are likely to realize [that understanding]; you get students to do the things that [support it]. Finally, the assessment tasks [measure it], so that you can test to see if the students have learned what ... they should be learning. All components in the system address the same agenda and support each other. The students are 'entrapped' in this web of consistency, optimizing the likelihood that they will engage the appropriate learning activities, but paradoxically leaving them free to construct their knowledge their way. ... This is deep learning by definition.
>
> (Biggs 2003: 27)

David Perkins and John Biggs acted as the international consultants on our ETL project and so influenced the thinking of a project team that included researchers from different universities and contrasting theoretical persuasions. We were working with course teams from 25 modules in five contrasting subject areas, and from 11 universities. The project thus produced a potent mix of ideas and experience that suggested new ways of thinking about teaching and learning in higher education, and ones that were firmly rooted in experiences of everyday academic work. Two of these ideas have already been discussed in Chapter 4, namely *ways of thinking and practising in the subject* and *threshold concepts*, while two more are explained in the next chapter – *the inner logic of the subject and its pedagogy* and *congruence within the teaching-learning environment*.

In this chapter we will concentrate on examples of how to encourage personal understanding both through direct teaching and through the design of the curriculum as a whole. The effects on learning from other aspects of the learning environment, such as feedback and assessment, will be discussed in Part 4.

▶ References

Biggs, J. B. (2003). *Teaching for Quality Learning at University* (2nd edn). Buckingham: SRHE & Open University Press (see, also, 3rd edn, 2007).

Perkins, D. N. (1998). 'What is Understanding?', in M. S. Wiske (ed.) *Teaching for Understanding: Linking Research with Practice* (pp. 39–57). San Francisco: Jossey-Bass.

Perkins, D. N. & Blythe, T. (1994). 'Putting Understanding Up Front', *Educational Leadership*, 51, 5, 4–7.

6 Research into Teaching for Understanding

As we saw in Chapter 3, a deep approach depends on the intention to understand for oneself, which brings into play learning processes more likely to lead to an integrative personal understanding. But the actual processes involved, and the type of academic understanding arrived at, differ in fundamental ways across the disciplines, hence the idea of there being an *inner logic of the subject and its pedagogy*. That is our starting point, developed further by using examples from contrasting subject areas to illustrate how teaching can be focused more directly on encouraging understanding, with other studies illustrating the importance of supporting direct teaching through the design of the curriculum as a whole.

▶ The inner logic of the subject and its pedagogy

In the original ETL research design, we had hoped to identify 'marker outcomes', essential syllabus elements found in a similar form across many undergraduate courses in a discipline. But our choice of course units was constrained by local circumstances and produced less direct overlap between course content across equivalent course units than we had expected. Only in electronic engineering were we able to look at a single major topic – analogue engineering – across several similar course settings. But that opportunity brought valuable insights into how the same topic area was being treated in different settings, showing broad similarities in the methods of teaching being used, but also marked differences in the ways it was carried out. Here we concentrate on the similarities while in Chapter 9 we consider the consequences of some of the differences.

Analysing the interview and questionnaire data collected, we found certain teaching and learning activities that were essential for students to be able to work confidently in analogue electronics. If any one of these was absent, or not well developed, students were likely to complain about difficulties in learning. The top half of Table 6.1 shows the main ways of thinking involved in solving circuit problems, a major requirement in all the courses. Each of these elements was essential for solving these problems satisfactorily, suggesting that they act together synergistically within a logical framework of learning processes in contributing to understanding. The lower half of the table shows the various teaching and learning activities that supported these specific ways of thinking. This strong connection between WTPs and teaching and learning activities

led to the notion of their being an *inner logic of the subject and its pedagogy*, reflecting its distinctive ways of thinking and practising, and indicating some of the necessary conditions for learning analogue electronics. To some extent, an effective

Table 6.1   A pedagogy for developing WTPs in analogue electronics

Ways of thinking in analogue electronics	• Appreciating the overall function of a circuit • Drawing on previous concepts and integrating them • Recognising the salient groups of components • Thinking logically in setting about circuit analysis • Developing the necessary analytic tools for solutions • Building up a memory bank of contrasting examples • Thinking intuitively in designing new circuits
Teaching and learning activities supporting understanding	• Circuits linked to real-life illustrations from industry • Main circuit components clearly highlighted in diagrams • Ways of thinking about circuits explained and exemplified • Working through sets of strategically varied examples • Ways of solving tutorial problems discussed • Worked examples provided at the appropriate time • Individual assistance with tutorial problems available • Progress monitored in tutorial work and tests

Source: Entwistle, Nisbet & Bromage, 2006: 48–9

pedagogy will have elements in common across most subject areas, but the nature of the subject must affect the particular forms of teaching and learning which suit that subject best and, in particular, the way in which common teaching methods are implemented.

(Entwistle, Nisbet & Bromage, 2006: 48)

While the idea of there being contrasting discourses across disciplines is already well established, as we saw in Chapter 4, the connection between ways of thinking and approaches to teaching has been less frequently discussed. The idea of an inner logic of the subject and its pedagogy is therefore used to draw attention to this necessary relationship. In studies that have looked in detail at the nature of the subject in relation to the approaches to teaching, a sense of this 'inner logic' holding together main ideas within the subject area can usually be seen, although this tight connection does not necessarily hold across whole disciplines. The recent work of Mia O'Brien is a good example of this. She invited university teachers to select what they saw as a threshold concept in their subject area and to discuss with a colleague its significance and how they taught it. This created discussions between teachers with similar knowledge and experience and showed the intimate connection between what they were trying to achieve and the specific approaches they used in their teaching. We shall consider the value of this approach in the final chapter.

The notion of an 'inner logic' has something in common with the notion of the *signature pedagogies of the professions*, introduced by Lee Shulman and his colleagues. They investigated several professional areas, including engineering, and pointed out that distinctive methods of teaching had evolved that were designed to encourage the kinds of thinking characteristic of each profession.

What I mean by 'signature pedagogy' is a mode of teaching that has become inextricably identified with preparing people for a particular profession. This means it has three characteristics: one, it's distinctive of that [specific] profession. ... Second that it is pervasive within the curriculum, so that there are certain continuities that thread through the program that are part of what it means to 'think like a lawyer' or 'think like a physician'. ... There are certain kinds of thinking that are called for in the rules of engagement of each course, even as you go from subject to subject. The third feature is another aspect of pervasiveness, which cuts across institutions and not only courses. Signature pedagogies have become essential to general pedagogy of an entire profession, as elements of instruction and of socialization.

(Shulman, 2005)

Although this description helps to make clearer the types of link to be expected between WTPs and essential elements of pedagogy, Shulman was focusing on special forms of teaching, such as clinical rounds in medicine or disputation sessions for lawyers. The teaching of analogue electronics was more commonplace, involving lectures, tutorials and laboratory sessions. But the teaching and learning activities were, nevertheless, being used in specific ways to encourage distinctive ways of thinking, hence the idea of an inner logic of the subject and its pedagogy.

While it was not possible to carry out equivalent analyses in the other ETL subject areas, the idea of an inner logic connecting WTPs to specific approaches to teaching still seems to be worth considering further. Looking at the WTPs within subject or topic areas, as we did in Chapter 4, it should generally be possible to see how specific teaching approaches are used to support the main aims of the course. Although the teaching methods adopted across the subject areas might seem to be the same – lectures, tutorials, set work and laboratory work, or working with e-learning or research materials – the specific ways in which these methods are being used will inevitably reflect the distinctive purposes of the discipline, the course team and the individual academic. This may seem entirely obvious, but recognition of this has been missing in many research studies. Researchers tend to look for general approaches that can be widely used, which may then be actively publicized, and even commercialized. University teachers may well resist these innovations, often for the very good reason that they are not appropriate for their own subject area. Although innovative methods used successfully in one subject area are worth considering in other areas, their success will be due in part to their match with specific subject matter and institutional context.

While WTPs were initially described in terms of a graduate-level goal at the end of a degree course, the example of analogue electronics shows that they also apply within separate subject domains, or even specific topic areas. And concentrating too much on the broadest level of WTPs may lose sight of the close connections that exist between teaching and learning within teaching domains. Within interdisciplinary studies, there are still likely to be important ways of thinking and handling evidence that underpin a group of subjects, and again these would be logically related to a specific set of teaching and learning activities that support them.

The following examples illustrate how university teachers in a range of subject areas have developed ways of helping students to understand the subject more deeply by drawing on theoretical principles that explain the links between teaching and learning.

▶ Examples of subject-specific teaching focused on understanding

Encouraging a deep approach to problem solving in electronic engineering

Our work in the ETL project had shown that many students found analogue electronics difficult to understand. The course teams we talked to suggested that the main difficulty came from having to combine the analytic skills of calculating the electrical output from a circuit with an 'intuitive' grasp of how each set of components affected the processes taking place. Analogue circuits are less transparent and predictable than digital ones, and consequently students have to build up experience of many different patterns of arrangement before they can recognize what is happening in any new circuit they meet. Students are thus given large numbers of circuit problems to solve. However, many of the students we interviewed were not engaging with the problems sufficiently deeply to develop any real understanding of problem solving; instead, they were following procedures blindly, hoping to reach correct solutions.

One of the striking features of the interviews was how many of the students showed what Max Scheja in Stockholm has described as 'delayed understanding'. Although some delay in understanding difficult topics is to be expected, its extent and consequences were particularly marked in the learning of analogue electronics. As a student in our own project said:

> In second year I got a better understanding of what I learned in first year. Now in third year I've kind of learned what I was supposed to know in second year. ... It's a shame that I've never felt that I've learned it in the actual year it was taught!

We found that about a quarter of the students were experiencing such problems and the failure rate in the end of year exam reflected their lack of understanding. Our questionnaire on experiences of teaching suggested that these problems were attributable to the teaching they had experienced. A substantial proportion of students in some units found the pace at which material was introduced much too fast for them; they also considered the content difficult to understand and rather boring (see Chapter 9 for details). In another university the main problem was not having sufficient feedback on the work completed. The issues raised by the students were not found to the same extent across all units, but where they existed, students said that they shifted their time and effort to courses where understanding was easier to achieve.

> I tended to do [the tutorial problems] blindly. I just knew if I did that, did that, did that, follow these steps, then I could come to an answer. ... I learned a routine: it wasn't so much understanding what it meant. ... When you work through ... the tutorials [in the different modules] – and they all take roughly the same time – the analogue ones you don't get any answers out of them. You have to focus your energy where it's [rewarded]. ... We scraped by but we probably would have got great marks had we actually understood what we were doing.

As the most consistent problem was that too many students were relying on a surface approach in solving problems, possible ways of improving that situation were discussed with the course teams. Research into how 'expertise' is developed in other fields suggested that the processes involved in problem solving should be made more explicit. Several changes were made in the course units, but in differing forms and to differing extents, depending on the circumstances. Lecturers were encouraged to talk through their own problem-solving strategies in lectures more frequently, and also to introduce tutorial workbooks in which students commented on any mistakes they had made and recorded how these had been corrected. Where possible, students also collaborated in problem-solving activities by discussing their own strategies with others. All of these changes were intended to strengthen the connection between the WTPs and the teaching and learning activities taking place, in other words *the inner logic of the subject and its pedagogy*. By making problem-solving strategies more explicit, and emphasizing the importance of thinking actively about the processes involved, students would be more likely to develop the understanding they need.

Establishing the critical features of a concept in computer studies

Marton's variation theory, described in Chapter 2, focuses directly on what a teacher wants students to learn and links that objective to specific approaches to teaching the topic. Within this theory, effective learning depends on being able to discern the critical features of a concept or topic, and to grasp in a holistic way the meaning of the patterns of variation that interconnect them.

> In general, a way of seeing can be characterized in terms of aspects discerned and taken into consideration. Or, even more simply, in terms of a particular pattern of aspects. ... Learning in terms of changes in or widening of our ways of seeing the world can be understood in terms of discernment, simultaneity, and variation. Thanks to the variation, we experience and discern critical aspects of the situations or phenomena we have to handle and, to the extent that these critical aspects are focused on simultaneously, a pattern emerges. ... [In research] there are new dimensions opened up [and] there is always a pattern arrived at eventually [with] meaningful relations between the parts and [the critical] features.
>
> (Bowden & Marton, 1998: 7–9)

These ideas are particularly valuable when dealing with a topic that students find difficult, such as the idea of an *information system* in computer studies. Chris Cope, working with Mike Prosser in Australia, decided to draw on Marton's ideas from both phenomenography and variation theory to find ways of teaching this topic more effectively. Phenomenography involves finding the different conceptions of a topic held by students and discovering the relationships between those conceptions: in so doing, it reveals the critical features as seen by the students. Cope and Prosser used this technique initially, and then reviewed the literature to find how academics described the idea of an 'information system'. In this way its critical features became clear, while the differing conceptions held by students indicated typical misunderstandings that existed. Some students saw an information system simply as a way of retrieving information, while others considered it to be no more than a computer system linking individuals within an organization. However, staff were looking for a much more complex conception that covered gathering, disseminating and communicating the varying kinds of information required to support different activities within an organization.

It was only when students could discern all the critical features and recognize the patterns of variation that allow new situations to be analysed, that they could really understand what an information system means to a computer scientist.

Students who had used surface approaches generally had reached only superficial conceptions, focusing on just one aspect, but those using deep approaches had come closer to the target understanding. A deep approach starts, as always, with an intention to understand for oneself and in this example depended on alertness to the importantly different ways of describing an information system, in other words its critical features. But being able to use a deep approach effectively depends encountering teaching and learning activities that focus on the critical features. Only then will students see the variations in information systems that have led to the concept in its full form, and so understand the purposes of those systems more clearly.

> To improve the quality of students' outcomes, the educationally critical aspects [of information systems] need to become explicit ... in ... the undergraduate curricula, textbooks, teaching strategies and learning activities. Importantly, students need to be aware, from the beginning of their studies, of the nature of the target level of understanding of the concept of an information system and how that understanding can be achieved. ... Learning tasks need to be designed ... [to] make students aware of *the experience of learning about an information system.*
> (Cope & Prosser, 2005: 366, emphasis in original)

In this study, students were asked to draw so-called 'Rich Pictures' to help students see the critical features and pattern of variation among them, using the technique developed by Peter Checkland at Lancaster for investigating the effectiveness of business organizations.

> The complexity of human situations is always one of multiple interacting relationships. A picture is a good way to show relationships, in fact it is a much better medium for that purpose than linear prose. Hence, as knowledge of a situation was assembled, ... [we] began to draw simple pictures of the situation. These became richer as enquiry proceeded ... [and] were found invaluable for expressing crucial relationships ... and [these] could be tabled as a basis for discussion. ... In making a Rich Picture, the aim is to capture, informally, the main entities, structures and viewpoints in the situation, the processes going on, the current recognized issues, and any potential ones.
> (Checkland & Poulter, 2006: 25)

In Cope and Prosser's study, students drew simple images to represent in a visually striking way the various aspects of information systems, with arrows joining the various activities and the nature of the relationships described alongside each link. Looking at the pictures enabled students to see the links between critical features simultaneously, with their meaning then being discussed in groups. In this way, a difficult topic became much easier to understand.

Helping students to understand threshold concepts in economics

The idea of threshold concepts originated in economics, as we saw in Chapter 4, and Peter Davies and Jean Mangan have recently been working with staff in several departments to discover better ways of teaching important concepts. However, initially it proved difficult to decide which of the concepts were really acting as thresholds by opening up the subject in important ways. The problem was resolved by describing different kinds of threshold that students encountered. In the early stages of the degree course, students were meeting *basic concepts* that opened up the subject for them by clarifying their thinking about economic issues, but these concepts were not integrative. Only later did students meet disciplinary *threshold concepts* that linked together several basic concepts, and so affected their ways of thinking more profoundly. By the end of their degree they were facing *procedural thresholds* that showed how knowledge and thinking were brought together to become ways of practising like an economist. Then students were able to identify and analyse novel situations using a range of concepts and simplifying assumptions to construct economic models.

By clarifying these different kinds of threshold, Davies and Mangan were able to suggest four principles designed to help students develop the ways of thinking and practising in economics. Staff were encouraged to:

- Ensure that there is a sufficient foundation of basic concepts to make it possible to work towards the acquisition of threshold concepts;
- Help students to integrate their understanding through re-working ... previously acquired concepts in the light of threshold concepts;
- Expose the way in which scholars in the discipline use procedural thresholds by highlighting the variation in the use of key procedures; and
- Help students to regard their understanding as provisional and to tolerate uncertainty.

One of the main criticisms of the early stages of undergraduate teaching in economics has been its over-reliance on formal lectures, which pass rapidly over a wide range of concepts without allowing students the opportunity to fully understand the meaning of the most important ones. If students are to really understand threshold concepts, a very different approach is needed. Davies and Mangan used variation theory to design learning materials that drew attention to critical features within everyday economic issues and also supported students' attempts to make sense of them in academic terms. Students initially answered several sets of multiple-choice items to show how they had tried to make sense of, for example, 'the economic case for introducing congestion charges'. They were then offered an economist's solution and graphs that represented the situation in terms of basic academic concepts. After trying to make sense of these diagrammatic representations on their own, students were provided with explanations of the economic reasoning involved, to help them evaluate the appropriateness of their own responses. In this way, the students' thinking was being 'scaffolded' (supported by a framework), as they were taken step-by-step through the stages of tackling an economic issue.

A key difference between lecturers' and students' analysis of economic problems lay in the number of different economic ideas which were brought coherently to bear upon the problem. However, the design of an exercise to support students' learning needs to be sensitive to their readiness: how many ideas are they currently capable of bringing together? Diagrams in economics are used to 'bring ideas together', but this may be lost on students who learn diagrams as fixed entities to be deployed in given circumstances, rather than as the expression of a particular set of ideas in a particular context.

(Davies and Mangan, 2008: 46–7)

Students also worked on economic case studies in groups, guided by suggestions about possible theoretical explanations that again helped to scaffold their thinking in the early stages. Finally, they were asked to consider which concepts were crucial to their solutions. All these exercises were intended to wean students away from passive rote learning by making the academic ways of thinking more explicit. The tasks also gave students opportunities to engage with realistic problems through group discussion. The intention behind this teaching was similar to that in analogue electronics, which had involved encouraging students to discuss problems in groups and to think more actively about the processes of problem solving, rather than mindlessly using formulaic routines.

Using concept maps to develop integrative understanding in history

In Chapter 4 we introduced David Hay's idea of *dialogic concept mapping*, which can now be seen as a more elaborate version of Checkland's 'Rich Pictures' with a greater emphasis on narrative explanation. It can be also used to draw attention to critical features and the pattern of variation among them. Hay's idea, as we saw, was to modify the usual concept-mapping procedure by allowing freedom in arranging the structure of the concept map and also by providing opportunities to explain the links between the concepts more fully. The method encourages internal dialogues about the student's existing knowledge of the subject, as well as external dialogues with teachers and other students about what the maps represent. It is thus more than a technique, it offers an important new way of thinking about teaching and learning.

Andrew Dilley, a historian now at Aberdeen University, used this approach while at Kings College, London to discover how his students went about making sense of a history course in which broad themes, such as the idea of Empire, were introduced in a range of differing contexts. A regular complaint from examiners had been that, in their answers to exam questions, students were not engaging with these themes sufficiently well. Dialogic concept mapping provided an opportunity to explore how students' understanding developed, and so suggest how to improve their grasp of the main aims of the course.

Students were asked to draw concept maps on three occasions during their first term at university and the relative complexity of these maps was assessed in terms of their structure (whether the maps showed chains or had a more complex structure – see Figure 6.1), their focus (whether it was on specific information or abstraction) and the nature of the links being made (whether incidental or theoretically important). Students were also asked to write about the meaning of their maps and to describe what they thought they had gained from drawing them. Some of the diagrams showed increases in complexity between the first and third maps, and in the number of concepts included. There were also examples of insightful commentary on the meaning of the maps.

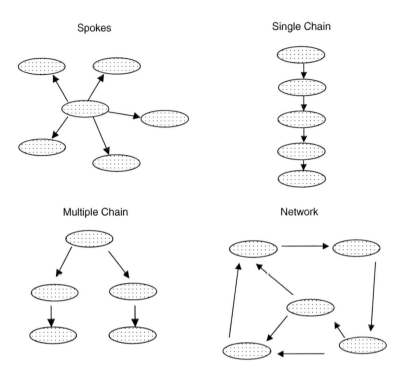

Figure 6.1   Generic concept map structures
Source: Hay, personal communication.

Figure 6.2 provides an example of the changes that occurred in the maps drawn by one of the students, with the structure evolving from a weak network into a more elaborate one, while the nature of the concepts changed from being somewhat vague to being more precise and better informed. They were then

> mostly abstract to do with broad manifestations of empire and the processes under-pinning it. ... Before and after maps show a willingness to think about the processes underpinning the history of Empire. The later map reveals matured reflection, but has many similarities [with the previous one].
>
> (Dilley, personal communication, emphasis added).

Students who produced maps that were well integrated and historically sensitive were more likely to be awarded higher assessment grades than the other students, although this was just a tentative finding. However, students who had drawn such maps at the end of the course had also used a similar structure on the first occasion, suggesting that they already had a way of thinking that enabled them to see the subject in more integrative ways.

Considering the implications of these findings, Dilley suggested that course designers should ensure an explicit focus on the broad themes running through the course and not just on the specific content of topics, again indicating the importance of helping students to achieve an overview of the subject, rather than implicitly inviting more atomistic approaches to learning.

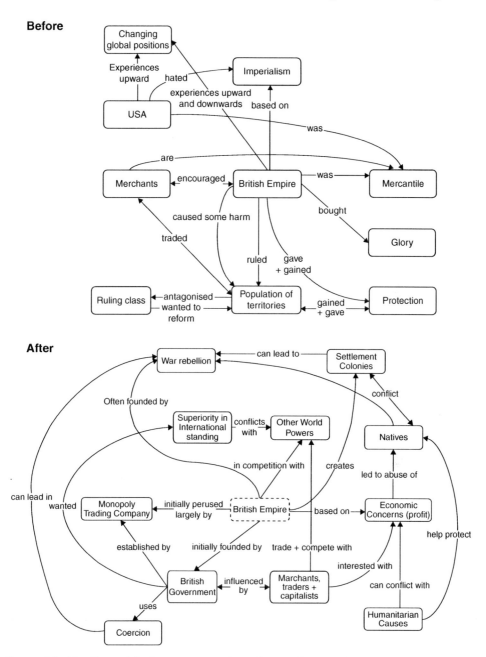

Figure 6.2   The first and third concept maps drawn by a student on a history course
Source: Dilley, personal communication.

▶ The teaching–learning environment as a whole

So far, we have been concentrating on specific sets of teaching and learning activities designed to help students understand particular topics or ways of thinking, but teaching that introduces students to new knowledge and ideas is only part of the process of learning. Commenting on what could be seen as high quality teaching one senior academic in Iceland commented:

> I feel that I have taught well when students are active, asking questions – it is an atmosphere – that they are 'with me'. … But I may have that experience and yet in the exam some students show no understanding, perhaps I didn't get them learning. … So quality in teaching has to depend on how much I get them to learn; and that is not just from teaching, but from the whole teaching–learning environment.
>
> (personal communication, interview by
> Anna Ólafsdóttir, University of Akureyri, Iceland)

Now we move on to the second aspect, that is, how the whole curriculum or teaching–learning environment can encourage and reinforce the idea that understanding is important. We shall use three studies to illustrate research studies that have taken this perspective. Two are taken from research in schools and the other from a university. In the schools, the innovations were intended to apply across subject areas, but at university level the example focuses again on a specific subject area, this time anatomy.

In each study a wider range of influences was arranged coherently to support the types of learning that staff wanted to encourage. But first we ought to consider what a 'teaching–learning environment' actually means. Figure 6.3 illustrates the components found in a typical teaching–learning environment in electronic engineering, along with the main purpose of each pedagogical activity. For completeness, the diagram includes some of the

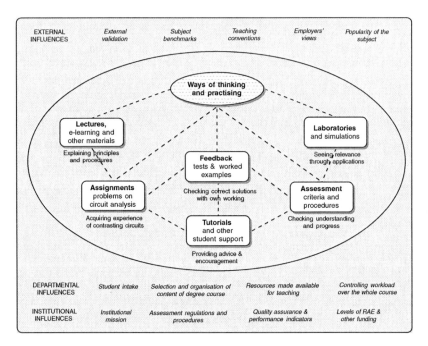

Figure 6.3 A typical teaching–learning environment within electronic engineering
Source: Entwistle, Nisbet & Bromage, 2006: 19.

external, departmental and institutional influences that also play a part, even though these are peripheral to the student's actual experience. The ways of thinking and practising in the subject, shown at the top of the diagram, are not part of the environment itself, but represent the target being set by staff within that environment. And that is the target on which all the teaching and learning activities are supposed congruently and coherently to focus.

Congruence within a teaching–learning environment

In the early stages of the ETL project we were thinking in terms of John Biggs' idea of constructive alignment, but later on we decided to introduce a somewhat broader description to represent the 'goodness-of-fit' between *ways of thinking and practising* in the subject and the whole set of teaching and learning activities provided. The term 'alignment' seemed to imply a straightforward sequential linkage between aims, teaching methods and assessment, whereas we were seeing a complex web of interconnections with a variety of time sequences involved. The idea of *congruence* serves the same purpose in emphasizing that teaching–learning environments act as systems, but allows additional aspects of the teaching–learning environment to be highlighted, in particular students' backgrounds, knowledge and aspirations and the course organization and management (see Figure 6.4).

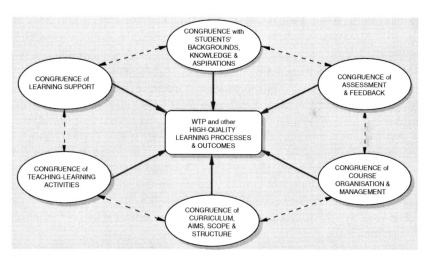

Figure 6.4   Differing forms of congruence within teaching–learning environments
Source: Hounsell & Hounsell, 2007: 101.

▶ Examples of whole teaching–learning environments supporting understanding

Teaching for understanding

As we saw in the Bridge Passage, researchers at Harvard had worked with teachers from a range of school subjects to decide how to change their curricula in ways that would 'put understanding up front', and the project culminated in a *Teaching for Understanding*

Table 6.2   Steps in creating a curriculum designed to teach for understanding

---

- Define *overarching goals* with a particular focus on broad aims for the whole course, related to developing forms of understanding crucial to the subject area.

- Describe and use *throughlines* – setting out the overarching goals in ways which are easy to keep in mind throughout the course and making clear how new topics relate to them.

- Select *generative topics* designed to be sufficiently open-ended to provoke thought and encourage active discussion.

- Design *understanding performances*, assignments that both develop and assess understanding. These are set at differing levels to suit the class and lead to 'culminating performances' that demonstrate how students' previous understandings interconnect.

- Specify *assessment criteria* that are closely related to the understanding goals, with frequent opportunities for feedback to help students improve their understanding.

- Encourage students to discuss their work among themselves and to revise drafts, culminating in a self-evaluation of the final product.

---

framework that progressively focused teachers' activities onto 'understanding'. The steps that teachers were encouraged to take, as described by Martha Stone Wiske, are outlined in Table 6.2. The starting point was setting up clearly defined *overarching goals*, stated in terms of the understandings expected, which were kept firmly in the students' minds through the use of *throughlines*, broad ideas or questions running through the whole course, about which students were regularly reminded. Teachers then devised open-ended *generative topics* that would provide opportunities for student activities and discussion.

> *Throughlines* need to capture the essence of a whole course … [and] are often rooted in deeply held but rarely articulated beliefs and values about both the subject matter and the teaching and learning processes. … They help students see the purposes that underlie their daily work, make connections among various topics and assignments, and track their own developing understandings.

> *Generative topics* are issues, themes, concepts, ideas, and so on that provide enough depth, significance, connections, and variety of perspective to support students' development of powerful understandings. … Generative topics … are central to one or more disciplines or domains, they are interesting … [and] accessible to students.
>
> (Blythe et al., 1998: pp. 18, 25, 41)

Examples of generative topics were 'The meaning of justice', or 'The definition of life', or 'How nineteenth century workplaces differed from current ones', while throughlines included questions like 'How does land shape human culture?', 'How do we find out "*the truth*" about things that happened long ago?', and 'How do we see through the bias in sources?' Such questions helped students to see important linkages between the topics and concepts they had met during the course.

Within the topics, assignments were chosen to encourage students to think critically and use evidence in trying to reach their own conclusions. These *understanding performances* developed students' own understanding, while their 'culminating perform-ances' were intended to show links with the overarching goals of the course. The main advantage of the framework, overall, is that

> it doesn't focus on just one aspect of the learning environment provided for students; it treats the curriculum as an interacting whole in its effects on learning. And this framework has been extensively used world-wide through setting up a web site to help teachers to apply its principles to their own practice.
>
> (http://learnweb.harvard.edu/ent/workshop/ccdt_framework.cfm)

This framework provides one of the most striking examples of an overall approach to curriculum reform that concentrates on helping students to achieve academically sound, personal understanding.

Powerful learning environments

The *Teaching for Understanding* framework showed teachers how to create conditions for learning that had a consistent focus on understanding, but the framework played down the role of expository teaching. In Europe, similar attempts have been made to develop a coherent set of conditions to encourage understanding, but with teachers actively showing students how to develop their learning strategies. Erik De Corte, at Leuven University in Belgium, based his approach on the psychological theory of *cognitive apprenticeship*, which sees the roles of teacher and student as analogous to master craftsman and apprentice. The teacher provides initial instruction and skill training, but then encourages students to become independent in their learning within what was called a *powerful learning environment* (see Table 6.3).

In such classrooms, there is a good deal in common with what is provided within the Harvard system, with an emphasis on open problems to arouse interest and provoke discussion. However, direct teaching is used extensively to model the thinking processes and learning strategies students are expected to follow. Students are also provided with step-by-step instructions to 'scaffold' effective learning strategies, but this support is then progressively removed to ensure that the students begin to use the strategies

Table 6.3 Teaching and learning activities creating powerful learning environments

---

- Provide authentic, open problems with learning materials in a variety of formats designed to make connections with students' previous knowledge and interests.

- Use teaching methods which arouse interest, activate prior knowledge, clarify meanings and model appropriate thinking strategies and reflective processes.

- Specify learning strategies in detail to provide *scaffolding*, with the guidance then gradually removed to encourage subsequent self-regulation of studying.

- Encourage students to monitor their own strategies and discuss these with other students, to produce a classroom culture that encourages reflection on process.

---

independently. They are also encouraged, increasingly, to monitor the effectiveness of their own learning and studying by themselves, adjusting their learning processes where necessary to achieve their goals, so becoming 'metacognitive' about their approaches to learning. Staff are urged regularly to discuss how people learn and so create a culture within which students feel more ready to explain to each other how they go about their own learning.

Powerful learning environments include several of the ideas introduced in the earlier examples of innovations in this chapter, particularly the choice of authentic, open problems and issues that engaged students' interest and invited the open discussion of meaning. But this approach also introduces the training of specific learning strategies, as they are required. Timing training in this way generally seems to be crucial to its effectiveness.

Designing a whole curriculum to encourage deep approaches

Whole curricula developed out of research findings or pedagogical theory are uncommon in higher education, where it is more usual to find innovations in specific methods of teaching or the use of new technology. In Australia, however, Norman Eizenberg was involved in helping an anatomy department to redesign its whole curriculum in response to Marton's ideas about approaches to learning. Owing to the sheer volume of rote learning entailed, students often find anatomy difficult, although this may be more a reflection of the teaching methods than the subject itself.

> The study of human anatomy may be attempted in either of two ways. One consists of collecting facts and memorizing them. The other way consists in correlating the facts, that is studying them in their mutual relationships. This leads inevitably to the apprehending of the underlying principles involved and the 'raison d-être' of such relationships. The student will thus learn to reason anatomically and will find the acquisition of new and related facts an easier task.
>
> (Grant, 1937, quoted by Eizenberg, 1988: 180)

Staff in this department realized that they had been following a traditional approach to teaching anatomy and decided to change their curriculum fundamentally, so as to encourage deep approaches to learning. The main changes they made are shown in Table 6.4, alongside the reasons for making them. To reduce students' reliance on rote learning, each element in the syllabus was given a 'star' rating to indicate how essential it was. The main change, however, was in the teaching, which was to put much greater emphasis on general anatomical principles and on explaining all topics in the course in relation to those organizing ideas.

Eizenberg was one of the first to argue that all the elements of the teaching–learning environment had to work together if deep approaches were to be effectively supported. He believed that even one important aspect out in line with the main aims could prevent the desired effects on learning.

> Since the interaction between the learner and the learning environment depends on perceptions ... the challenge in any educational programme is to prevent misperception and mismatch. ... Inappropriate approaches to learning are simply induced

Table 6.4 Changes introduced into an anatomy curriculum

Changes introduced in the curriculum	with the purpose of
Course content and structure	
Linking to faculty goals explicitly	making the aims clear to staff and students
Matching curriculum, teaching, assessment	keeping all teaching in line with aims
Incorporating applications in the syllabus	making the subject explicitly relevant
Identifying the essential knowledge	limiting the pressure on memorization
Selecting appropriate textbooks	ensuring understanding was encouraged
Teaching	
Analysing the derivation of new terms	showing meaning rather than just definition
Emphasizing principles and concepts	encouraging linking facts with principles
Using recent graduates as tutors	reducing authority and formality
Focusing on problem-based discussions	actively engaging students in the issues
Assessment	
Providing trial oral exams with feedback	reducing the stress otherwise experienced
Using structured assessment tasks	enabling students to monitor progress
Helping staff to assess open answers	rewarding understanding through marking

Source: Eizenberg, 1988: 186

> by teaching: just one piece of the 'jigsaw' that is out of place ... may interfere with the relation between the learner and the content. ... Encouraging students to adopt deep approaches and to employ them holistically is ... difficult because [all] the pieces need to fit together.
>
> (Eizenberg, 1988: 196–7)

Students appreciated the changes introduced into this anatomy course and staff found that the students afterwards showed a firmer grasp of the subject as a whole. This example shows how an influential research finding can help university teachers see their teaching in a new light, leading to important changes in how they plan the curriculum as a whole.

▶ Concluding summary

This main purpose in this chapter was to illustrate how teachers, working with educational researchers, can adapt theoretical ideas about encouraging understanding to the specific needs of their own subject or topic areas. The starting point was to explain the origin of the idea of an *inner logic of the subject and its pedagogy*. This concept underlines the crucial importance of taking into account the differing kinds of understandings and ways of thinking that are found across contrasting disciplines and professional areas. In the examples which followed we addressed the apparent paradox between the existence of general principles of teaching and learning, and yet a need for subject specificity. It became clear how a theory, or an earlier research finding, could be reinterpreted to suggest teaching innovations within a particular subject area or departmental setting.

Initially, we saw how several teaching and learning activities can be brought together to encourage students to help them think more consciously and strategically about the processes of problem solving in analogue electronics. Concept maps have been used in history to help students to broaden their own understanding by reflection, and also through discussion with other students and feedback from the teacher. While experienced students find it relatively easy to discern and make sense of the critical features of the topics or concepts they meet, other students find this process much more difficult. Variation theory has been used to help students understand the complexity of the concept of an 'information system'. It has also been used to design learning materials that help students come to terms with threshold concepts in economics that integrate lower-level concepts.

The next step was to consider how research could contribute to using a whole curriculum or teaching–learning environment to foster student understanding. Research in schools pointed up well-established ideas of teaching through arousing interest, clarifying meanings, scaffolding new skills and strategies for students and modelling thinking strategies and reflective processes. It also showed the value of designing *understanding performances* that both developed and demonstrated understanding, and of creating classroom cultures that made discussion of learning processes an accepted part of classroom activity. Reviewing a whole curriculum seems to be essential to ensure that a deep approach is consistently encouraged; even one component out of kilter with the rest may divert students from that goal.

These ideas need to be kept in mind as we move into Part 4, where we consider the idea of a teaching–learning environment in a more systematic and practical way. A heuristic model of teaching and learning in higher education will be used to point up some of the critical features that influence the quality of student learning. Those aspects are then considered in turn, focusing initially on the characteristics of the learners, then on the organization and presentation of the content and finally on the other aspects of the learning environment that influence the approaches to studying used by students.

▷ Further reading

Biggs, J. B. (2003). *Teaching for Quality Learning at University.* (2nd edn) Buckingham: SRHE & Open University Press (now available as a third edn, 2007).

De Corte, E., Verschaffel, L., Entwistle, N. J. & van Merriënboer, J. (eds) (2003). *Powerful Learning Environments: Unravelling Basic Components and Dimensions.* Oxford: Pergamon.

Hay, D. B. & Entwistle, N. J. (under consideration). 'Ideas Made Personal: Visualising and Explaining Understanding through Dialogic Concept Mapping', *British Journal of Educational Psychology.*

Hounsell, D. J., & Entwistle N J. (2005). 'Enhancing Teaching–Learning Environments in Undergraduate Courses', final report on the ETL project to the ESRC and TLRP, retrievable at http://www.tlrp.org/.

McCune, V. & Hounsell, D. J. (2005). 'The Development of Students' Ways of Thinking and Practising in Three Final-Year Biology Courses', *Higher Education*, 49, 255–89.

Novak, J. D. (1998). *Learning, Creating and Using Knowledge: Concept Maps as Facilitative Tools in Schools and Corporations.* Mawah, NJ: Lawrence Erlbaum.

O'Brien, M. (2008). 'Threshold Concepts for University Teaching and Learning: A Study of Troublesome Knowledge and Transformative Thinking in the Teaching of Threshold Concepts', in J. H. F. Meyer, R. Land & J. Smith (eds) *Threshold Concepts in the Disciplines* (pp. 289–306). Netherlands: Sense Publishers.

O'Brien, M. (2008). *Teaching as Translation: An Investigation of University Teachers' Pedagogical Content Knowledge, Reasoning and Intention*, doctoral thesis, School of Education and Professional Studies, Griffith University, Australia.

Wiske, M. S. (ed.) (1998). *Teaching for Understanding: Linking Research with Practice.* San Francisco: Jossey-Bass.

▶ References relating to quotations

Blythe, T. and associates (1998). *The 'Teaching for Understanding' Guide.* San Francisco: Jossey-Bass.

Bowden, J. & Marton, F. (1998). *The University of Learning: Beyond Quality and Competence in Higher Education.* London: Kogan Page.

Checkland, P. & Poulter, J. (2006). *Learning for Action: A Short Definitive Account of Soft Systems Methodology and its Use for Practitioners, Teachers and Students.* Chichester: Wiley.

Cope, C. & Prosser, M. (2005). 'Identifying Didactic Knowledge: An Empirical Study of the Educationally Critical Aspects of Learning About Information Systems', *Higher Education*, 49, 345–72.

Davies, P. & Mangan, J. (2008). 'Embedding Threshold Concepts: From Theory to Pedagogical Principles to Learning Activities', in R. Land, J. H. F. Meyer & J. Smith (eds) *Threshold Concepts within the Disciplines* (pp. 37–50). Rotterdam: Sense Publishers.

Eizenberg, N. (1988). 'Approaches to Learning Anatomy: Developing a Programme for Preclinical Medical Students', in P. Ramsden (ed.) *Improving Learning: New Perspectives* (pp. 178–98). London: Kogan Page.

Entwistle, N. J., Nisbet, J. B. & Bromage, A. (2006). *ETL Subject Area Report on Electronic Engineering* on the project web site at www.etl.tla.ed.ac.uk/publications. html.

Hounsell, D. J., & Hounsell, J. (2007). 'Teaching–Learning Environments in Contemporary Mass Higher Education', in N. J. Entwistle & P. D. Tomlinson (eds) *Student Learning and University Teaching* (pp. 91–111). Leicester: British Psychological Society.

Shulman, L. (2005). 'The Signature Pedagogies of the Professions of Law, Medicine, Engineering and the Clergy: Potential Lessons for the Education of Teachers', paper presented at a workshop held at the US National Research Council's Center for Education, 6–8 February 2005, and posted at the website of the Carnegie Foundation for the Advancement of Teaching at http://hub.mspnet/index.cfm/11172.

Part 4

Providing Teaching and Assessment to Support Learning

A Heuristic Model of Teaching and Learning

In the 1970s, Lee Cronbach and Richard Snow in the USA introduced a new research field into educational psychology called aptitude-treatment interaction. Previously, research into learning had looked for general cognitive processes, while research into ability and personality concentrated on finding a variety of traits. Research into memory and learning was carried out with small samples under controlled experimental conditions, while ability and aptitudes were investigated though large-scale surveys using tests or questionnaires that related to everyday experience. Cronbach and Snow brought the two approaches together, recognizing that learning could not be seen as independent of either different aptitudes or contrasting ways of teaching. And this idea was broadened even further as abilities and personality characteristics were found to be affected, to a greater extent than originally expected, not just by experiences but by people's ways of interpreting them.

> When we describe ... current behaviour in terms of person-situation interaction processes, ... the problem is not how the person and the situation, as two separate parts, ... interact. It is, rather, ... how individuals, by their perceptions, thoughts, and feelings, function in relation to their environment ... [including their] conceptions of the external world ... [and their] self-conceptions.
>
> (Magnusson, 1984: 231)

At that time, no systematic attempt had been made to describe environments in detail. While research into ability and personality had identified many different characteristics, there had been no equivalent attempt to discover which aspects of the environment were affecting human development or learning. And that seemed to be a necessary next step in our own research.

The work carried out into student learning by the 1980s had already shown links between approaches to learning and perceptions of various aspects of teaching, and so it was possible to use this research, along with the new ideas in psychology, to describe the complex set of influences on learning in university settings. Around the same time, a colleague of mine in Lancaster, Peter Checkland, was developing *soft systems analysis* as a way of analysing business organizations. He argued that effective change depended on analysing businesses as whole interacting systems, identifying problems and weaknesses and then negotiating with staff the types of change most likely to improve the situation. This approach seemed to offer possibilities for describing teaching and learning in higher education as part of an interacting system and looking for improvements.

A first step involved mapping the main influences on learning within an overall framework. The result was a 'heuristic model' of influences on learning within higher

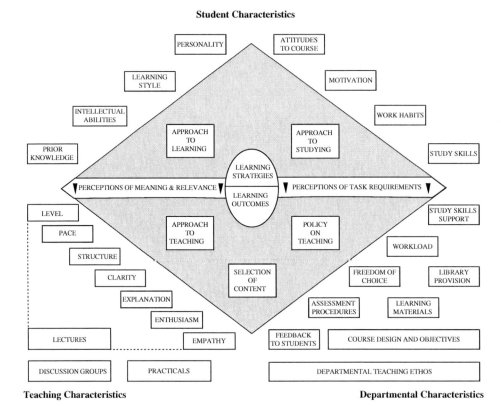

Figure 7.1   A heuristic model indicating influences on student learning
Source: Adapted from Entwistle, 1987: 23.

education (Figure 7.1). It was 'heuristic' in the sense that it was designed to guide thinking, rather than as a computable model to predict the outcomes of learning. The framework draws attention to four main influences on learning – the characteristics of students, the nature of the subject matter, the teaching carried out by staff and the learning environment provided by the department. The top half of the model shows the characteristics of students, with the relatively more consistent individual differences, such as abilities and personality, shown on the left, and those more likely to be affected by experience, like attitudes and study skills, on the right. The lower half of the model describes influences on learning coming from approaches to teaching on the left and the learning environment on the right, with selection of content being placed between them. Aspects of teaching that help students to learn were positioned, as far as possible, so as to suggest links with the student characteristics immediately above them. For example, 'level' is immediately below 'prior knowledge', 'pace' below 'intellectual abilities', and 'study skills support' under 'study skills'. Such direct linkages could not, however, be established for all the aspects shown.

The connections between students' characteristics and approaches to teaching are shown across the centre of the model through their *perceptions of meaning and relevance*, while those from teaching policies are linked with *perceptions of task requirements*.

John Biggs developed a similar model of teaching and learning as a system. He introduced a *3P model* – **p**resage, **p**rocess and **p**roduct – that was based on the three stages found in bringing about learning. It described what comes before learning takes place, namely prior knowledge, study habits and the teaching arrangements; the strategies students use while learning; and the outcome of these strategies. The main purpose of each of these models was to provoke reflection and discussion about the nature of the subtle interactions that, together, influence the quality of student learning.

Figure 7.1 reflected the state of research into student learning in the late 1980s, but since then much more has been learned about how teaching–learning environments affect the quality of student learning, as we have seen in earlier chapters. Following these developments, the model evolved through various forms, leading eventually to the version shown in Figure 7.2. This diagram shows a similar pattern to the earlier

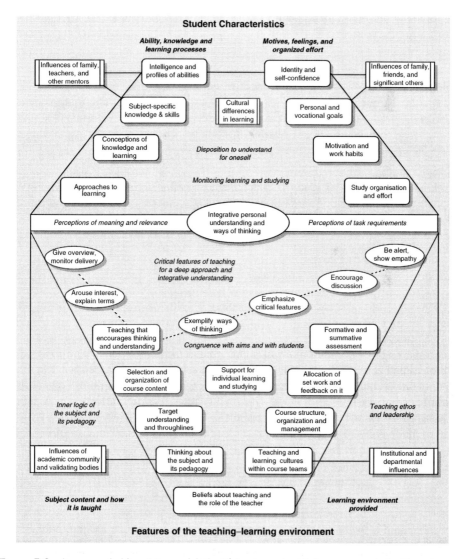

Figure 7.2   An expanded heuristic model identifying important influences on student learning

one, with student characteristics in the upper half and the influences of teaching and the learning environment below, but it became more complex as new influences were added. The separation of teaching from the rest of the teaching–learning environment can now be justified in terms of the *inner logic of the subject and its pedagogy* that binds together content and teaching approaches. Certain parts of the overall teaching–learning environment are certainly more directly related to the actual subject content than others, and these are shown down the left-hand side of the model. The influences from the rest of the learning environment are indicated on the other side, although some of these, like assessment, also involve content.

The labels given to the various boxes cannot indicate the specific ways in which each component of the model influences student learning or suggest how teaching and learning activities affect their outcome. The ideas presented in the previous chapters, along with suggestions coming from other research and professional experience, will be used in the next two chapters to tease out some of the practical implications for teaching and learning. These will still not describe 'what works' or indicate 'best practice' in any general way for reasons already made clear, but they do open up discussion about which specific teaching and learning activities are most likely to encourage the forms of understanding and ways of thinking and practising being developed within particular degree courses or course units.

Admittedly, the diagram is too complex to be easily understood as a whole (and even too small to be easily read), and so each part of the model will be considered separately over the next two chapters. At this stage in the book, a fuller referencing system is being introduced to make it easier to track down more detailed descriptions of the main studies and methods of teaching being discussed.

▶ References

Biggs, J. B. (1978). 'Individual and Group Differences in Study Processes', *British Journal of Educational Psychology*, 48, 266–79.

Biggs, J. B. (1993). 'From Theory to Practice: A Cognitive Systems Approach', *Higher Education Research and Development*, 12, 73–86.

Checkland, P. (1981). *Systems Thinking, Systems Practice*. London: Wiley.

Cronbach, L. J. & Snow, R. E. (1977). *Aptitudes and Instructional Methods: A Handbook of Research on Interactions*. New York: Irvington.

Entwistle, N. J. (1987). 'A Model of the Teaching–Learning Process', in J. T. E. Richardson, M. W. Eysenck & D. Warren Piper (eds) *Student Learning: Research in Education and Cognitive Psychology* (pp. 13–28). Buckingham: SRHE & Open University Press.

Entwistle, N. J. (2003). 'Concepts and Conceptual Frameworks Underpinning the ETL Project', Occasional Report 3 from the ETL Project, accessible at www.tla.ed.ac.uk/etl.

Magnusson, D. (1984). 'The Situation in an Interactional Paradigm of Personality Research', in V. Sarris & A. Parducci (eds) *Perspectives in Psychological Experimentation: Towards the Year 2000* (pp. 211–33). Hillsdale, NJ: Erlbaum.

7 Research Guiding Teaching

In previous chapters we have been using research findings to suggest a way of thinking about teaching and learning that can help with decisions about how to teach in specific subject areas. This chapter, and the next, look again at some of the many influences on student learning, starting with a brief review of differences among students, and continuing with a more detailed consideration of how teaching affects learning. We have covered many of the aspects already, so these are summarized briefly; others are described more fully to fill out the overall picture presented in the heuristic model.

▶ Student characteristics influencing learning

Figure 7.3 shows the top half of the full heuristic model from the Bridge Passage to remind us of the main concepts introduced in earlier chapters. The left-hand side shows abilities, knowledge and learning processes, while the other side brings in feelings, motives and organized effort. It is impossible to point out all the interconnections between the various concepts, but intelligence, profiles of abilities and subject-specific knowledge and skills are all strongly affected by family, teachers and other mentors, as well as by the wider culture. Experiences within the family also affect identity, self-confidence and personal and vocational goals, but these are also strongly influenced by friends and peers. Individual teachers and the teaching ethos of a school can also affect the willingness to learn, and those influences continue in higher education. The other characteristics in Figure 7.3, like conceptions of learning and motivation, are more directly linked to experiences of teaching and the learning environment at university, and so represent even stronger influences.

Of course, it is impossible to bear all these characteristics in mind while teaching, or even in planning a course, although they may be needed when advising, or guiding, an individual student. Generally, university teachers have to think in terms of groups of students for whom only a profile of characteristics can be known, and so simplifying assumptions have to be made. University teachers will usually find out from experience the range of their students' abilities and prior knowledge, but research findings suggest that other aspects are at least as important. In planning teaching, it may also be useful to think about how to develop a *disposition to understand* in your students, and the alertness necessary for *monitoring learning and studying* for themselves. These characteristics are likely to have a strong overall effect on producing a deep approach to learning and thus lead the way towards integrative personal understanding. But this will happen only if the teaching and the learning environment consistently support these forms of learning and understanding.

We now come to the bottom line of the diagram, which forms the interface between the student characteristics and the teaching–learning environment. The cognitive elements on the left side affect most directly students' perceptions of the meaning and relevance within

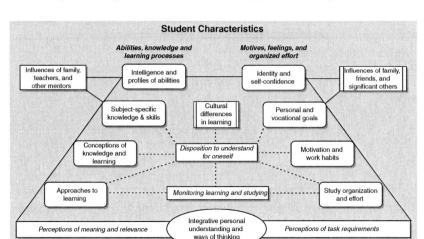

Figure 7.3 Student characteristics influencing learning

the teaching, while motives and organized effort are more closely linked to their perceptions of the task requirements. The ellipse at the centre represents the high quality learning that is a consistent goal of university education, and that should lead to a continuing disposition to develop understanding further and to seek ways of using that understanding in creative ways as Perkins (2008) argues.

One limitation in the model is that it presents a static view of what is a continuing process. Students go through repeated cycles of learning as they try to understand the content they meet. These cycles involve distinct phases in learning, for example, preparing to tackle the course material, acquiring the necessary information, relating it to previous knowledge, practising new skills and working on assignments that bring together ideas into integrative personal understanding whenever time and opportunity allow. These activities, and the balance among them, will naturally differ across subject areas and among students, but each phase needs to be actively encouraged and supported through the teaching provided, in ways we come to now.

▶ Subject content and how it is taught

Figure 7.4 shows the lower left-hand side of the overall heuristic model. The external influences in this part of the diagram come from the academic community and also from validating bodies in professional areas. Just as there are different phases in student learning, so are there logical phases in thinking about teaching, bound together by the inner logic of the subject and its pedagogy. Initially, there is a logical progression from the bottom to the top of our model describing phases involved in planning a course and teaching it. Thinking about the subject and its pedagogy stems from fundamental beliefs about teaching and the role of the teacher. Together these influence the target understandings set, the form of any 'throughlines' offered to students and the selection and organization of course content. Then come decisions about how best to carry out the teaching.

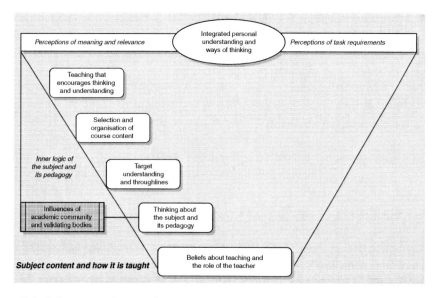

Figure 7.4   Influences on learning from the subject and how it is taught

Once we reach this stage, there is another logical sequence, which suggests some of the key teaching and learning activities (see Table 7.1) that follow the phases of learning described earlier.

Although this set of teaching and learning activities offers a handy 'check-list' of steps in supporting learning, it cannot show how to bring together the parts into a meaningful whole. Teaching is not just a set of activities; much more is involved. The 'excellent'

Table 7.1   Activities designed to support each phase of a student's learning cycle

• **orientating**	setting the scene and explaining what is required
• **structuring**	providing a 'map' of the knowledge within the subject domain
• **motivating**	pointing up relevance, evoking interest and encouraging effort
• **presenting**	introducing new knowledge within a clear logical progression
• **explaining**	clarifying important ideas, with examples to promote understanding
• **elaborating**	providing other material to broaden and deepen understanding
• **guiding**	making clear how to use that material to develop understanding
• **stimulating**	encouraging individual reflection, along with group discussion
• **consolidating**	providing opportunities to develop and test personal understanding
• **commenting**	offering clear and timely advice about completed work
• **supporting**	giving encouragement and bolstering confidence whenever needed
• **confirming**	ensuring the adequacy of the knowledge and understanding reached

university teachers, mentioned in Chapter 5, emphasized the need for academic rigour in teaching at a level appropriate for the students, but also saw themselves as conveying feelings, arousing interest and creating a supportive learning ethos, all based on their beliefs about what is involved in learning at university.

That brings us back to our model of teaching, and using it to draw together research findings and the experiences of outstanding university teachers to think about the stages involved in planning a course and teaching it. These will be considered with a continuing concern about what is likely to encourage integrative personal under-standing. We shall need to keep in mind that teaching is not just a matter of 'giving' students knowledge and ideas but also showing them how to think in disciplinarily appropriate ways, and encouraging the development of a disposition to understand for oneself.

▶ Planning a course

This section looks, in turn, at the four aspects within the heuristic model relating to planning a course, before moving on to consider ways of ensuring that the teaching itself promotes high quality learning.

Beliefs about the role of the teacher

In designing a course, several issues have to be considered, many of which can be looked at through the lens of research findings. Course teams obviously have to discuss which topics are to be included and in what sequence; they also need to think about how this material should be taught, for example, through lectures or through materials for independent study, on the net or through book lists. Then there are issues about who should be respon-sible for each topic, about providing opportunities for collaborative working or discussion groups and so on.

There may well be substantial differences of opinion underlying such discussions about the nature of the subject and how it should be taught (Hativa & Goodyear, 2002; O'Brien, 2008a). In Chapter 5 we highlighted the differing beliefs of lecturers about the nature of teaching and the role of the teacher, whether seen from the perspective of the subject specialist – a *teacher-focus* – or with a *student-focus* that placed more emphasis on the students' conceptual development and understanding. Course teams are unlikely to discuss openly their views about the role of the university teacher or their own learning styles (preferred ways of learning), and that may lead to misunderstandings and disagree-ments. Also, if lecturers rely entirely on their own preferred styles of learning, these are unlikely to suit the wide range of preferences existing among students for learning in, say, serialist or holist ways (Pask, 1988). Holists are much more likely to respond to the whole picture and to the personalizing of subject matter, while serialists prefer step-by-step progression and clear logical developments. Of course, it is implausible to offer alter-native pathways, but we can cater for both preferences within the teaching and supportive learning materials provided (Entwistle, 1988). This alertness to such differences among students is one facet of teaching that is 'multipli-inclusive' (Entwistle & Walker, 2002 and Chapter 5).

Discussion among colleagues of approaches to teaching is clearly desirable, but increasing time pressures make it difficult to fit in meetings where fundamental issues of pedagogy can be explored. Yet they offer an important way of sharing innovative ideas.

> When university teachers start looking at their colleagues' ways of dealing with the same content that they themselves have taught, and when ways of dealing with content become a topic of conversation for them, then an important step towards the improvement of university teaching and learning will have been taken.
>
> (Marton, 2007: 28)

Course teams often arrange informal meetings that could be used for this purpose, while general reviews of departmental teaching create an opportunity for discussing the kinds of teaching and learning needed to encourage a deep approach to learning in that subject. This was what Eizenberg (1988) and his colleagues did in revising their anatomy curriculum (see Chapter 6).

Thinking about the subject and its pedagogy

The model shows a direct link between thinking about the subject and the traditions of teaching within the academic community, again drawing attention to the inner logic of the subject and its pedagogy. Besides sharing ideas with colleagues, it is helpful to think carefully about the nature of learning in the discipline and how students come to understand it. A good starting point is to talk to students about their ways of studying to make sure that what is involved is clear from the student's perspective. The whole thrust of the research into student learning has been to try to shift the way of thinking about teaching and learning away from a teacher-focus or 'transmission' model to a student-focus, one that emphasizes active student involvement in their own conceptual development. And that is what outstanding university teachers already say they are doing, as Bain (2004) reported from an extensive interview study in the USA.

> We found that our subjects have at least an intuitive understanding of human learning akin to the ideas that have emerged from research in the learning sciences. ... They often use the same language, concepts, and ways of characterizing learning that we found in the literature. While others, for example, talk about transmitting knowledge and building a storehouse of information in the students' brains, our subjects talk about helping learners to grapple with ideas and information to construct their understanding. Even their conceptions of what it means to learn in a particular course, bears the mark of this distinction. While others might be satisfied if students perform well on the examinations, the best teachers assume that learning has little meaning unless it produces a sustained and substantial influence on the way people think, act, and feel.
>
> (Bain, 2004: 16–17)

Paul Walker (discussed in Bridge into Chapter 5) described a similar view when explaining his approach to teaching physics.

> I wanted to share with my students my realization that knowledge … could be seen as a collection of models of the world, invented by individuals, rather than as indisputable facts, which had to be swallowed like so much castor oil. … This outlook [proved] … to be a potentially powerful catalyst for stimulating interest and inquiry among my students. … It did not imply the need for a radical change in the curriculum, but simply sought to engender inquiry in the broad majority of students, rather than in the small minority who may already have happened upon it. … I began to design and use questions in class to foster engagement, rather than … obtaining the 'right answer' from those who already knew it. Responding to students' questions (and to the 'questions behind the questions') in ways which encouraged critical thought and dialogue, was equally important … to keep directing attention to issues that are just beyond the current horizon of students' awareness and thus stimulate an expansion of that awareness.
>
> (Entwistle & Walker, 2002: 28–9)

▶ Target understanding and throughlines

'Target understanding' is used here as shorthand for what staff expect students to learn. In some subject areas students have to reach conceptions that are closely similar to those of the teacher, but in others, independent interpretations are the target. In most disciplines evidence of such critical thinking is valued, but within accepted explanatory frameworks.

In Britain the initial framework for deciding what to include in a degree course has been provided by 'benchmark' statements decided for each major subject area by working parties organized by the Quality Assurance Agency. As their website explains:

> Subject benchmark statements set out expectations about standards of degrees in a range of subject areas. They describe what gives a discipline its coherence and identity, and define what can be expected of a graduate in terms of the abilities and skills needed to develop understanding or competence in the subject. Subject benchmark statements do not represent a national curriculum in a subject area, rather they allow for flexibility and innovation in programme design, within an overall conceptual framework established by an academic subject community.
>
> (QAA, 2008)

These benchmark statements are now familiar reference points in the planning of new courses and the revision of old ones, although they concentrate only on minimum degree requirements. Building on these guidelines, the specific ways of thinking and practising in the discipline can then be used to guide subsequent planning. The curricula in professional areas necessarily reflect the requirements of the validating bodies, some of which exert considerable influence on the content. The sense of what counts as 'good teaching', however, is usually developed informally through experience and discussion among colleagues. And it is this sense of the nature of the subject and how it should be taught that reflects the inner logic of the subject and its pedagogy.

Quality assurance procedures in British universities now generally require staff to use a common framework in producing *intended learning outcomes* for every course unit. However, as already argued, this procedure may fragment students' ways of perceiving what has to be learned. The procedure was introduced to create more uniformity in course descriptions and to increase efficiency in higher education, but has had unintended consequences. Behaviourist psychologists were the first to argue for the use of precisely defined behavioural objectives to shape students' learning. Later there was an attempt to describe academic and professional learning in terms of similarly narrow 'competences', which lost the sense of how these came together to produce the essence of professional competence (Bowden & Marton, 1998). Intended learning outcomes follow this same path, as part of a process that controls and, as a consequence, restricts outstanding teaching. The advantage in making clear what has to be learned is unarguable, but in some degree courses students face literally hundreds of such descriptions of the component outcomes, which encourages students to 'tick the boxes' and move on. In so doing they are left with no real sense of what the underlying nature of the discipline involves and may also fail to use past knowledge to build up integrative understandings. James (2005), among others, has spelt out the disadvantages of this narrow approach.

> Although learning outcomes can be useful, their adoption for the purposes of control has distorted them so that they become vacuous … at best useless, at worst damaging. The key objections are (1) that learning outcomes have a largely spurious clarity, explicitness and objectivity; (2) that they bring to bear an unwarranted homogeneity across academic disciplines, which have within them different ideas of level and necessarily different concepts of what skills are appropriate at what stage; (3) that they can, and in all likelihood do, restrict learning, either by helping students to aim at only threshold passes, or by undervaluing all-important emergent, less predictable educational outcomes.
>
> (James, 2005: 89)

The ETL project suggested that it would be better to focus more broadly on the ways of thinking and practising (WTPs) found in the discipline or professional area (Entwistle, 2006; Hounsell & Anderson, 2008). The *Teaching for Understanding* (TfU) report argued along similar lines for 'overarching goals' to provide an overall framework within which to develop school curricula (Wiske, 1998). Some of the teachers in this study began their planning by producing a concept map to show how the various topics related to each other, and this strategy has also proved useful in higher education (Hay, 2007). Multiple interconnections within such a map draw attention to clusters of concepts that play an important role in understanding a topic and may also indicate the presence of threshold concepts.

Table 7.2 draws on the *TfU* framework to suggest how target understandings might be presented to students. Its intention is to put the emphasis on broad aims, rather than specific, lower-level processes and objectives, and on repeatedly reminding students about the main purposes of the course. It also indicates how the course requirements and the teaching and learning activities reflect those aims.

Table 7.2   Ways of emphasizing the broader aims of a module

- Explain how the module relates to the overall degree programme, why the area covered is important, and what makes it interesting.

- Introduce the main ideas and ways of thinking in the module as an overview to show how they interrelate and also link with the more general WTPs of the discipline.

- Develop these aims further in the course handbook by introducing *throughlines* in the form of broad questions that will provide a continuing thread for the module.

- Introduce *generative topics*, or intriguing issues, that encourage students to take a broader view and to think critically, particularly in coursework assignments.

- If 'intended learning outcomes' are used, make them subordinate to the overall purposes of the module and to the main intellectual and professional issues covered.

Selection and organization of course content

Because they know the subject so well, university teachers often argue that they <u>have</u> to include all the main aspects of a topic to ensure 'thorough coverage'. But the sheer volume of content may then obscure the essential features of the subject through an overemphasis on detail or incidental aspects or confusing qualifications. Staff themselves may well feel better about having given a full exposition of the topic, but what really matters is the general level of understanding reached by the students. Critical questions need to be asked about how appropriate each topic or concept is at that stage of the degree course and how much time will be needed for the majority of students to grasp these ideas thoroughly. It is also worth considering whether the content has to be presented during lectures or can be made part of required, and monitored, independent work by the students. One way of dealing with 'coverage' was described in the preceding chapter, where a star rating was used with anatomy students to indicate the relative importance of each part of the syllabus, thus allowing students to allocate time and effort for themselves more efficiently.

In the sciences especially, the continued introduction of new material has meant that many students struggle to keep up with the pace and volume of material presented. Some science students, for example, describe substantially *delayed understanding* (Scheja, 2007), due to the pace and volume of material covered in lectures. And this delay can have repercussions on attitudes to studying and the distribution of effort between modules, as we saw in Chapter 6. Reducing coverage provides more time for spending on difficult topics and allows students more chance of reaching a thorough understanding. Thinking carefully about the demands made by different concepts or organizing ideas within a module may indicate where more time might be needed.

The organization of course material also involves deciding the order in which the topics are to be introduced, and this should not be decided simply on the basis of the disciplinary logic but also on the psychological principles that indicate how to maintain interest and motivate students (Ausubel, 1985). And interest depends, in part, on keeping the ideas 'fresh', drawing on the latest developments in the subject and involving students, wherever possible, with ongoing research in the department (Brew, 2006). As the philosopher Alfred North Whitehead (1932) once commented: 'For successful education there must be a certain freshness in the knowledge dealt with: … knowledge does not keep any better than fish'. And that brings us to the final aspect shown in Figure 7.4.

Teaching that encourages thinking and understanding

It is possible to 'unpack' each of the concepts shown in the heuristic model to show its critical features. 'Teaching that encourages thinking and understanding' was opened up in this way in the full model as an example of this process, and is shown again as Figure 7.5. These critical features are drawn mainly from the examples provided in Chapter 6, although other aspects could well have been included. The choice was designed to provide an appropriate range of features, and also to bring together a coherent set of ideas, all of which focused on encouraging students to use a deep approach in constructing their own understanding, based on academically accepted concepts and theories that satisfy the conventions of the discipline or professional area.

Although the illustrations in the sections that follow are drawn mainly from traditional methods of teaching, many of the principles apply to other approaches, although in modified ways.

Giving an overview and monitoring delivery

Advice on lecturing often starts by emphasizing that a lecture needs a beginning, a middle and an end. Students need to be reminded about what has come before and alerted to what is to come, so 'activating prior knowledge' to make future linkages easier. 'Through-lines' can then be used to keep the main aims of the course repeatedly in students' minds. The middle is where the main exposition and discussion of ideas takes place, leading to a conclusion that summarizes the main points covered, and also anticipates what is to come in the next lecture, while reminding students about the work they should be doing in the meantime. This basic structure of lectures is, of course, part of the common lore of teaching, but research findings take us further.

In Chapter 4 we saw how students could reach an integrative personal understanding of academic topics, while the following chapter showed how university teachers who had

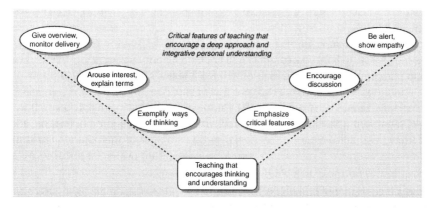

Figure 7.5 Aspects of teaching found to encourage thinking and understanding

a holistic understanding of their subject were likely to display this also in their teaching. Seeing the logic underlying the way knowledge has been organized in a subject also makes it easier for students to follow the reasoning involved. Above all, it helps to keep students engaged in meaningful learning, rather than seeing the course as a set of unconnected elements inviting the mindless regurgitation of rote-learned detail.

Many years ago, Bruner (1960, 1966) argued that students should be helped to develop the kind of understanding that requires the use of deep, reflective, adventurous and intuitive modes of thinking within a discipline.

> Mastery of the fundamental ideas of a field involves not only the grasping of general principles, but also the development of an attitude toward learning and inquiry, toward guessing and hunches, toward the possibility of solving problems on one's own. ... To instil such attitudes by teaching requires ... a sense of excitement about discovery – discovery of regularities of previously unrecognized relations and similarities between ideas, with a resulting sense of self-confidence in one's abilities. ... The cultivation of a sense of interconnectedness is surely the heart of the matter. For if we do nothing else, we should somehow give to [students] a respect for their own powers of thinking, for their power to generate good questions, to come up with interesting informed guesses, ... to make ... study more rational, more amenable the use of mind in the large rather than mere memorizing.
>
> (Bruner, 1960: 20; 1966: 96)

Nowadays concept maps are being used to make visible connections between concepts or other aspects (Hay, 2007) and also to encourage students to reflect on critical features and their linkages. But a concept map used to present a topic must avoid undue complexity, as its purpose is to make clear an overall pattern and structure. Often it may be better to start by encouraging students to draw their own concept maps and to reflect on them with other students, before introducing the teacher's view of the subject. Circumstances, and the nature of the subject, will decide what strategy to follow.

In his 'cognitive' educational psychology, Ausubel emphasized the importance of helping students to develop a well-structured and well-ordered cognitive structure. In teaching a topic, he argued that students must be reminded of the 'anchoring ideas' they have already met, to which new knowledge can subsequently be linked. Ausubel also suggested the need for 'advance organizers', broad integrative ideas that show the links between the new ideas that follow (Ausubel, Novak & Hanesian, 1978). These might be theoretical frameworks or what we now see as threshold concepts. However, on occasions it may be better to allow the excitement of the chase to develop, with the discovery of new ideas or ways of thinking being followed through all its stages.

In teaching the crucial thing is to monitor its effects on the students. Some aspects are self-evident, such as making sure that the whole class can hear what is being said, and can see clearly any visual material being used. But it is not just a matter of being heard. What is said has to be intelligible, and that depends on using straightforward language without unnecessary use of technical or abstruse language. As one of the 'excellent' Australian teachers mentioned in Chapter 5 said:

> I'm very careful about choosing the terminology I'm going to throw at students, ... [as] the terminology can often hinder an understanding of a process; so, I try to concentrate on what's

actually happening and not overuse the terminology. I try to explain concepts in simple, everyday terms.

And in the USA study we met earlier in this chapter, Bain (2004) found that his teachers thought carefully about how they would present their ideas before they started teaching, and about ways of keeping attention and maintaining interest as it progressed. Above all, they remained fully aware of their audience.

> The most effective speakers used conversational tones but projected their voices to include everyone present. ... There was within this conversation/performance a sense of the dramatic, a sense of when to stop talking and let key ideas land. That slight change of pace became the exclamation behind a key point, a trigger for thought, for calculation, or for the construction of understanding. ... Every ten or so minutes, they change the rhythm and content of their delivery, shifting direction or focus, altering activities or subject, punctuating an explanation with stories or questions. ... Some teachers sprinkle humour; others move from concrete to abstract ... yet no catalogue of such abilities and preparations can capture fully the ingredient that made these teachers so effective in reaching their students: a strong intention to help them to learn.
>
> (Bain, 2004: 119–20)

Monitoring the pace of delivery is also important. As we have seen, too much material presented too quickly will leave many students with little chance of thinking about the meaning or developing their own understanding.

> At the beginning I was all [at sea], sort of too much information at one time. But ... when he went back to it later on to revise it, it was a lot easier to understand. ... I just think that we're given too many different concepts at one time. ... It seemed that once we'd gone over one specific [topic] we weren't really given enough time to absorb the information before we were given another one, and the difficulty level increased as you went onwards. It really was step by step and, if you hadn't taken the first couple of steps, it was harder to grasp the more difficult ones.
>
> (Electronics student in the ETL project)

Given the limitations in short-term memory, there are inevitable consequences for student learning if too much information is provided at the same time, or if too many new ideas are included in quick succession (van Merriënboer, Kirschner & Kester, 2003). There are also difficulties created by introducing detail too soon, bringing in unnecessary qualifications, or making too many links between ideas. We have to be aware of how information is processed if we are to avoid unnecessary overload.

Arousing interest, explaining terms and encouraging understanding

While arousing and maintaining interest and attention comes initially from the organization and presentation of the material, the feelings aroused in the students may be the single most powerful influence on learning, and stemming from perceptions of the lecturer.

> Looking back to my own experience as a learner, the teachers who really helped me were the one's who obviously were in love with teaching and ... with the material that they taught. These teachers had many different styles. They weren't all up front, open wide, outgoing types of people, but they all had the same passion for what they were teaching. They had a way of conveying a love of learning, a love of knowledge that was infectious.
>
> Good teaching, first of all, means making the subject interesting for the students – capturing and maintaining interest in the subject area. I think that's the biggest hurdle you've got to overcome. ... I always try to be enthusiastic, no matter how boring the topic. If you can't transfer that interest and inspiration to the students, it's a bit of a lost cause, isn't it?
>
> (Lecturers' comments in Ballantyne, Bain, & Packer, 1997)

These comments, and a substantial body of research, suggest that the impact of teaching in encouraging conceptual understanding comes not from a particular method or style of teaching, but mainly from the teacher's attitude towards the subject matter and to the students. It may amount to a passion, not just for the discipline but also for conveying that enthusiasm to students in ways which make them want to understand for themselves. And a feeling that you understand strongly affects judgements made by students about whether the teaching has been 'good' or not. In one study, Bliss and Ogborn (1977) asked university students to explain what they found helpful or unhelpful about lectures, and separated out 'good stories' from 'bad stories'. The good stories involved a

> strong element of reacting well to the personal human qualities of the teachers as well as their teaching ability as such. ... Running like a thread through both 'good' and 'bad' stories are both involvement and understanding. Essentially, all 'good' stories mention interest, enthusiasm, and so on, if they mention nothing else. Essentially, all 'bad' stories mention their gloomy opposites. Again, both kinds stress understanding, or not understanding, as the single most frequent reason for feeling 'good' or 'bad'.
>
> (Bliss & Ogborn, 1977: 114)

In another study, Hodgson (1997) found that students experienced different forms of relevance in the lectures. 'Extrinsic relevance' came from the information needed to pass exams, while 'intrinsic relevance' depended on thinking about the meaning and trying to relate it to their own previous knowledge or experience. Extrinsic relevance was more likely to lead to a surface approach, while intrinsic relevance encouraged a deep approach. Hodgson also introduced an additional category to explain how some lecturers were able to shift a student's approach from surface to deep through a *vicarious experience of relevance* that came from the lecturer's own enthusiasm.

> In the course of a lecture, students whose experiences might normally be largely extrinsic may find their interest kindled by the lecturer's enthusiasm or, through the medium of a vivid example or illustration, see the content of the lecture as having meaning in the real world. ... Through vicarious experience of relevance, therefore, it becomes possible

for the lecturer to go beyond the outward demands of a learning situation and make connections between the content of the lecture and their understanding of the world around them.

(Hodgson, 1997: 171)

Nevertheless enthusiasm alone cannot overcome poor organization or other deficiencies in presentation; technical aspects of lecturing also have to be done well and explanations have to be effective.

Good explanations depend on ensuring that new terms are understood and getting the level right, having a clear idea of what the students already know and making explicit links to that prior knowledge. With a large, heterogeneous class, it can be extremely difficult to decide on the right level, but there are ways of getting a sense of what students know already and where there may be unexpected gaps or misunderstandings. At the start of a module, giving students a series of short-answer questions on the main ideas or concepts to be introduced helps in judging the right level. The responses also indicate where remedial material may be needed on the intranet or through special tutorial support. Any serious lack of prior knowledge makes it impossible for students to adopt a deep approach, since they cannot make the linkages necessary for constructing personal understanding.

In his USA study, Bain (2004) found that the best teachers deliberately oversimplified the topic they were teaching to begin with, and then gradually introduced detail and complexity once the basic idea seemed to have been grasped. One of the teachers explained:

> I often begin with an explanation … that will help students begin to grasp something, to build their conceptions. Later, as we add more information and ideas, they begin to realize that our initial way of thinking was too simplistic and even misleading. But if I started with the more complex way of explaining something, they would never understand it.

Bain comments:

> Notice her intention is to help students to understand, not to impress them with the sophistication of her knowledge. … Good explanations start with ways to help the learner begin to construct a good understanding; they are not necessarily the most accurate and detailed way of putting something. … Good explanations come from people who realize that learners must construct knowledge rather than simply absorb it.
>
> (Bain, 2006: 124–6)

Questions during lectures, or in e-learning material, help to keep students alert, but in large classes there is little prospect of expecting individual answers. One way of dealing with this problem was described by Mazur (1997, Crouch & Mazur, 2001). He had been concerned that his physics students said they were bored, and tried to find out why that was so. He found that students were concentrating on learning 'recipes' or problem-solving routines, which allowed them to arrive at solutions, but with little understanding of the underlying principles, leading to inexplicable mistakes even by 'bright' students. He decided that the traditional form of lectures was the main cause of what we would now see as surface approaches to learning. So he tried to make students more actively involved in their own learning during lectures, and eventually devised what he called *peer instruction*.

This approach transformed traditional lecture-based instruction by interspersing the lecturer's presentation with occasional five-minute, short-answer or multiple-choice *concept tests*. Typically, students are required to write an individual answer and then justify their answers to other students sitting nearby. These discussions are designed to increase student activity and involvement, although the time involved reduces content coverage. Mazur puts any omitted material on the web and requires students to demonstrate that they have used it. This technique has been adapted to work with the Personal Response System (PRS) in which students can respond to questions using a hand set (like a remote control), now called 'clickers', with a computer analysis providing a display of the proportions of the different answers given by the class.

The great advantage of this technology is that both lecturers and students are shown immediately the extent of any misunderstanding; staff can use the pattern of responses to explain the topic more carefully, while students will see how their own response fitted in with the overall range (Caldwell, 2007; McCune, 2008). Being wrong feels more comfortable if you are in good company. The use of clickers has created a burst of interest in student understanding, particularly in the physical and life sciences, and this has led to a closer concern with the nature of the subject and how it is taught. It has been used extensively in several countries now, with interesting studies being carried out by Carl Wieman (2007) in the Universities of British Columbia and Colorado, who comments:

> The reason I have been a strong proponent of clickers is that I have seen them to be the easiest route into a much more interactive student-centered instruction in university science classrooms. ... We see continually a remarkable disconnect in large science courses between what the faculty think the students are thinking and learning, and what is the reality, [as well as] a total lack of formative assessment. The use of clickers is the best way I have found to bridge the disconnect. The clickers themselves actually play only a minor role; what is really happening is the faculty are developing a more sophisticated view of teaching and learning. The clickers simply provide a vehicle to encourage [them] to find out what their students are thinking, and as they do that, they start to rethink their views about teaching, and come to teach in very different and more effective ways. So I have come to see the most important use of clickers is as a tool for faculty professional development.
>
> (Wieman, e-mail message)

'Clickers' certainly provide a valuable way of checking how well students have understood the main concepts. But there are many other ways of getting feedback about students' understanding, from an awareness of glazed expressions or nods of agreement, to asking students to note down at the end of a lecture, or on a message board, the most important point made in a lecture.

Because certain theories or threshold concepts are so important in allowing students to make sense of new ideas, it is worthwhile spending time making sure that these are thoroughly understood before introducing new material.

> Discipline experts understand the material in a certain way, but I think an expert educator understands material in a way that is a little different. An educator identifies the 'sticking

points' (difficult points). For example, I had taught frequency modulation a few times and I kept getting ridiculous answers back from the students. I couldn't work out why, and then suddenly I realised there was one concept they weren't understanding. So I introduced an analogy to help them grasp the concept, and the problem didn't recur to the same extent. To do this, I had to cut back on time spent on some other content, but overall their understanding improved because the focus was on what they needed most to understand.

(Lecturer in communication engineering from Ballantyne, Bain, & Packer, 1997)

Exemplifying ways of thinking and practising

Bain (2004) found that the teachers he had interviewed attempted to convey a way of thinking about the subject through an overall ethos that focused on critical thinking, just as De Corte had done in trying to produce 'powerful learning environments' (see Chapter 6).

More than anything else, the best teachers try to create a natural critical learning environment: 'natural' because students encounter the skills, habits, attitudes, and information they are trying to learn embedded in questions and tasks they find fascinating – authentic tasks that arouse curiosity and become intrinsically interesting; 'critical' because students learn to think critically, to reason from evidence, to examine the quality of their reasoning using a variety of intellectual standards, to make improvements while thinking, and to ask probing and insightful questions about the thinking of other people.

(Bain, 2004: 99)

This context, rather like that described earlier in relation to tutorial teaching (Chapter 5; Anderson, 1997), encourages critical thinking in a climate of mutual trust, without anxiety about being 'put down'. In Bain's study it involved five elements: an intriguing question or problem as a starting point, guidance in helping the students to understand the significance of the question, engaging them in some higher-order intellectual activity (as in T/U project's 'understanding performances'), challenging them to develop their own explanations, and encouragement to look for further questions or issues to be dealt with. Bain's teachers also made their own thinking transparent.

Perhaps the most significant skill ... wherever they met with students was the ability to communicate orally in ways that stimulated thought. ... More than anything else, ... [they] treated anything they said to their students – whether in fifty-minute lectures or in two-minute explanations – as a conversation rather than a performance.

(Bain, 2004: 117)

Such 'conversations' also take the form of thinking aloud while looking at issues or problems, a practice that is particularly effective in bringing the discourse of the subject area to life for students. Students are then able to 'catch' the ways of thinking for themselves, and so model their own explanations along disciplinarily accepted lines.

Emphasizing critical features and patterns of variation

The art of developing an effective explanation depends, above all, on imagining what it is like not to understand the topic and seeing the steps through which understanding can be developed. Striking examples or illustrations, as well as personal anecdotes, all allow students to see the topic from a variety of complementary perspectives and instances. That is a well-established tradition in lecturing, but the ideas of Ference Marton on variation theory offer a more systematic way of deciding which examples are most likely to lead to a deep understanding of a topic or concept (Bowden & Marton, 1998; Marton, 2007). As we saw in Chapter 2, students must *discern* the *critical features* and distinguish them from other more incidental aspects, but the ability to recognize what is most important does not come easily. So the teaching has to be carefully designed to bring out the critical features and to show how the pattern of variation among these dimensions affects what happens.

Aspects of variation theory were used in two of the examples given in the previous chapter. When a concept or a topic proves difficult, it is helpful to explore the different understandings that students have of it. This can be done, thoroughly, using phenomenography, as in the study on computer studies by Cope and Prosser (2005), or simply by asking students in a class to write down their own understandings and marking the responses in relation to the target understanding. A simple approach would be to find the ten best answers, ten in the middle range and ten at the bottom, and list the aspects covered in each group and also any major misunderstandings that emerge. In Cope and Prosser's study it was clear that the weaker students not only mentioned fewer of the critical features of an information system, but failed to look for the ways in which features fitted together into patterns of variation (Bowden & Marton quoted in Chapter 6).

The task of the teacher is to help students to discern the critical features for themselves, which can be done by explaining how the critical features combine to create a concept that can be used to explain certain phenomena in a more revealing way. Listing the critical features or requiring students to learn a definition is not sufficient, if we want students to be able to think in more academic or professional ways about the subject. To establish an effective conception, as we saw in Chapter 2, people must experience a range of examples of the concept in differing situations and also be able to discriminate the meaning of the concept from that of other similar ones. In many disciplines this process has been widely used, but the choice of examples may be somewhat haphazard. Often students are expected to learn simply by doing numerous examples, but this is not an efficient strategy. In developing problem-solving skills, for example, it is better to provide a systematic choice of examples designed to draw attention to variations in the critical aspects of the process, and so to lead students to a deeper understanding of what is involved (Marton & Pang, 2006; Thuné & Eckerdal, 2009).

Marton (2007) has suggested that variation will become clearer if the variation in one dimension is exemplified, while holding all the other critical features constant. This technique has been demonstrated to be effective in school settings (Marton & Pang, 2006) and can also be used in higher education. But at university level, we are mainly trying to establish a way of thinking and practising that will enable students to discern for themselves the critical features of future concepts or in novel situations, and this depends on making the patterns of variation more explicit through discussions of the interplay of the critical features seen as whole, and to understand how these patterns come about (Davies & Mangan, 2008; Thuné & Eckerdal, 2009).

There will inevitably be only a limited number of concepts that could be treated in this way, given the time involved, but some important threshold concepts could well be taught along these lines. Such overarching concepts draw attention to how simpler concepts work together to make sense of phenomena. In a recent study of how university teachers were using what they considered to be threshold concepts, O'Brien (2008b) illustrated the different ways in which these had been conceptualized. A clear example came from a physics teacher who was describing the teaching of 'inertia' to illustrate the importance of the interconnections between concepts. The following extract starts with O'Brien's commentary:

> While teachers identify the composite elements of the threshold concepts, some give emphasis simply to their existence, while others emphasize, by deliberate articulation, the relatedness and particular interplay that must occur between the constituent parts, if the threshold concept is to be mastered.
>
> I think that [inertia] is a sort of web of ideas that all fits together. Once you can see how it fits, it makes sense. ... Once you accept it as an idea, you have a much more powerful way of analyzing things moving. ... So instead of blind acceptance, ... that this is the way the world is ... it actually gives you ... a rationale for saying, 'This is why it happens'. ... It gives you a way of explaining what it is that causes a change in motion.
>
> In [his] descriptions there is a deliberate de-emphasising of the 'formula' [approach to teaching physics] in favour of conceptual understanding and explanations of phenomena.
>
> (O'Brien, 2008b: 65)

Of course, in many subject areas, the patterns of connection between ideas remain actively disputed, and so students have to create their own patterns and consider their plausibility in relation to evidence and critical commentary. And this process, as we saw in the previous chapter, can be supported through the use of dialogic concept mapping, which enables students to see the interconnections all at the same time.

One of the students explained how she used dialogic concept maps in reading and thinking about articles she was reading, and her description emphasizes the aspects discussed earlier. She identifies what Marton sees as the critical features and organizes them into a form of integrative personal understanding through reflecting on repeated versions of a concept map. In the process she creates something like a knowledge object which allows her to see the relationships between parts and whole simultaneously, and in a very personal way.

> I do my reading in three phases: the first to get the gist of the paper and to make a map of this; the second to extract new information; and the third to make sure that what I am reading fits with what I understand and need to know. In the first and second phases, what I try to do is to unravel the structure that the author made and I search and scan for things that help me to see the arguments and data they have drawn together. ... In the third phase, I will play about with the relationships in my map and tie in what I have just read with knowledge that I am already confident about – I will also leave things out on purpose. That's because I don't want to remember things if they're not important ... because otherwise ... [Otherwise they get] fixed in my mind, just by the mapping. ... So mapping is a means of reading and remembering, and it's more useful than note-taking line-by-line because it lets you read the

whole paper simultaneously. It lets you get control of what you read. ... It takes a lot of work to actually get to that understanding. And I have to be able to see them. The ideas have to come to be represented for me in my visual space. I don't mean I will necessarily see things as objects, but they have to be coloured somehow, coloured and arranged spatially according to how I know them, how I can picture them and which ones are closer to me or further away – that is ... making friends with ideas.

Hay, 2009

Encouraging individual reflection and group discussion

What distinguishes dialogic concept mapping from previous approaches is not just the commentaries that students are expected to provide on their maps but also the ways in which the maps are used in teaching and learning. Students are asked to reflect on the initial understandings shown in the maps and see how they can be developed. Teachers also comment on how successful the maps are in capturing the target understandings being expected. Students are also given opportunities to discuss with others what their maps represent and so to arrive at better understandings for themselves. And this interplay between individual understanding and group discussion, guided by feedback from teachers, has a crucial role to play, generally.

The increased use of intranet message boards or 'blogs' makes it possible to encourage students to share their ideas and get feedback on them. And the intranet can also be used to encourage students to reflect on the effectiveness of their own learning, as well as on the ways in which their understandings have been changing over time. It is difficult to help students to think for themselves about their ways of learning, and to be ready to adapt those approaches when necessary, and yet this skill is crucial; giving them opportunities for 'meta-learning' in differing settings and circumstances helps them to think in this way, habitually.

Tutorial teaching has continuing importance in many subject areas, but sometimes it proves difficult to get students to talk, and then it may become a mini-lecture by the tutor. In Chapter 5 we saw what students believed to be the most effective tutorials, where there was a climate of mutual trust and encouragement, and the importance of creating this climate has been echoed by many academics.

I think collaborative learning structures establish a class cohesion, a more caring atmosphere. They help to bridge the gap between the teacher and the learner.

(Educational psychology lecturer from Ballantyne, Bain, & Packer, 1997)

But effective tutorials also depend on good preparation by the tutor, preparing helpful materials and thinking about ways of stimulating discussion. One common approach is to pose a question or a problem and ask students to spend some time thinking about it and then writing down their ideas or a proposed solution. This is then shared with another student and discussed. Sometimes the pairs are then joined together before sharing their ideas in a plenary discussion (think/pair/square/share). In successful group teaching

[s]tudents generally don't fear being wrong because everyone is wrong at some point as they collectively struggle to understand and because they know [the tutor] emphasizes understanding over reaching correct answers. In contrast, many less successful teachers

play a game that might be called 'guess what's on my mind'. In that game there is only one right answer. Some students play it well while others cringe, fearing they might get it wrong and often refusing to contribute. Ultimately, discussions work well both because the students feel comfortable with one another and the instructor, and because the conversation is part of a larger attempt to create what [was earlier] called a 'natural critical learning environment'.

(Bain, 2004: 131–2)

Although it is becoming increasingly difficult to run tutor-led small-group discussions, at least in large departments in British universities, it is still possible to build student-led discussions into the timetable. Encouraging students to discuss the <u>process</u> of learning or problem-solving, and so making that process explicit, helps to develop understanding. The practice of sharing ideas and discussing how to tackle problems or issues remains a crucial part of higher education that has lasting value for students after graduating, both in employment and in their everyday lives.

Being alert while teaching and showing empathy with students

Alertness comes in different forms. It involves monitoring the impact you are having on the students, being aware of the amount of interest being shown (or increasing boredom) and picking up any general lack of understanding.

> There are a number of ways in which I monitor whether students are learning. In lectures, all those crowd control sort of things tell you whether students are learning or not. You can see the glazed-eye look, you can see if they're not interacting with the material or not interacting with you, if they're not attempting the extra questions or if they're talking.
>
> (Finance and economics lecturer from Ballantyne, Bain, & Packer, 1997)

But such impressions may not help to discover the source of the reactions. Standard evaluation forms come too infrequently to provide useful feedback, and are also too general. More detailed feedback is required from informal discussions with students to explore fully what are the main sources of difficulty. Where dissatisfaction seems widespread, a more detailed evaluation questionnaire, such as the one shown in Appendix B, can provide a clearer idea of where the problems lie.

A quite different form of alertness is also important, one that monitors opportunities to develop a particular idea further or correct faulty thinking. It depends on building on a chance event while teaching, or a comment by a student, to develop interest or explain ideas more clearly. The experiences of Paul Walker (discussed in Bridge into Chapter 5), led to the idea of *strategic awareness*, as a consequence of a sophisticated conception of teaching (Figure 5.1).

> Involving the students more actively in some of the 'big ideas' of the discipline ... led to what we might call a *strategic alertness*, capitalising on chance events in the classroom to create springboards to significant learning. Such opportunistic reactions to classroom events can provide 'teachable moments' or 'learning moments' (Woods & Jeffrey, 1996; Trigwell & Prosser, 1997; Forest, 1998). McAlpine and her colleagues (1999), in a study of exemplary university teachers, found that almost two-thirds of changes to teaching

method and content were unplanned, carried out while teaching was taking place, rather than in preparation for it, ... seizing an opportunity arising during the process of teaching – 'not the monitoring of student response to their teaching, but monitoring for openings to teach provided by the students'. (McAlpine et al., 1999, p. 120).

(Entwistle & Walker, 2002: 35)

A more general way of helping students see some of the 'big ideas' of the discipline is through involving them in ongoing research, either through meeting active researchers or through carrying out small-scale studies themselves. The strong motivational effect of helping students to see themselves in a professional role was seen in our ETL project when final-year students were actively involved in thinking about research issues arising in ongoing projects (McCune, 2009).

Some of the students were describing a profound shift in their learner identities, which seemed to have a marked impact on the effort they subsequently put into their studies and their disposition to understand for themselves. The key shift seemed to be toward feeling genuinely able to engage critically with research findings, and this was associated with feeling like a scientist, rather than like a student of the sciences. The students also described certain authentic learning experiences that seemed to support this shift. These experiences were described by students variously as: similar to how they imagined scientists work in the 'real world'; involving their engagement with open ended research questions, contradictory findings and contested interpretations; [leading to] their social integration into research communities, and being trusted to approach tasks independently and responsibly.

(Entwistle & McCune, 2009)

Brew (2006) goes further in arguing strongly for bringing research to the forefront of undergraduate teaching and learning in universities. She sees the university of the future as being more ready to bring students into the research community through involvement in authentic research in collaboration with staff and professionals and provides examples of where this is already happening.

When students engage in undergraduate research schemes they become research associates and as such tend to be treated quite differently to the way they are treated in their courses. They are perhaps more likely to be engaged in discussions of a more democratic nature. ... Their relationship with their teachers, and with each other, changes. There is a shift in status, as they are listened to by experts in the field. ... Academic communities share a common purpose, namely, to come to understand an aspect, or aspects, of the world better. As such, higher education becomes a participatory activity, where people are enabled to develop their identity through their particular contributions to the knowledge-building enterprise.

(Brew, 2006: 173, 177–8)

Another key aspect in teaching is the *empathy* shown to students, as the interviews with the Australian teachers (Chapter 5) brought out clearly. Part of this involves being authentic in the relationship established with the class, letting them see you as a person with your own interests and personality. It is also important to try to put yourself in the position of the student, to anticipate what might be found difficult and letting students know that some learning is difficult and that learning it may well take more effort than usual.

> I tell students that discomfort is a sign that learning is happening. 'If you're confused, you're on the threshold of an opportunity to learn, and let's move towards it rather than away from it'. The main thing, I think, is to let them know that you know they're anxious, or you know they're cross, to hear what they say and to acknowledge it. ... You don't just ... ignore their concern and hope it will sort itself out later.
>
> (Business Studies lecturer from Ballantyne, Bain, & Packer, 1997)

Empathy, above all, comes from a warm relationship with students that is openly expressed and a readiness to respond to students' own ideas.

> I believe a good relationship between teacher and learner is crucial for effective learning. ... I try as much as possible to get to know individual students, to communicate that I care for that student as an individual. ... Of course, you can't care for three hundred, but you can communicate that you value their contribution to a discussion, and you can communicate a sense of yourself as an individual. ... I may not know all of the students as individuals, but they feel they can relate to me.
>
> (Educational psychology lecturer from from Ballantyne, Bain, & Packer, 1997)

The reaction to students' difficulties is one of the main ways in which students judge empathy. Perkins (2007) has described how teachers differ in their reactions to what he calls 'trouble spots'.

> The least helpful response to trouble spots [*blame*] locates them outside the content and the teaching-learning process itself, blaming the students and blaming the conditions. So the teacher continues to teach in the same way and the students to learn in the same way, and both suffer the consequences of ... plenty of frustration but no adaptation. ... A range of responses to the trouble spots [that involve *trying harder*] along the same lines ... zoom in on the difficulties with more time and attention. And that certainly helps. ... [But] for *really good pedagogy*, we need ... [to identify] the trouble spots in that particular content, strive to explain them, and point toward adjustments in the teaching-learning process to help with them.
>
> (Perkins, 2007: 44–5)

▶ Technological aids, e-learning and blended learning

The impact of advances in educational technology on higher education over the last decade has been extraordinary, affecting the ways in which universities are administered, courses organized, materials provided for students, e-learning, contacts through e-mails and 'blogs', and so on. It has played an important part in helping staff to manage large classes and the assessment demands these create, and to provide learning materials for students through the intranet, in various forms. Lectures can be provided as 'pod-casts' so that students can catch up on any they have missed, or go over ones they attended but found difficult. Some of these advances, however, have done little more than move information around in more efficient ways. In looking at influences on the quality of student learning, we have to try to identify what the new technology can offer that goes beyond the compass of traditional teaching methods. Laurillard (2002, 2006) has discussed the use of the new learning technologies in a way that balances enthusiasm with caution.

> The nature of the medium has a critical impact on the way we engage with the knowledge being mediated. The oral medium has the strength of having greater emotional impact on us, which enables action through motivation; the written medium has the strength of enabling a more analytic approach to action. ... The interactive computer provides a means for representing information and ideas not simply as words and pictures, but as ... an information system, which embodies a working model with which the user can interact – not just analysing and reworking, but testing and challenging. ... Yet the ... focus has been on the presentation of information to the user, not on the tools for the user to manipulate information. ... Those of us working to improve student learning, and seeking to exploit e-learning to do so, have to ride each new wave of techno-hype, and drive it towards the quality agenda. We have to build the means for e-learning to evolve and mature as part of the educational change process, so that it achieves its promise of an improved system of higher education.
>
> (Laurillard, 2006: 71, 77, 78)

The weakness of information technology for university education is that it is often used as a convenient way of 'delivering' knowledge and understandings to students as 'packages' to be deposited within their memory banks. What we know about student understanding warns against this conception, drawing attention to the importance of students engaging with topics and interacting with ideas. So we have to look carefully at any e-learning techniques to see how likely they are to have this effect. Of course, as we saw with 'clickers', where the use of new information technology puts an emphasis on student understanding, it can lead to more general changes in how staff view teaching and learning.

Although the literature described in this book has derived mainly from traditional approaches to teaching, many of the main principles emerging also contain important messages for those devising e-learning environments, but ones not widely recognized so far (Ginns & Ellis, 2007). Interactive models, particularly in the various areas of medicine and the sciences, are regularly used alongside traditional teaching to great effect. 'Second Life' has been used to introduce students to experiences that they might not otherwise meet, or to explore interpersonal relationships, but the program is essentially an adventure game that has addictive properties, for good or ill. Adapting such programs for educational purposes, or the designing of interactive models, is time consuming and expensive; the potential value has thus to be carefully justified within limited resources.

Perhaps the most important development has been the recognition of the value of *blended learning*, with its concern to find the most appropriate ways in which e-learning and traditional teaching can work together to support deep and meaningful learning (Laurillard, 2002; Garrison & Kanuka, 2004). This seems the best route to follow in conventional universities and colleges. The widespread use of e-learning to deliver content knowledge no longer seems desirable, except where courses have been designed specifically for distance or part-time students, or to teach e-learning techniques. In publications on e-learning

> a lot of the hype has vanished and ... the talk of '*death of traditional educational methods*' ... has been replaced by a renewed realism about the importance of blending face-to-face methods with e-learning, and that real learning is hard whatever methods are used – there are no 'silver bullets'. ... [Also it shows that] individual innovation by academic staff does not lead automatically to real educational progress, as it is random and not strategically focused. Nor does it lead to containment in costs but rather to an escalation in them.
>
> (Haywood, 2004)

The most obvious technological influence on face-to-face teaching has been the use of Powerpoint slides which, if designed well, can certainly support students' understanding (McKeachie & Svinicki, 2006: 243). But the technique also has considerable dangers. Putting too much information on a slide destroys the main purpose, which is usually to provide a supportive framework for a description or an explanation. Including too many slides in a lecture can become bemusing and tedious for the audience, while the inclusion of background designs or unnecessary images or logos distracts attention from the main message. There is also a problem created by the linearity of presentation, which detracts from the sense of interconnection between ideas that is crucial for understanding (Hay, 2007). But the technology itself can be used to highlight interconnections and so overcome the pervading sense of linearity.

The Powerpoint program is also widely used to create handouts, but again there is a drawback; students often find them difficult to follow when they look back at them later on, as they lack the accompanying descriptions and explanations. Supplementary material can, however be provided on the web to remind students of the explanations, and to pose questions that encourage students to develop their personal understanding.

The advantages of technological advances in teaching are well worth exploring, but the pedagogical value of any new program or device needs to be established thoroughly, and judged against what is known about student learning, before being widely adopted. As in all approaches to teaching, it needs to be clear how any new technique helps students understand and encourages disciplinary ways of thinking and practising. And no matter what the advantages, information technology inevitably lacks the sense of the person, the explanations tailored to a specific group of students, the enthusiasm for the subject that can be catching and the empathy that shows that the teacher wants the students to share an enthusiasm about the ideas presented. Blended learning allows e-learning to play its part within an overall teaching–learning environment that fully supports student learning.

▶ Concluding summary

This chapter used component parts of a heuristic model to focus on the subject content and how it is taught. It brought together the experience of outstanding university teachers and research findings to make it easier to think about teaching and learning within specific subject areas and institutional contexts. And the selection of examples reflected a continuing concern about how best to encourage students to understand ideas for themselves.

As it is crucial to keep the students, and what affects the quality of their learning, firmly in mind, the chapter began with a brief summary of the concepts describing learning that had been described earlier. Given the difficulty in keeping in mind the many different characteristics, we focused on just two aspects that bring together several other influences on learning. The *disposition to understand for oneself* can be seen as a continuing preference for using a deep approach to learning. It involves a willingness to use whatever effort is needed to achieve a deep level of personal understanding, and also an alertness to opportunities for developing understanding further and for using existing understandings in imaginative and worthwhile ways. The other aspect highlighted was *monitoring learning and studying*, being continuously alert to the learning strategies being used, and changing them when necessary. This form of self-awareness is sometimes described as *meta-learning*.

If we are to encourage these aspects through our teaching, we ourselves have to monitor the effects of our teaching on student learning. We focused on the five main components of the heuristic model that represented steps in developing and teaching a course: beliefs about the role of the teacher, thinking about the subject and its pedagogy, target understanding and throughlines, selecting and organizing content and teaching that encourages thinking and understanding. All these steps were seen in terms of the need to prepare students for the independent understanding and critical thinking so crucial in current society.

Other ideas and research evidence were used to look at the teaching practices likely to encourage this type of learning: giving an overview and monitoring delivery; arousing interest, explaining terms and encouraging understanding; exemplifying ways of thinking and practising; emphasizing critical features of concepts and topics and the patterns of variation among them; encouraging individual reflection and group discussion; and being alert to 'teachable moments', while showing empathy with students and their difficulties. Finally we considered the value of using technological aids and e-learning, and the opportunities presented by 'blended learning' to capitalize on the relative strengths of both conventional methods of teaching and e-learning, within the broader learning environment that we explore in the next chapter.

▶ References

Anderson, C. (1997). 'Enabling and Shaping Understanding through Tutorials', in F. Marton, D. J. Hounsell & N. J. Entwistle (eds) *The Experience of Learning* (2nd edn) (pp. 184–97). Edinburgh: Scottish Academic Press – available at www.tla.ed.ac.uk/resources/EoL.html.

Ausubel, D. P. (1985). 'Learning as Constructing Meaning', in N. J. Entwistle (ed.) *New Directions in Educational Psychology. 1. Learning and Teaching*. London: Falmer Press.

Ausubel, D. P., Novak, J. D. & Hanesian, H. (1978). *Educational Psychology: A Cognitive View*. (2nd Edn). New York: Holt, Rinehart & Winston.

Bain, K. (2004). *What the Best College Teachers Do*. Cambridge, MA: Harvard University Press.

Ballantyne, R., Bain, J. & Packer, J. (1997). *Reflecting on University Teaching: Academics Stories*. Canberra: Australian Publishing Service.

Bliss, J. & Ogborn, J. (1977). *Student Reactions to Undergraduate Science.* London: Heinemann.

Bowden, J. & Marton, F. (1998). *The University of Learning: Beyond Quality and Competence in Higher Education.* London: Kogan Page.

Brew, A. (2006). *Research and Teaching: Beyond the Divide.* Basingstoke: Palgrave Macmillan.

Bruner, J. S. (1960). *The Process of Education.* Cambridge, MA: Harvard University Press.

Bruner, J. S. (1966). *Towards a Theory of Instruction.* Cambridge, MA: Harvard University Press.

Caldwell, J. E. (2007). 'Clickers in the large classroom: Current research and best-practice tips', *Life Sciences Education*, 6, 9–20.

Cope, C. & Prosser, M. (2005). 'Identifying Didactic Knowledge: An Empirical Study of the Educationally Critical Aspects of Learning about Information Systems', *Higher Education*, 49, 345–72.

Crouch, C. & Mazur, E. (2001). 'Peer Instruction: Ten Years of Experience and Results', *American Journal of Physics*, 69, 970–7.

Davies, P. & Mangan, J. (2008). 'Embedding Threshold Concepts: From Theory to Pedagogical Principles to Learning Activities', in R. Land, J. H. F. Meyer & J. Smith (eds) *Threshold Concepts within the Disciplines* (pp. 37–50). Rotterdam: Sense Publishers.

Eizenberg, N. (1988). 'Approaches to Learning Anatomy: Developing a Programme for Preclinical Medical Students', in P. Ramsden (ed.) *Improving Learning: New Perspectives* (pp. 178–98). London: Kogan Page.

Entwistle, N. J. (1988). *Styles of Learning and Teaching: An Integrated Outline of Educational Psychology.* London: David Fulton.

Entwistle, N. J. (2006). 'Ways of Thinking and Ways of Teaching Across Contrasting Subject Areas', *Education-on-line* at http://www.leeds.ac.uk/educol/documents/156501.html.

Entwistle, N. J. & McCune, V. (2009). 'The Disposition to Understand for Oneself at University and Beyond: Learning Processes, the Will to Learn, and Sensitivity to Context', in L-F. Zhang & R. J. Sternberg (eds) *Perspectives on the Nature of Intellectual Styles.* New York: Springer.

Entwistle, N. J. & Walker, P. (2002). 'Strategic Alertness and Expanded Awareness within Sophisticated Conceptions of Teaching', in N. Hativa & P. Goodyear (eds) *Teacher Thinking, Beliefs and Knowledge in Higher Education* (pp. 15–39). Dordrecht, The Netherlands: Kluwer Academic Publishers.

Forest, J. J. F. (1998). 'University Teachers and Instruction: Important Themes for a Global Discussion', in J. J. F. Forest (ed.) *University Teaching: International Perspectives* (pp. 35–72). New York: Garland.

Garrison, D. R. & Kanuka, H. (2004). 'Blended Learning: Uncovering its Transformative Potential', *The Internet and Higher Education*, 7, 95–105.

Ginns, P. & Ellis, R. (2007). 'Quality in Blended Learning: Exploring the Relationships Between On-line and Face-to-Face Teaching and Learning', *The Internet and Higher Education*, 10, 53–64.

Hativa, N. & Goodyear, P. (2002). *Teacher Thinking, Beliefs and Knowledge in Higher Education.* Dordrecht, The Netherlands: Kluwer Academic Publishers.

Hay, D. B. (2007). 'Using Concepts Maps to Measure Deep, Surface and Non-Learning Outcomes', *Studies in Higher Education*, 32, 39–57.

Hay (in press). 'Facilitating Personal Understanding in Higher Education: The Role of Dialogic Concept-Mapping', *Psychology Journal (of Greece)*.

Haywood, J. (2004). 'A Short Review of E-Learning in UK Higher Education', internal document, University of Edinburgh.

Hodgson, V. (1997). 'Lectures and the Experience of Relevance', in F. Marton, D. J. Hounsell & N. J. Entwistle (eds) *The Experience of Learning* (2nd edn) (pp. 159–71). Edinburgh: Scottish Academic Press, available at http://www.tla.ed.ac.uk/resources/EoL.html.

Hounsell, D. & Anderson, C. (2009). 'Ways of Thinking and Practising in Biology and History: Disciplinary Aspects of Teaching and Learning Environments', in C. Kreber (ed.) *The University and its Disciplines: Teaching and Learning within and Beyond Disciplinary Boundaries* (pp. 70–83). London: Routledge.

James, D. (2005). 'Importance and Impotence? Learning Outcomes and Research in Further Education', *The Curriculum Journal*, 16, 83–96.

Laurillard, D. (2002). *Rethinking University Teaching: A Conversational Framework for the Effective Use of Learning Technologies* (pp. 71–84). London: RoutledgeFalmer.

Laurillard, D. (2006). 'E-Learning in Higher Education', in P. Ashwin (ed.) *Changing Higher Education: The Development of Learning and Teaching*. London: Routledge.

Marton, F. (2007). 'Towards a Pedagogical Theory of Learning', in N. J. Entwistle & P. D. Tomlinson (eds) *Student Learning and University Teaching*. British Journal of Educational Psychology, Monograph Series II: Psychological Aspects of Education – Current Trends (pp. 19–30). Leicester: British Psychological Society.

Marton, F. & Pang, M. F. (2006). 'On Some Necessary Conditions of Learning', *The Journal of the Learning Sciences*, 15, 193–220.

Mazur, E. (1997). 'Understanding or Memorization: Are we Teaching the Right Thing?', in J. Wilson (ed.) *Conference on the Introductory Physics Course* (pp. 113–23). New York: Wiley.

McCune, V. (ed.) (2008). 'Effective Use of Clickers in the College of Science and Engineering', accessed at http://www.scieng.ed.ac.uk/ltstrategy/clickers_effectiveUse.html on 8 January 2009.

McCune, V (2009). 'Final Year Biosciences Students' Willingness to Engage: Teaching–Learning Environments, Authentic Learning Experiences and Identities', *Studies in Higher Education*, 34, 347–61.

McAlpine, L., Weston, C., Beauchamp, C., Wiseman C. and Beauchamp, J. (1999). 'Building a Metacognitive Model of Reflection', *Higher Education*, 37, 105–31.

McKeachie, W. J. & Svinicki, M. (2006). *McKeachie's Teaching Tips: Strategies, Research, and Theory for College and University Teachers*. Boston, MA: Houghton Mifflin.

O'Brien, M. (2008a). 'Threshold Concepts for University Teaching and Learning: A Study of Troublesome Knowledge and Transformative Thinking in the Teaching of Threshold Concepts', in J. H. F. Meyer, R. Land & J. Smith (eds) *Threshold Concepts in the Disciplines* (pp. 289–306). Netherlands: Sense Publishers.

O'Brien, M. (2008b). 'Teaching as Translation: An Investigation of University Teachers' Pedagogical Content Knowledge, Reasoning and Intention', doctoral thesis, School of Education and Professional Studies, Griffith University, Australia.

Pask, G. (1988). 'Learning Strategies, Teaching Strategies and Conceptual or Learning style', in R. R. Schmeck (ed.) *Learning Strategies and Learning Styles* (pp. 83–100). New York: Plenum Press.

Perkins, D. N. (2007). 'Theories of Difficulty', in N. J. Entwistle & P. D. Tomlinson (eds) *Student Learning and University Teaching*. British Journal of Educational Psychology, Monograph Series II: Psychological Aspects of Education – Current Trends (pp. 31–48). Leicester: British Psychological Society.

Perkins, D. N. (2008). 'Beyond Understanding', in R. Land, J. H. F. Meyer & J. Smith (eds) *Threshold Concepts within the Disciplines* (pp. 3–19). Rotterdam: Sense Publishers.

Quality Assurance Authority (2008). 'Subject Benchmark Statements', accessed on 10 January 2008 at http://www.qaa.ac.uk/academicinfrastructure/benchmark/default.asp.

Scheja, M. (2006). 'Delayed Understanding and Staying in Phase: Students' Perceptions of their Study Situation', *Higher Education*, 52, 421–45.

Säljö, R. (1979). *Learning in the Learner's Perspective. I. Some Common-sense Conceptions* (Report 76). Gothenburg: University of Gothenburg, Department of Education.

Thuné, M. & Eckerdal, A. (2009). 'Variation Theory Applied to Students' Conceptions of Computer Programming', *European Journal of Engineering Education*, (in press).

Trigwell, K. & Prosser, M. (1997). 'Towards an Understanding of Individual Acts of Teaching and Learning', *Higher Education Research and Development*, 16, 241–52.

Van Merriënboer, J. J. G., Kirschner, P. A. & Kester, L. (2003). 'Taking the Load off a Learner's Mind: Instructional Design for Complex Learning', *Educational Psychologist*, 38, 5–13.

Whitehead, A. N. (1932). *The Aims of Education*. London: Benn.

Wieman, C. (2007). 'Why Not Try a Scientific Approach to Science Education?', *Change*, 9–15 September/October.

Wiske, M. S. (1998) 'What is Teaching for Understanding', in M. S. Wiske (ed.) *Teaching for Understanding: Linking Research with Practice*. San Francisco: Jossey-Bass.

Woods, P., & Jeffrey, B. (1996). *Teachable Moments*. Buckingham: Open University Press.

Assessment the Driver, but in Which Direction?

In the research we carried out in Lancaster in the 1970s it was already clear that certain aspects of the teaching seemed to affect students' approaches to learning. Students experiencing 'good teaching' and 'freedom in learning' tended to describe deep approaches to their learning, while those reporting a 'heavy workload' and less freedom in learning mentioned surface approaches. A majority of students who had adopted deep approaches obtained at least an 'upper second' class degree, whereas those using a surface approach were less likely to do so.

Assessment, too, had a marked influence on how students went about their studying, as students are strongly influenced by rewards or criticisms. The grades and written comments students receive, as well as oral remarks or suggestions from teachers, all affect learning. Assessment is generally seen as most direct 'driver' of study behaviour, not only of the amount of time and effort students put into their work, but also their ways of studying. Students find that deep approaches take more time and effort than surface approaches, and consequently they have to persuade themselves that the 'pay-off' is worth the effort.

The following extracts from Paul Ramsden's interviews illustrate how students act strategically in writing essays or preparing for exams, as they keep in mind the specific types of questions expected and what kind of answer the examiner expects.

> I look at [the topic] and I think to myself, 'Well, I can do that if I can be bothered to hunt through hundreds of textbooks and do the work' – and you sort of relate that to these are student quotes and should be put in the smaller Arial light typeface as usual the value of the work in the course, which is virtually zero because it's so much exam assessment. ... I just don't bother with it until the exams come around ... [and] my revision is basically aimed at passing the exams without bothering too much about studying the subject. (Physics student.)

> With that essay ... I wrote it with the image of the marker in mind, the personality, the person. I find that's important, to know who's going to be marking your paper. ... You see an essay is an expression of thought, really, but that's not what they're after; they're after a search through the library, I think, and a cribbing of other people's ideas. (Psychology student.)
>
> (Ramsden, 1997: 198, 204)

Such comments showed how students' perceptions of assessment affect their approaches to learning, and this link was reinforced by research carried out by Patrick Thomas, who spent part of a sabbatical with us. He had been conducting an experimental study of approaches to learning in which the method of assessment was changed from an essay-type examination to a multiple-choice format (MCQ), and then back again. The introduction of MCQs led the class as a whole to show more marked surface approaches along with reduced deep approaches; reintroducing the essay exam reversed that effect. In spite of this overall effect, students who had the highest levels of deep approach on essays had a similar approach to the other method of assessment. In other words, the whole class moved down as a result of the shift to MCQs, but the relative scores of individual students stayed much the same. Similar findings have been reported since, but recent work suggests that the relationship may not be as straightforward as that.

Around the same time in Lancaster, Dai Hounsell was looking at the effects of assessment on students, concentrating on what students believed essay writing to entail. Some thought that it involved little more than finding relevant content and describing it, while others realized the importance of using evidence to support a carefully constructed argument. Students with a restricted conception of essay-writing were, not surprisingly, given lower marks, and were also more likely to find comments made by tutors unhelpful. Staff found it difficult to imagine why such students failed to take notice of suggestions for improvement, but the research provided an explanation.

> Where students' conceptions of essay-writing are qualitatively different from those of their tutors, communication cannot be readily taken for granted because the premises underlying the two disparate conceptions are not shared or mutually understood. Students misconstrue a tutor's comments or guidance, or fail to grasp the import of these, because they do not have a grasp of ... the academic discourse underlying what is being conveyed to them. Similarly, tutors fail to acknowledge the subtle interplay between what is said and what is taken for granted and so do not seek to close the gap between their own and their students' understanding of expectations.
>
> (Hounsell, 1987: 114)

This failure to make sense of feedback from tutors can be found in all subject areas, and it is hardly surprising. Students only gradually begin to understand the ways of thinking within differing academic disciplines, and the conventions for interpreting evidence and developing arguments. They have to be guided towards ways of improving their reasoning and evidence base; effective and prompt feedback is essential for completing the learning cycle mentioned in the previous chapter. Without this to guide learning, academic progress is likely to be slow.

The perceived nature of the assessment thus affects the <u>direction</u> learning takes (towards understanding or reproduction), while the effectiveness of the feedback determines how much the learning strategy can be improved in the future. But assessment and feedback are just two of the influences on the quality of learning within a learning environment; other influences also have to be taken into account in planning a learning environment that will evoke and support deep approaches to learning, as we saw in our ETL project, and will become clear in the following chapter.

▶ References

Hounsell, D. J. (1987). 'Essay Writing and the Quality of Feedback', in J. T. E. Richardson, M. W. Eysenck & D. Warren Piper (eds) *Student Learning: Research into Education and Educational Psychology* (pp. 109–19). Milton Keynes: SRHE & Open University Press.

Ramsden, P. (1997). 'The Context of Learning in Academic Departments', in F. Marton, D. J. Hounsell & N. J. Entwistle (eds) *The Experience of Learning* (2nd edn) (pp. 198–216). Edinburgh: Scottish Academic Press, available at http://www.tla.ed.ac.uk/resources/EoL.html.

Thomas, P. R. & Bain, J. D. (1984). 'Contextual Dependence of Learning Approaches: The Effects of Assessments', *Human Learning*, 3, 227–40.

8 Influences of the Learning Environment

We now come to the remaining influences of the teaching–learning environment on the quality of student learning. This broader context includes external influences on universities coming from government and from changes in society and employment, but here we concentrate on those found within institutions. These were shown down the right-hand side of the heuristic model, and are shown again as Figure 8.1. Each of these aspects will be considered in turn, following a logical progression that moves from broader contextual influences to those more directly impinging on the quality of students' under-standing, such as set work, feedback, assessment and support for individual learning.

▶ Institutional and departmental influences

Higher education, certainly in the UK, has become more tightly controlled by government policies over recent years, with universities being required to develop, and submit to funding agencies, strategic plans for all aspects of their work. Universities have to provide a general mission statement and then set out their development plans in the form of objectives, strategies and specific targets in various areas. These can then be judged against defined indicators of progress. Table 8.1 provides an example of part of one such plan, but without specific targets or indicators. Schools and departments also have to

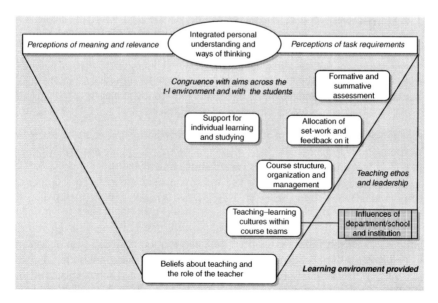

Figure 8.1   Influences on learning from other components of the learning environment

Table 8.1   Extracts from a university strategic plan in relation to education

Our Mission	*The University's mission is the advancement and dissemination of knowledge and understanding. As a leading international centre of academic excellence, the University has as its core mission:*

- to sustain and develop its position as a research and teaching institution of the highest international quality and to benchmark its performance against world-class standards
- to provide an outstanding educational environment, supporting study across a broad range of academic disciplines and serving the major professions
- to produce graduates equipped for high personal and professional achievement, and
- to contribute to society, promoting health, economic and cultural well-being.

Objectives   *In pursuing excellence in education we will:*

- continue to enhance the quality of, and maintain breadth in, our educational provision
- ensure fair access and progression for all who can benefit while maintaining the high quality of our student intake and graduate output
- produce graduates equipped for both personal and professional achievement at the highest levels
- provide programmes that are relevant to the needs of students and society
- increase the proportion of postgraduate students
- increase opportunities for, and participation in, lifelong learning.

Strategies   *Our strategies for achieving our objectives include:*

- responding to recommendations identified through quality enhancement activities
- developing the professional capability of all those involved in the delivery of teaching and learning
- ensuring that all those with the potential to study with us are not deterred from applying
- improving support for more vulnerable students
- developing more flexible ways of learning, teaching and assessing and exploiting new technologies
- ensuring our research and scholarship feeds directly into the learning experience
- providing flexible and better informed curriculum choice
- making administrative processes more efficient and cost-effective both for students and teachers
- working with employers and professional bodies to develop new programmes, keep current programmes up-to-date and provide more opportunities for students to develop transferable skills
- expanding access to postgraduate and CPD provision through e-distance courses.

present plans that describe how funds will be allocated to support their various activities, including research and teaching.

Strategic plans are designed to relate directly to national priorities outlined in policy documents issued by government and funding agencies, and are increasingly written in the language of business management. This language, and the thinking underlying it, expressed in terms of supply, demand and output, filters down into departments, but there meets a different set of priorities and contrasting ways of describing issues; university teachers think in terms of courses, academic content and the progress of individual students.

> The UK universities have traveled a much longer distance than their US counterparts from ... a collegial character towards a marketized system yet with considerable state intervention. ... There has been a discernible movement towards 'academic capitalism' in which market-like behaviours become common at both institutional and academic staff level ... [and] 'chasing the dollar' (or Euro) has become an increasingly important part of the academic's role. ... In the face of these pressures universities are required to develop more creative, adaptable, and efficient means of organizing academic work, ... [which] have led to the commodification of knowledge ... as a 'thing' capable of being bought and delivered in module-sized chunks, with learning outcomes being the unit of currency. ... Managerialism involves a framework of values and beliefs about social arrangements and the distribution and ordering of resources. It provides a guide and justification for managers' and leaders' behaviour – behaviour that is oriented to efficiency, economy and market responsiveness and which calls for the direction of employee activities towards these ends by managers.
>
> (Becher & Trowler, 2001: 9–10)

Even quality assurance of teaching has to fit in with the overall business plan, leading to a concentration on 'output measures' that are only crude indicators of the achievements of students. Quality assurance procedures are typically more concerned with output measures than with any clear conceptual view of a high-quality teaching–learning environment. The current procedures protect students from the least effective teaching, but are unlikely to promote 'excellence', while being caught between the contradictory aims of satisfying external economic considerations and encouraging the more supportive teaching–learning environments that are almost inevitably less economic.

Within departments, institutional strategic plans and related policy changes are generally applied top-down, often without full consultation. Even if the changes are explained, they may continue to be stated in terms of business plans, with a lack of correspondence between that rhetoric and the realities of everyday teaching, thus creating murmurings of discontent and passive resistance to the imposed change, as Paul Trowler explains:

> In a heavily top-down and authoritarian context the significance of backstage and under-the-stage talk and practices is increased. ... There is a public arena, front-of-stage, in which formal proclamations are made in, for example, mission statements and speeches by vice-chancellors. This front-of-stage presentation may have little to do with actual practices, values, attitudes and meanings on the ground. ... The back-stage

area is where deals are done: individuals and small groups make decisions and take actions away from the public eye. ... Finally, the under-stage arena is where gossip is purveyed ... and critical comments are exchanged.

(Trowler, 2008: 59)

In departments, the focus of concern, necessarily, has to be on developing up to date courses designed to suit specific intakes of students and also to reflect disciplinary and professional requirements. Quality assurance of teaching thus needs to balance the demands made by government against the aspirations and current knowledge base of the students.

University policies usually seek to impose uniformity of approach across the disciplinary and professional divides, partly for administrative convenience and the requirements of information systems, but also to ensure perceived fairness across courses. Such policies have made departments reassess what often had become unconsidered practices, based more on tradition than on pedagogical requirements, but these policies can also constrain the necessary diversity involved in fitting teaching and assessment methods to the differing requirements of contrasting subject areas. The imposition of top-down policies may also inhibit innovation. The ETL project found that the substantial time lag created by extensive quality assurance procedures substantially delayed the introduction of desired changes in teaching. Moreover, staff had come to resent procedures that introduced more elaborate paperwork, and so discouraged experimentation.

Naturally, the current situation varies enormously across institutions within the UK, and is different in other countries, but the problems created by planning at system level without careful consideration of the impact on departments and teachers exist everywhere. The alienating effects of inappropriate managerialism and 'business-speak' can be strong, and damaging to the quality of teaching (Allen, 2009).

▶ Teaching and learning cultures within course teams

The heuristic model shows teaching–learning cultures emerging out of differing beliefs about teaching and the role of the teacher. In the previous chapter we saw the effect of such differences in terms of the subject content, but here we shall be thinking about it in its social context. Decisions about content are generally taken within course teams, and even where there is a single teacher both the content and the proposed approaches to teaching have to be justified to colleagues. Over time, departments develop a particular ethos, based on beliefs about how students should be taught and what priority should be given to research. They also establish norms relating to particular teaching methods, class size, student support, assessment procedures and marking criteria. Sometimes, the ethos may be strongly affected by a charismatic leader, and so change over time. But the prevailing ethos affects discussions within course teams and the decisions of individual teachers about their approaches to teaching, even though staff may not necessarily be aware of these influences.

A good deal of interest has been shown recently in how groups of individuals act together in what have been termed *communities of practice* (Wenger, 1998). Some of these are informal, for example, in recreational activities where shared interests help to form social bonding and friendships, but others are also found in work groups, with university teachers taking part in several of these groups, all of which may affect their sense of identity as academics. Disciplinary specialisms and departments create strong communities of practice with shared knowledge, values and attitudes. And effective collaboration within these groups is crucial, not just for the smooth running of departments but also for 'keeping the peace', avoiding potentially destructive tensions.

Ideally, experienced staff share their expertise with newer staff in a collegial way to help them become part of the 'team'. But in most departments there are schisms in beliefs about the subject and how it should be taught; several communities of practice may thus coexist and are as likely to create tensions and dispute as to contribute to collegial agreement. Trowler (2008) has been exploring how these work groups function within teaching–learning environments, teasing out the sociological aspects seen to govern their activities. He identified what he called *teaching and learning regimes*, using the term 'regime' not to reflect rigid authority but rather the working relationships that lead to mutual understanding, although not necessarily agreement. In exploring the nature and practices of the workgroups related to their teaching activities, Trowler comments:

> I was looking for different *communities of practice* … interacting with each other. What I found surprised and puzzled me. The problem was summed up by one head of department who said, 'There are more factions than people in my department'.… One reason for choosing [the] word ['regime'] is to be deliberately provocative. While the currently popular term 'community of practice' has connotations of consensus and harmony, 'regime' has … overtones of oppression, power and, usually, resistance. … The meanings workgroups attribute to their projects and the ways they define their situation are themselves partly formulated within the regime that develops. Meanings and intentions are not always shared though: … teaching and learning regimes are almost always sites of contest. However, there is often a degree of consensus too … and, crucially, a shared social context in which these tensions are played out.
>
> (Trowler, 2008: x, 52, 60)

Attempts to introduce innovatory ways of teaching depend, in part, on the extent to which consensus can be reached across a department or teaching organization. Without such agreement, individuals may find themselves isolated in trying to change their approaches to teaching, creating difficulties for themselves and possible confusion for their students, through apparently contradictory perspectives on teaching and learning.

▶ Course structure, organization and management

Our focus now shifts closer to the experiences of students. Course teams have to consider not only aspects of content, such as those described in the previous chapter, but others such as the allocation of teaching roles among staff, arrangements for setting course work for students, support for individual students, providing criteria for deciding grades and collating those grades from different markers. In Chapter 6 we introduced the importance of ensuring congruence with the aims of the course, with the students taking the course, and among all the various components of a teaching–learning environment. And in Figure 8.1 we drew attention to some of the main aspects that have to be kept in mind in designing a learning environment to support student learning.

Course organization and management are relatively straightforward in small classes with a single teacher but, as classes get larger, this aspect becomes increasingly important and potentially problematic. Done well, organization and management become invisible to both staff and students, but done badly they can cause dissatisfaction and markedly interfere with student learning.

In the first phase of the ETL project we analysed the reports on teaching quality from a range of departments rated as 'excellent' in national evaluations to identify the main criteria used in deciding ratings. The full set of characteristics regularly mentioned as outstanding in the reports is shown here in Table 8.2 for completeness, although only a subset of them is specifically related to this section.

Table 8.2   Characteristics of departments rated as 'excellent' in national evaluations

Course organization and administration	• Effective quality assurance procedures • Course handbooks detailing aims, teaching, learning resources, assignments and assessment • Well-managed staff appraisal and active encouragement of staff development • Well-designed, well-maintained and accessible accommodation, equipment and facilities
Curricula, teaching, learning and assessment	• Overall programme design, including a wide but coherent choice of options • Structure of module/course, and of individual teaching sessions, made clear and linked to aims • Content chosen to match students' prior knowledge, abilities, interests and understanding • Challenging content focusing on understanding and academic and generic skills • Good teaching, making appropriate use of supporting resources and teaching/learning technologies • Careful control and monitoring of student progress, particularly in the early stages • Encouraging progressively more self-regulation in learning • Stressing relevance of content to aims/vocational value, interplay between theory and practice • Wide range of appropriate and varied assessment, backed up by timely, helpful feedback • Small-group teaching/tutor-student closeness
Student support	• Staff-student relationships showing mutual respect and good rapport • Identifying and supporting specific learning needs, including language, maths and study skills • Seeking and acting on student feedback on courses and teaching • Meeting 'personal tutors' regularly

In the main phase of the ETL project, there were several large first-year courses where students were experiencing difficulties. In the biology departments, for example, there were course teams of up to 26 people directly involved in the teaching, with a mix of backgrounds that included departmental academics, staff with teaching-only contracts, post-doctoral students and postgraduate teaching assistants. Such staff differ in their roles, experience of teaching, and the amount of time spent working on the course; some have a responsibility for organization of one or more parts of the course, while others may give a set of lectures or act as tutors or laboratory demonstrators. Distributing responsibility in this way draws in a valuable range of backgrounds, knowledge and interests, but can also create difficulties (Hounsell et al., 2008).

Students in such courses often complained about a sense of impersonality and distance because they could not get to know lecturers who appeared on only a few occasions. With large teaching groups, conflicting messages may come from different teachers, tutors may not be fully aware of what is being taught in the lectures and lecturers may not see at first hand the difficulties faced by students in carrying out their work. In our own study, students were particularly concerned about perceived inconsistencies in the marking and feedback of coursework by tutors. Although staff accepted these problems, they explained how difficult it was to ensure common practices and good communication with so many people involved.

Team-taught courses have their pluses and minuses. Students are often very worried by team-taught courses because they find it hard to carry material over from one lecture into the next, ... hard to see the thread that runs through the course. If you are aware of that, and you work hard at trying to pull things together, then I think that team-taught courses are very good, because you can have somebody who really knows about some particular topic. ... But one has to bear in mind that there are cracks in between that people can fall through.

I'm not sure all of us have a complete view of the unit. The course coordinators have to [have one], to some extent, ... [but] I'm not convinced we spend enough time as a body, getting everyone together to review where we are and where we're going. ... You try to go along to meetings when meetings are called, but you're not always available, and since it's such a large course with so many people, having everyone there every time is not feasible.

(Hounsell et al., 2008: 36–7)

Based on our research, the support of less experienced staff seems to be crucial, in particular, for marking assignments or exams. This can be done by providing detailed criteria to indicate what is to be expected for each grade level, supported by examples of student work graded in this way. Explanations of how the criteria have been used also helps, as do opportunities to discuss the lectures with those delivering them and the function of assignments and tutorials in supporting student learning with experienced markers (Hounsell et al., 2008).

▷ Allocation of set work and feedback on it

As we saw in the previous chapter, there is a cycle in student learning that progresses through several distinguishable phases: preparing to tackle the course material, acquiring the necessary information, relating it to previous knowledge, practising new skills and working on assignments that bring together ideas into integrative personal under-standing. In this book our concern is, of course, not so much about specific techniques, as with their effects on the quality of student learning. From this perspective, the main function of assignments is to develop ways of thinking, although this will be done in rather different ways across disciplines. In the humanities and social sciences students write essays to explain their ideas, while in the sciences problem solving demonstrates how understanding has been put to work. In medicine and similar areas students use their understanding to interpret evidence from individual case histories. But in all these different ways, work is set that requires students to both develop and demonstrate their understanding.

The *Teaching for Understanding* framework (Chapter 6) explained the importance of designing *understanding performances* to evoke the types of thinking necessary for understanding, building towards a 'culminating performance', such as an end-of-unit assessment, to demonstrate what has been achieved. The *TfU* researchers found that

> [as] teams of teachers and researchers attempted to define and design performances that would develop and demonstrate students' understanding of important goals, they had to distinguish performances of understanding from other kinds of activities. They recalled the project's definition of understanding as 'going beyond the information given' to extend, synthesize, apply, or otherwise use what one knows in creative, novel ways. Performances that fulfil this definition include explaining, interpreting, analyzing, relating, comparing and making analogies, … [and remind] teachers that students can undertake a much more varied range of activities than is encompassed by typical assign-ments. If students use the full spectrum of [their multiple] intelligences, not just the verbal and mathematical ones, … they may perform their understandings in a myriad of creative ways.
>
> (Wiske, 1998: 73)

Within this *TfU* framework, the notions of understanding goals and throughlines were used to guide the allocation of set work, but there are other guiding principles that serve this purpose. For example, research stemming from the work of Ference Marton implies that we need to look carefully for the *critical features* of a topic or concept and how these can be used to evoke learning processes that will help to build integrative personal understanding. In areas where manual skills or problem-solving tasks are involved, and extensive repetition is essential, varying the critical features will make its effects stronger. It is not the number of occasions or examples that hones the skill but the experience of *systematic variation* in differing situations and contexts, as well as the readiness to reflect on the effects of that variation.

Once assignments have been completed they have to be judged according to predetermined criteria, possibly with quite elaborate scoring procedures for reaching an overall grade. Wherever possible, the mark should explicitly reward students' attempts to understand the material for themselves. The research discussed in Chapter 4 provides a broad framework for evaluating the quality of understanding shown. In essays, for example, this quality can be judged in terms of breadth (how much material has been brought together), depth (how well the ideas have been integrated with other work), structure (how logical and individual the arrangement of ideas is) and explanation (how well the answer deals with the question or topic set). Of course, specific frameworks will also be needed for each essay topic while other kinds of work will require altogether different ways of judging quality. Nevertheless, in whatever subject area, making the criteria explicit will influence the approach to learning that students use in carrying out an assignment.

Finally, to complete the learning cycle, there has to be effective *feedback* that reinforces the importance of thinking for oneself. Feedback is not just a matter of pointing up inadequacies; it provides an opportunity to give encouraging comments and suggestions about how to improve future work. As one of psychology's original 'laws of learning' made clear (Chapter 2), feedback powerfully shapes future behaviour.

> [A] major law of skill acquisition involves *knowledge of results*. Individuals acquire a skill much more rapidly if they receive feedback about the correctness of what they have done. If incorrect, they need to know the nature of their mistake. It was demonstrated long ago that practice without feedback produces little learning. ... One of the persistent dilemmas in education is that students spend time practising incorrect skills with little or no feedback. Furthermore, the feedback they receive is often neither timely nor informative. For the less capable students, unguided practice can be practice in doing tasks incorrectly.
>
> (Pelligrino et al., 2001: 87)

> Feedback is probably the best-tested principle in psychology. It has been shown to be most effective when it is timely, perceived as relevant, meaningful, and encouraging, and also offers suggestions for improvement that are within a student's grasp.
>
> (Brown, 1997: 51)

In the US, Wilson and Scalise (2006) found that students who were not given adequate feedback became alienated and ceased trying to understand for themselves. And in Britain, the National Student Survey (NSS, 2008) found 'feedback' to be the least satisfactory aspect of students' learning experience. Criticism was not uniform across all institutions or subject areas, but it was widely reported and strongly felt. Feedback seems to have become a major casualty of the substantially increased ratio of students to staff in UK higher education. In Table 8.3, students' interview comments from the ETL project are used to illustrate some consequences of inadequate feedback.

The comments about analogue electronics showed a mismatch between how students wanted to use worked solutions and what staff believed they would do with them. In biology, the comments drew attention to the problems created by feedback not fulfilling its purpose or being provided too late to be useful. From the staff perspective, the main problem is lack of time, given an increasing workload; however, within these constraints, there may be better ways of offering feedback. Hounsell (2008) has suggested how to make feedback more effective in mass higher education through *whole class feedback*, which points out general weaknesses or limitations and indicates better ways of dealing with the questions set. This approach can also suggest how students can improve their work in the future (Hounsell, 2007; Hounsell, Xu & Tai, 2007).

> The aim is to increase the value of feedback to the student by focusing comments not only on the past and present [work] ... but also on the future – what the student might aim to do, or to do differently, in the next assignment. ... [Prior to exams], in addition

Table 8.3 Students' comments on problems encountered with feedback

Electronic engineering	**Context** *In analogue electronics most of the assignments involved solving circuit problems, with staff available in large-group tutorials to give advice. Students tended to rely on worked solutions being provided.*

I think it's essential to get worked examples to get solutions, [but] some courses are not giving them out. That's all very well if people know what they're doing, but [if they don't], then worked solutions are possibly the only option they've got for passing. But some lecturers refuse to give them out because they say, 'If we give you worked solutions, you'll just sit back and a week before the exam you'll try and memorize the solutions to a question'. ... I just think that's wrong the way they withhold these from you: I don't think they should do that.

[There were] no tutorial solutions. We were refused any. We were told we had to approach the lecturer and ask for help rather than get solutions. But there are 80 students for that course and ... it's not so easy, especially if you live away from [town] ... I think our lecturer's opposed to giving solutions actually 'cause he thinks we'll just learn it parrot fashion.

Biological Sciences	**Context** *In biological sciences, problem solving was again important, but written work was carried out as well.*

For [that assignment], I totally got the wrong end of the stick. ... I read the instructions, and I felt there were hidden things that you had to put [in] that they didn't explain. I got 8 out of 20, and I've got nothing written on my [feedback] sheet at all. ... And they tell you to do it in double-spacing, so they can write things in, but they never do. ... I mean, if we're getting half marks, it must have a lot wrong with it. But it's not telling us anything.

If you get [your coursework assignment] back then you should be able to learn from your mistakes. But they come back too late for you to learn from your mistakes, to help you with your actual exam. That happened last year: ... it was right up until about the last week before we got some information back, and I thought, 'Well, what's the point'?

I understand that they have so many to mark in a short space of time, but it would be nice if they could put more information into the marking. But if they can't, if you have a question regarding your lab report that needs further explanation, it would be good to know who to go to.

Source: ETL subject area reports on the project website.

to giving students access to past papers, the lecturer [can provide] a commentary in note form on how past questions were and could be tackled, what potential traps might lie in wait for the unwary, and the comparative advantages and limitations of different approaches to a particular question.

(Hounsell, 2008: 5–6)

Such information can also be provided on the intranet, along with opportunities to carry out self-assessment exercises in multiple-choice format that provide immediate feedback on students' current knowledge.

Other valuable approaches involve using either *self-assessment* or *peer-assessment* (Boud, 1995; Brew, 1999; Falchikov, 2001). Students can be encouraged to use self-assessment by looking critically at their own work and marking it, using the same criteria used by staff. Students can also read each other's work, using the criteria in peer-assessment and then considering what comments to make. This process can also be used after first drafts have been produced to stimulate discussion among the students about the whole process of writing, and to help students recognize the importance of revising drafts.

These procedures would not normally be used in formal grading, but rather as a way of helping students to become clearer about what is being expected in a piece of work, and about the function of feedback. In the early stages of a degree course, many students seem to be confused about the purpose and importance of tutors' comments. As we saw in the Bridge Passage, however, this may not be due to any fault of the student; staff may not have explained what they meant in a sufficiently straightforward way. And even intelligible comments may miss an important opportunity to guide future learning. They can be used to encourage a deep approach, for example by asking what a concept really means to the student, suggesting where ideas might be developed further or where additional evidence might be found, or what alternative interpretations there might be. In such ways, feedback can guide thinking into paths that are critical, curious and imaginative.

Formative and summative assessment

From a student perspective, what is expected of assessment is, above all, *transparency*, being able to see why the grade was awarded, and *fairness*, feeling that the grades make understandable distinctions between different levels of performance. Students judge fairness by comparing their work with that of other students, and their ability to make that judgement depends on the quality of the comments they have received on their assessed work. Staff necessarily have to view assessment rather differently, with an emphasis on the standards needed to certify the level of performance reached. They may, of course, also see assessment as a way of supporting learning, but there is an inevitable tension between assessment for certification and for encouraging learning.

Assessment that comes at the end of a course is called *summative*; when it is part of the learning process it is described as *formative*. Assessment being used to certify a standard of performance has to be *valid*, in other words it must measure what was intended. It also has to be *reliable*, so that an equivalent grading would be given if marked again shortly afterwards, or by another person. If any form of assessment is not reliable, it cannot be valid; but an assessment can be reliable and yet be invalid, by accurately measuring the wrong thing.

In the 1980s, concerns about unreliability in traditional methods of assessment, such as essay questions, led to an increased use of tests with multiple-choice questions (MCQs). These can be marked quickly and easily with little marker inconsistency, and can even be computer-marked. But they do not generally tap the same qualities as do essay questions, testing mainly information or simple forms of knowledge. It is possible to design MCQs that require understanding, but often they do not; and this limitation becomes particularly worrying where a substantial proportion of assessment is carried out in this way (Gardiner, 1994). Short-answer questions (SAQs) offer an alternative: they are less reliable than MCQs but more likely to tap advanced ways of thinking. The types of exam not only differ in reliability and validity but as we saw in the Bridge Passage, they can markedly affect the approach to learning that students adopt, and therefore the quality of understanding reached. Generally students believe MCQs require only rote learning, and so tend to adopt surface approaches, while essay assignments are perceived as demanding understanding, and so are more likely to lead to deep approaches (Thomas & Bain, 1984; Scouller, 1998). Thus trying to improve the reliability may adversely affect not only the validity of the technique, but also the approach to learning.

The differences between MCQs and SAQs point up the value of using a combination of methods to utilize their strengths while limiting their side effects. We came across a good example of this while collaborating with an economics department during the ETL project (Reimann & Xu, 2005). Departments at one university had been required to introduce MCQs and SAQs to reduce the time spent on marking, but the staff in this department were well aware of the possible effects of these tests, and so gave considerable thought to the design. They explained to students that the MCQs would test their understanding as well as their breadth of knowledge, while the SAQs would involve solving problems by making explicit use of appropriate concepts and techniques. Examples of the problems were discussed in tutorials and specimen papers were provided, with e-mail reminders also being circulated shortly before the exam. Questionnaire responses showed that students had accepted the advice, revising widely for the MCQs and trying to understand economic principles in preparation for both tests. Table 8.4 illustrates the reactions of staff and students to the changes in the assessment procedure, with the general conclusion being that this combination of assessment methods had been successful in guiding students' learning towards deep approaches.

Table 8.4   Comments made by staff and students about a combined MCQ/SAQ exam

Staff:	One of the reasons for introducing the tests was ... it saves on staff time, [but] [MCQs] are quite time-consuming and costly to set up, and they can become [no more than] multi-guess. So you have to be very careful in selecting questions that have plausible wrong answers ... and mean the students have to think and calculate to get the right answer. It's very time consuming ... [but] all of them were analytical in the sense that you've got to understand economics theories to understand the question and select the right answer. ... We decided that the SAQs ... would require them to apply a concept to a specific situation.
Student:	I reckon [the exam's] probably harder this year than in previous years. ... In other years you had to do two essays ... so you could afford to not revise a couple of topics if you wanted. But [this year], because we had twenty MCQs, then five SAQs, you had to know pretty much everything to be confident. ... Trying to answer the short answer questions, it's a case of applying understanding: it's not just knowledge – drawing a diagram and explaining it requires understanding – it's not just what you can learn, but what you can actually understand, [and] show that you understand.

Source: Reimann & Xu, 2005.

Varieties of assessment

There are now many different assessment methods being used and these vary widely in the skills and ways of thinking they are measuring; they also have different effects on student learning. Besides the possible effects of MCQs, noted earlier, other approaches contain implicit messages to students about the kinds of learning they are expected to use. Brown (1997) described a range of common assessment methods and their likely effects, and these are shown here in a modified form (Table 8.5).

Table 8.5   Commonly used assessment methods and some of their characteristics

Essays assess differences in the levels of understanding of complex material. Questions are relatively easy to set and impressionistic marking can be carried out fairly quickly, but variations in the marks awarded by different assessors can be large. Grading according to criteria takes longer, but improves consistency, while providing thorough feedback is time-consuming. Essays nevertheless encourage a deep approach.

MCQs allow a wide range of knowledge to be tested quickly with high reliability and fast feedback. They can cover analysis and problem-solving skills as well as understanding, but such questions are more difficult to design. It is too easy to test trivial aspects of the subject, which convey the wrong impression to students and encourage a surface approach to learning.

SAQs can be used to assess analysis, application of knowledge, problem-solving and evaluative skills and model answers can be used to increase consistency in marking. Feedback can be provided quite easily.

Problems can indicate strengths in application and analysis as well as problem-solving strategies. Routine problem solutions can be easily and quickly marked or even self-marked, but providing feedback is time-consuming, and repetition of similar problems proves boring and may seem unrelated to the real world. Authentic problems are more difficult to mark, but are more likely to encourage deep approaches.

Cases encourage reflection and personal interpretation, as well as thinking and communication skills specifically related to professional contexts, all of which develop understanding. They are also engaging, but there need to be well-designed marking schemes to avoid inconsistent marking.

Orals probe the level of understanding and test the capacity to think quickly under exam conditions, but can create considerable anxiety, which affects performance differentially. Standardization of the procedure and criteria for marking are needed, but subjectivity remains an issue.

Peer-assessment can be used in the humanities and social sciences to help students understand the criteria being used in judging essays and also to provoke discussion about the processes of thinking and writing involved.

Practicals are used in laboratory subjects to link theory with practice and are assessed by written reports. Marking can be relatively fast and accurate if structured forms are used, but otherwise substantial variation between markers is generally found.

Projects are increasingly used as assessment towards the end of degrees. Work on individually selected projects encourages deep approaches, as well as developing skills relating to identifying information and evidence, and using it in developing an argument, but marking of reports can become very subjective. Group projects are particularly valuable in developing collaborative work.

(Continued)

Table 8.5   (Continued)

Presentations develop skills in retrieving information and analysing and integrating it. Explaining that an effective presentation depends on understanding encourages a deep approach. Feedback can be provided immediately both by a tutor and other students, and can be used to moderate the grading process. There is a danger that this assessment procedure may encourage slick presentation without adequate substance, but using explicit criteria should avoid this problem.

Examinations in the traditional three-hour essay form take time to mark with problems of inconsistency. Providing revision time allows some students to use it to develop personal understanding, but simply encourages rote learning in others. Questions can be designed, however, to reward and encourage personal understanding. End-of-unit exams usually depend on revision during the unit, and discourage synthesis across units. Open-book exams have been used to avoid undue anxiety and reliance on memorization, but create difficulties in ensuring equal access to resources. Advance notice exams decrease anxiety, but may encourage memorized answers.

Source: Based on Brown, 1997: Table 4.3.

Table 8.6   Principles involved in developing integrative and sustainable assessment

Alignment	Given that aims are rarely unidimensional, a range of assessment methods will usually be required in any course to cover differing skills and ways of thinking. It is also important to look for complementarity between them in their likely effects on approaches to learning, as well as ensuring that the methods have been carefully adapted to the particular needs of the subject.
Inclusivity	Bearing in mind the increasingly diverse range of student backgrounds, it is important to ensure that assessments take into account the differing kinds of educational and cultural experience among the students, as well as of forms of disability that may be affecting some.
Feedforward	Assignment and assessment tasks are built into a recursive cycle to allow comments on completed work to be [used] in later work. Where possible, comments can be made on drafts which can be used to improve the quality of submitted work.
Cumulation	Instead of a small number of major pieces of work, students are given shorter pieces which can be either on paper or sent electronically, with feedback [provided] that leads towards a more demanding assignment or assessment.
Progression	The assignments and assessments are strategically planned across a whole degree course to follow the type and level of knowledge and skills that are expected to be developed. Course teams use this model in deciding the specific tasks to be set in their units.
Expectations	Students and the markers have to be equally clear about what the tasks require and what criteria are being used to determine grades.
Feedback	Students need to be shown how important it is to use feedback to work more effectively, while staff have to ensure that it is given promptly, that it will be seen to be relevant and to contain suggestions for improvement that students can be expected to manage.
Economy	Assignments take substantial time and effort, with students balancing these against the perceived importance and pay-off. Assessments and feedback also take markers' time, meaning that staff have to weigh tasks and grading procedures against time and cost.

Source: Based on information provided in QAA, 2007.

With assessment taking many different forms, and also being more widely distributed among tutors with differing experience, assessment procedures have to be brought together systematically. In Scotland, a series of booklets has been prepared to help staff devise *integrative and sustainable assessment* that interweaves various strands in a coherent way and indicates manageable ways of coping with them (see Table 8.6).

Effects of assessment on study strategies

In Chapter 5 and in a previous section, we described students' perceptions of assessment and discussed how these affected their studying. But differing assessment methods not only affect the approaches to learning that students use, they also affect distribution of effort across different assignments. Several studies show this effect. For example, a psychology department asked an educationalist to provide a 'speed reading' course because their students were not doing enough background reading (Gibbs, 1981). The researcher decided it would be better to ask the students, first of all, why they were not doing much reading. Apparently, they believed writing up their practical work would determine whether they passed or failed, and so they spent many hours perfecting their laboratory reports. In reality, marks on practical work counted only at the margins, and when students realized this, they spent more time on reading, avoiding the need for a 'speed reading' course.

Another example comes from medicine. Staff were concerned about the low reliability of their clinical oral examinations and replaced them with ward appraisals by supervisors. Students soon found that the supervisors were passing almost everyone and so they spent more time on the theory part of the course, which they were more likely to fail. When staff realized the effects of the new assessment procedure, they returned to a clinical examination, but in a modified form that made it more reliable (Newble & Jaeger, 1983). Students then divided their time along the lines that the staff wanted.

These examples, along with the earlier ones, show just how strongly and directly assessment procedures affect the ways in which students study.

▶ Support for individual learning and studying

Many of the ideas discussed in the last two chapters are intended to support student learning and encourage a deep approach, but there are aspects of studying that can get overlooked. Students face two distinct sets of skills that they have to develop, those required to master the knowledge and understanding within the subject area they are studying, and those that are involved in carrying out the work they have to do – their *study skills* (Janssen, 1996).

As students now have such a wide spectrum of social, cultural and linguistic backgrounds, universities are offering a range of additional courses and guidance to ensure all can benefit from the teaching. Although students will usually have been given some study skills training at school or college, university education demands another set of skills, such as taking lecture notes, writing essays, discussing with other students in tutorial settings, solving problems of various kinds and preparing for different kinds of examinations. Training for skills works most effectively when introduced immediately before it is needed. So workshops for students with non-traditional backgrounds are needed at the beginning of their degree. However, such teaching is inevitably generic, provided by study skills specialists, and cannot be equally suitable across a wide range of subject areas. Students will therefore look to departmental staff to provide the more specific advice they need. However, university teachers often find difficulty in providing such advice, so help must then be sought from educational developers who can provide the necessary advice.

From the research on student learning it may seem that we could just explain to students that they need to adopt a deep approach, but telling does not lead to doing. Nevertheless it is useful to alert students to possible problems in their current ways of studying, and there are several questionnaires available that provide profiles of scores on study strategies. The simplest of them show the balance between deep, surface and strategic approaches or organized effort, while others offer a more detailed profile (Entwistle & McCune, 2004). Well-tested questionnaires are *ASSIST* (Approaches and Study Skills Inventory for Students) (available at http://www.etl.tla.ed.ac.uk/publications.html) or *RoLI™* (Reflections on Learning Inventory). ASSIST provides scores on 13 sub-scales, but these can be reduced to the three main factors described in Chapter 3 – deep, surface and strategic (organized effort) (Tait, Entwistle & McCune, 1998). RoLI was developed by Meyer (2004) and produces a profile of 16 aspects online, drawing attention to scores that are problematic, but also intended to encourage students to become more alert to their own studying (meta-learning). Either of these instruments can be used either to check the relative extent of differing ways of studying in a whole class or to encourage individual students to consider their pattern of scores and the implications for the effectiveness of their studying. Providing students with opportunities to discuss their strategies with others, in relation to theoretically sound frameworks, is likely to be particularly valuable.

In earlier research Janssen (1996) identified what he saw as the main interacting capabilities needed to become an expert student. They included intention, ability, exertion, planning, study discipline and alertness to application and transfer. All of these affect the extent to which students feel comfortable with the process of learning and confident about their academic progress. This set of attributes includes all those described earlier within a disposition to understand for oneself, with its combination of thinking strategies, willingness to put in effort and alertness to possibilities for developing or using understanding. But becoming an expert student with a disposition to understand is not something that is easily or quickly developed; it builds slowly through experiencing high-quality teaching of the kinds described throughout this book, and on those individual characteristics that are also needed to make the most of the teaching provided.

▶ Concluding summary

Teaching for understanding depends not just on the teaching approaches discussed in the previous chapter but also on the broader learning environment within which it takes place with all its institutional, social and educational aspects. This chapter considered it, initially, in broad social and institutional terms, before concentrating on those aspects that more directly affect student learning. The heuristic model again shaped the discussion and drew attention to the importance of ensuring that the teaching–learning environment as a whole is congruent with the students' capabilities and aspirations, and with the aims of the course.

In Britain, as in many other countries, government policies determine what universities are expected to provide for students and influence the language through which activities are described. Nowadays, each institution has to define its mission and objectives before describing the strategies to put these into practice, and this creates a framework within which teaching and learning take place. Adopting the language and practice of business management alters the nature of higher education by focusing attention on quantitative measures of student output and standardized course structures. This focus is at variance with that of academics, who are much more concerned about the ways of thinking and practising they hope students will acquire. And where the management message is too uncompromising, the disparity can lead to alienation and disaffection among staff, and thus affect the quality of teaching.

Course teams are generally responsible for designing new courses, and given the variety of conceptions of teaching and learning described earlier, it is not surprising that there can be substantial disagreements within these groups about the content to be included and the teaching approaches to adopt. Competing teaching–learning cultures may thus develop within a department, but a consensus is usually possible, which allows the allocation of teaching and the organization and management of courses to be carried out without dispute. When dealing with large classes, however, course management can become problematic, if a large number of people with very different experience are involved in the teaching. Students and tutors alike become confused if they hear contradictory ideas about what is required from the more experienced teachers. Such problems can be avoided as long as organizers have sufficient time and resources to provide guidance on what is required, to monitor the teaching–learning activities closely and to provide opportunities for discussing any problems that emerge.

Within this institutional and social milieu, staff allocate set work to students, give feedback to them and mark assessments. And all these activities have a direct impact on the quality of student learning. Theoretical frameworks, such as *Teaching for Understanding* and *variation theory* can suggest ways of designing assignments that support integrative personal understanding. But the quality of student learning also depends on obtaining, not just timely and carefully constructed feedback on assignments but also helpful suggestions about how subsequent assignments can be improved. Within mass higher education it is proving difficult to maintain the quality of feedback that students receive, but there are ways of improving it. Whole-class feedback of common weaknesses and better ways of studying can be supplemented by peer discussion of assignment drafts or problem-solving strategies, while self-assessment helps students to monitor their own ways of studying.

Whereas assessment was traditionally *summative*, carried out only at the end of a course, *formative assessment* is now widely used during the course to guide student learning. When assessment is being used to certify the standards reached, it is crucial that the methods used are reliable, with markers agreeing on the level reached by students, and that tests are valid, measuring what they are intended to cover. The unreliability in traditional methods led to the development of tests using multiple-choice questions, which can be easily and accurately marked. However, any overemphasis on facts and detail in such tests leads some students to adopt surface approaches. The range of methods of assessment now being used taps different academic qualities, and also influences students' approaches to learning in contrasting ways, as well affecting the time and effort they put into assignments. *Integrative and sustainable assessment* techniques test a wide variety of ways of thinking and encourage understanding, while being chosen to make realistic demands on staff time.

Finally, a learning environment has to provide support for student learning by offering, when required, training in the study skills needed to take full advantage of the teaching they experience. Study skill courses are now often introduced at entry, particularly for students who are not well prepared for higher education. Staff with specialist knowledge of study skills usually run these workshops, but the specific techniques needed in the courses students meet later have to be introduced by departmental staff, who may not be confident about teaching study skills. It is important that staff are given opportunities to find out how to give such help. Students can be asked to complete questionnaires to indicate their current study strategies, with profiles of scores being used to promote reflection and discussion about ways of improving their studying. But the outcome of learning ultimately depends on the interaction between the teaching and the individual, with all the components of the heuristic model, and many more besides, coming into play.

▶ **References**

Allan, J. (2009). 'The Civic and the Civil in Professional Education', *Aberdeen University Research Papers*, 18, 27–39.

Becher, T. & Trowler, P. R. (2001). *Academic Tribes and Territories: Intellectual Enquiry and the Culture of the Disciplines*. Buckingham: SRHE and Open University Press.

Boud, D. (1995). *Enhancing Learning Through Self-Assessment*. London: Kogan Page.

Brew, A. (1999). 'Towards Autonomous Assessment: Using Self-Assessment and Peer-Assessment', in S, Brown & A. Glasner (eds) *Assessment Matters in Higher Education*. Buckingham: SRHE & Open University Press.

Brown, G. (1997). *Assessing Student Learning in Higher Education*. London: Routledge.

Entwistle, N. J. & McCune, V. S. (2004). 'The Conceptual Bases of Study Strategy Inventories in Higher Education', *Educational Psychology Review*, 16, 325–46.

Falchikov, N. (2001). *Learning Together: Peer Tutoring in Higher Education*. London: Routledge-Falmer.

Gardiner, L. F. (1994). *Redesigning Higher Education*. (ASHE-ERIC Higher Education Reports). Washington: George Washington University, Graduate School of Education and Human Development.

Gibbs, G. (1981). *Teaching Students to Learn: A Student-Centred Approach*. Milton Keynes: Open University Press.

Hounsell, D. J. (2007). 'Towards More Sustainable Feedback to Students', in D. Boud and N. Falchikov (eds) *Rethinking Assessment in Higher Education* (pp. 101–13). London: Routledge.

Hounsell, D. J. (2008). 'The Trouble with Feedback: New Challenges, Emerging Strategies', *TLA Interchange*, 2, Spring 2008, 1–9, accessed at http://www.tla.ed.ac.uk/interchange.

Hounsell, D. J., Xu, R. & Tai, C. M. (2007). *Monitoring Students' Experiences of Assessment*. (Scottish Enhancement Themes, No. 1). Gloucester: Quality Assurance Agency for Higher Education (http://www.enhancementthemes.ac.uk/publications)

Hounsell, D. J., McCune, V., Litjens, J. & Hounsell, J. (2008). ETL Project *Subject Overview Report: Biological Sciences*, accessed at http://etl.tla.ed.ac.uk/publications.html

Janssen, P. J. (1996). 'Studaxology: The Expertise Students Need to be Effective in Higher Education', *Higher Education,* 31, 117-142.

Meyer, J. H. F. (2004). 'An Introduction to the RoLI', *Innovations in Education and Teaching International*, 41, 491-7.

National Student Survey (NSS) (2008). Results available at http://www.hefce.ac.uk/learning/nss/data/2008/.

Newble, D. I. and Jaeger, K. (1983). 'The Effect of Assessments and Examinations on the Learning of Medical Students', *Medical Education*, 17, 25–31.

Pellegrino, J., Chudowsky, N. & Glaser, R. (2001). *Knowing What Students Know: The Science and Design of Educational Assessment.* NCR Center for Education. Washington, DC: National Academy Press.

Quality Assurance Agency for Higher Education (QAA) (2007). *Integrative Assessment: Balancing Assessment of and Assessment for Learning*, available at www.enhancementthemes.ac.uk.

Reimann, N. & Xu, R. (2005). 'Introducing Multiple-Choice alongside Short Answer Questions into an End-of-Year Examination: The Impact on Student Learning in First-Year Economics', paper presented at the 11th biennial conference of the European Association for Reseach into Learning and instruction, Nicosia, Cyprus, August, 2005. Available at http://etl.tla.ed.ac.uk/publications.html

Scouller, K. (1998). 'The Influence of Assessment Method on Students' Learning Approaches: Multiple Choice Question Examination Versus Assignment Essay', *Higher Education*, 35, 453–472.

Tait, H., Entwistle, N. J. and McCune, V. (1998). 'ASSIST: A Reconceptualisation of the Approaches to Studying Inventory', in Rust, C. (ed.) *Improving Student Learning: Improving Students as Learners*, Oxford Centre for Staff and Learning Development, Oxford. The inventory itself can be found at www.etl.tla.ed.ac.uk/questionnaires/ASSIST.

Thomas, P. R. & Bain, J. D. (1984). 'Contextual Dependence of Learning Approaches: The Effects of Assessments', *Human Learning*, 3, 227–40.

Trowler, P. R. (2009). *Culture and Change in Higher Education.* London: Palgrave Macmillan.

Wenger, E. (1998). *Communities of Practice: Learning, Meaning and Identity.* Cambridge: Cambridge University Press.

Wilson, M. & Scalise, K. (2006). 'Assessment to Improve Learning in Higher Education: The BEAR Assessment System', *Higher Education*, 52, 635–63.

Wiske, M. S. (ed.) (1998). *Teaching for Understanding: Linking Research with Practice.* San Francisco: Jossey-Bass.

Part 5

Monitoring the Effectiveness of Teaching

Measuring Students' Approaches and Perceptions

In thinking seriously about how we are teaching, it is essential to know how students are going about learning in our courses, and how they are reacting to our teaching. My interest in trying to monitor and measure students' study activities and experiences goes back to the work I did in Aberdeen in the late 1960s. At that time I developed a questionnaire to assess pupils' academic motivation in schools, and then one that measured motivation and study habits at university. Then I was drawing on ideas mainly from educational psychology but later on, influenced by Ference Marton's ideas, I began to use concepts more closely linked to students' own experiences. I also had discussions with John Biggs about a questionnaire he was developing at that time. Subsequently, Paul Ramsden and I produced two questionnaires, one to measure study strategies – the *Approaches to Studying Inventory (ASI)* – and the other to indicate students' reactions to teaching – the *Course Perceptions Questionnaire (CPQ)*, mentioned earlier.

Later on, in Edinburgh, I worked with Hilary Tait and Velda McCune to develop a revised version of the ASI, followed by a complete re-conceptualisation. The resulting *Approaches and Study Strategies Inventory for Students (ASSIST)* included sections on conceptions of learning and preferences for different types of teaching to show the links these have with approaches to studying. Sophisticated conceptions of learning are related to deep approaches, and students showing these characteristics prefer student-focused teaching. Students with less sophisticated conceptions and adopting surface approaches are satisfied with the teacher-focused approach, even though it is unlikely to support high-quality learning. This created a dilemma about whether such students should be offered teaching considered to be less effective. While we can encourage a deep approach, we cannot expect every student to adopt it. If we are to satisfy all students, we need to provide easily assimilated material for those who are not prepared to use deep approaches, while at the same time stretching the understanding of those who are. Again we come back to the idea of a *multi-inclusive* approach to teaching.

While these questionnaires and inventories were used initially to explore variations in the ways in which students learned and studied, they have been used subsequently to monitor the effectiveness of teaching. Paul Ramsden produced a revised version of the CPQ, called the *Course Experiences Questionnaire (CEQ)*, which has been used widely in Australia and other countries to evaluate courses. The ETL project used two questionnaires, one mainly to assess approaches to studying and the other to monitor students' reactions to teaching–learning environments. Sari Lindblom-Ylänne and her colleagues are now using the second questionnaire (ETLQ) to evaluate courses throughout the University of Helsinki, with encouraging results.

The research-based inventories differ from standard evaluation questionnaires in the thoroughness with which they have been designed and developed; also, the wording of items is based on comments made by students during interviews, and so relates directly to their experiences. These inventories also contain scales that have a strong conceptual and psychometric basis. Most of the evaluation forms used in universities, in contrast, are more functional; they provide evidence for quality assurance purposes of students' satisfaction with the courses, but generally no more than that. They do not indicate how teaching might be improved. As one lecturer commented:

> You get a whole bunch of quantitative measures ... [with] little bar charts all over, an answer for each question, ... which were mostly good. And that was great fun, in a way. But what they didn't say is, you could improve by doing this, or these ten people thought you were [awful]. ... All I got was, most of the people think you are doing alright, ... [so] I was not able to use that information to change the way I teach at all.
>
> (Åkerlind, 2007: 30)

We shall see in the following chapter how a short, research-based questionnaire can be used to provide information that <u>does</u> suggest implications for teaching. In the ETL project we also used group interviews with students to complement the information provided by the questionnaires. This combination of quantitative and qualitative approaches provides valuable guidance to university teachers on how to 'fine-tune' their courses. It can also be used to carry out research into how students learn in different subject areas, and how specific aspects of teaching affect that learning. And this move beyond the local evaluation of teaching becomes one part of what has been called the *scholarship of teaching*, leading to discussion among university teachers about the effects of their teaching, and more widespread dissemination of the ideas.

▶ References

Åkerlind, G. (2007). 'Constraints of Academics' Potential for Developing as a Teacher', *Studies in Higher Education*, 32, 21–37.

Biggs, J. B. (1987). *Student Approaches to Learning and Studying*. Melbourne: Australian Council for Educational Research. (Describes SPQ.)

Entwistle, N. J. & Ramsden, P. (1983). *Understanding Student Learning*. London: Croom Helm. (Describes ASI and CPQ.)

Entwistle, N. J. & Tait, H. (1990). 'Approaches to Learning, Evaluations of Teaching and Preferences for Contrasting Academic Environments', *Higher Education*, 19, 169–94.

Parpala, A., Lindblom-Ylänne, S., Komulainen, E., Hirsto, L. & Litmanen, T. (in press). 'Students' Perceptions of the Teaching–Learning Environment, Approaches to Learning, and their Relationship, among First- and Third-Year Students', *Studies in Higher Education*.

Ramsden, P. (1991). 'A Performance Indicator of Teaching Quality in Higher Education', *Studies in Higher Education*, 16, 129–50. (Describes CEQ.)

Ramsden, P. & Entwistle, N. J. (1981). 'Effects of Academic Departments on Students' Approaches to Studying', *British Journal of Educational Psychology*, 51, 368–83.

Tait, H., Entwistle, N. J. & McCune, V. (1998). 'ASSIST: A re-conceptualisation of the *Approaches to Studying Inventory*', in C. Rust (ed.) *Improving Student Learning: Improving Students as Learners* (pp. 262–71). Oxford: Oxford Brookes University, Centre for Staff and Learning Development. (Describes ASSIST, full version available at http://www.etl.tla.ed.ac.uk/publications.html.)

9 Monitoring and Developing Teaching

We have already looked at the series of stages involved in planning and implementing a course unit, but two other steps are also involved – reviewing the success of the teaching and deciding any changes that might be needed next time. As we have seen, formal evaluations for quality assurance purposes provide only an indication of students' satisfaction with the teaching. It is thus helpful, periodically, to carry out a more thorough evaluation of teaching using a research-based questionnaire, discussing the findings with colleagues and a group of students, and talking at some length to one or more students. This more thorough feedback can then be used to fine-tune the teaching, either during the course or in preparation for the next occasion.

In this chapter we shall be looking at these methods of obtaining feedback, and at ways of developing, over time, more effective approaches to teaching. The starting point is the short questionnaire mentioned in the Bridge Passage, before moving on to the use of interviews to explore how students go about their learning. This then leads on to teaching development and the idea of there being a *scholarship of teaching*.

▶ An evaluation questionnaire to monitor teaching

A much abbreviated version of the *Experiences of Teaching and Learning Questionnaire* used in the ETL project can be found in Appendix B, while fuller versions can be downloaded from the project website (http://www.etl.tla.ed.ac.uk/publications.html). It allows staff to judge to what extent students are adopting deep approaches and whether the teaching seems to be encouraging these approaches, taking no more than ten minutes to fill in, either during a teaching session or online, towards the end of a specific course unit or module. Students indicate the relative strength of their agreement or otherwise with each statement on a five-point scale; the ratings given on each dimension are then added together to produce a score.

The first part of the questionnaire indicates the main approaches to learning and studying discussed in Chapter 3, while the rest of it monitors students' reactions to their experiences of the course unit and provides a self-rating of the knowledge and understanding acquired. The main dimensions have been identified statistically, using factor analysis to separate out sets of statements that together represent a distinguishable facet of students' experience. These dimensions are described briefly in Table 9.1, while the scoring procedure and other details are in Appendix B. A more general discussion of various inventories currently in use can be found elsewhere (Entwistle and McCune, 2004).

Table 9.1 shows, first, the three dimensions describing approaches to learning and studying, but at the end of this section of the questionnaire a final statement has been

Table 9.1   Scales and typical items describing approaches to studying and experiences of teaching

Scales	Typical items
Approaches to studying	
Deep approach	I've looked at evidence carefully to reach my own conclusion about what I'm studying.
	Ideas I've come across in my academic reading often set me off on long chains of thought.
Surface approach	I've just been going through the motions of studying without seeing where I'm going.
	Much of what I've learned seems no more than unrelated bits and pieces in my mind.
Organized effort	I've organized my study time carefully to make the best use of it.
	I have generally put a lot of effort into my studying.
Experiences of the teaching–learning environment	
Congruence and coherence	What we were taught seemed to match what we were supposed to learn.
	The topics seemed to follow each other in a way that made sense to me.
Teaching for understanding	The teaching encouraged me to rethink my understanding of aspects of the subject.
	The teaching helped me to think about the evidence underpinning different views.
Staff enthusiasm and support	Staff tried to share their enthusiasm about the subject with us.
	Staff were patient in explaining things which seemed difficult to grasp.
Constructive feedback	The feedback given on my set work helped to clarify things I hadn't fully understood.
	The feedback on my work helped me to improve my ways of learning and studying.
Support from other students	Students supported each other and tried to give help when it was needed.
	Talking with other students helped me to develop my understanding.
Interest and relevance	I found most of what I learned in this course unit really interesting.
	I enjoyed being involved in this course unit.

added – 'When I look back, I sometimes wonder why I ever decided to come here'. This item indicates a negative attitude to the university experience, one that may substantially affect students' ways of tackling their work. In some analyses it has proved to be a valuable indicator of alienation in a whole class. Table 9.1 then shows the six factors that emerged from analysing students' experiences of the teaching–learning environment, both in our own analyses and in those carried out in the University of Helsinki (Parpala et al., in press), mentioned earlier. The table also shows typical items for each scale, while the whole set can be found in Appendix B. As all the factors are related to each other, there is a strong first factor, which can be used by summing all the scores, as an overall indicator of what Richardson has described as 'academic quality' (Richardson, 2005).

The questionnaire also covers the 'perceived demands' experienced by students, such as the previous knowledge expected, and asks them to rate the 'knowledge and ways of thinking' they believe they have acquired. These do not form conceptually valid scales and so the items are treated separately. How the inventory can be used to explore the effects on teaching will be discussed later, but now we come to the use of interviews to explore why students adopt particular study strategies.

▷ Interviews to explore student learning

Informal interviews with students can help staff to understand the differences that exist in the ways in which students learn, and they can also be used in more detailed ways to investigate the effects of teaching on learning. The Bridge Passage into Chapter 3 mentioned the development of *phenomenography* (Marton & Booth, 1997; Bruce & Gerber, 1997) as an approach to exploring aspects of student learning. This research approach adopts a distinctive style of interviewing that develops a natural conversation with a student, although it focuses on a specific topic, such as an approach to studying or the understanding of a particular concept or topic.

A series of questions is decided in advance to encourage a logical progression in the interview (such as that shown in Appendix A), while allowing students opportunities to describe, fully and freely, their experiences of studying or ways of understanding (Entwistle, 1997; Marton & Booth, 1997). A typical interview on approaches to learning focuses initially on a specific instance, such as a piece of work that has been recently completed. Students might be asked what they thought was required of them, how they began the work, what resources they found in the library or on the web, how they carried out the task and how they felt about what they had written. At each stage they are encouraged to explain more fully what they had done and why, with the interviewer pushing for more detailed explanations and exploring any comments that seem particularly inter-esting. From time to time interviewers reflect back to the student their understanding of what has been said, to check that their interpretation is what was intended. Through such interviews it is possible to understand not just what approach has been used but also why it has been adopted.

Even informal discussions with students often reveal unexpected variations in how they go about their studying, as well as the familiar differences in approaches to learning. And it is also valuable to discuss how they try to understand new ideas. This may throw light on the specific processes of learning involved in the deep approach in that particular area of study, or indicate what students are failing to do. Staff may find it quite difficult to understand why some apparently obvious strategies are not being used.

Table 9.2 provides an illustration of an interview in which a final-year student was asked about an essay she had written. At one level, it may seem to explore just the process of planning and writing the essay, but the main intention was to see how

Table 9.2   Extract from an interview about an essay assignment in economic history

---

The student was in her final year of Economic History, and the interview focused on the development of understanding and any imagery related to it.

I   *I'd like to talk to you about how you tackled this particular essay.*

S   Right, well, you're given a reading list, so really the way I always do my essays is I try to find a basic book that's going to cover everything and which is on the reading list. And then the articles get more and more specialised and bring in more and more points, so I'll try to read the book first, and then I will try and read all the articles. I know some people read a few of them, but I always feel as though I'm missing out on something, and actually by the time I get to the end of the reading, most of the articles are repeating what has already been said, so the reading gets faster. I generally take notes from all the books and articles, then I go back to the title and read through it, and decide what they're looking for. Then I make a little schedule, and go back and read through my notes again, highlighting all the relevant points. Next, I'll go back and make a more detailed plan of what I want to do, and then I'll just write it all up using my notes.

I   *How much detail was there in the notes you took from the articles you read?*

S   A lot of detail, actually, especially the first couple of books or articles I read, because I'm never quite sure exactly what I'm looking for until I've read a couple of things. Then it's easier to start picking out what you need and what you don't need, but I guess it's one of my faults that I do take too many notes, and I know that. But then I feel that I have to do it to get a grip with the subject; then it's just a matter of reducing them and taking down what you need.

I   *And when you've got all these notes, you said you reduce them, but how do you do that from what sounds like quite a stack of notes?*

S   It usually takes me a day just to read them and highlight them and then see what I need. I think about the title of the essay and what the lecturer said about that topic and try to decide what is important for the essay.

I   *And having read through the notes, what have you got?*

S   I see what everybody is talking about; the kind of things they're getting at, and then I ask what the question is looking for. … You just take the question apart: … I look through my notes, highlight them and usually I change the structure of what I'm going to write about because I actually write out a more detailed plan and I bring in more bits, so I can see where they fit in.

I   *So when you are writing, you have your plan close by; it's there just as a sort of general guide, but as you're writing, how do you know where to go next?*

S   The further I get into an essay the more I know exactly what I'm trying to get at. When I'm writing, I know if it is going to be a good essay, because it just seems to flow.

I   *What you mean by 'flow'?*

S   Well, it just seems that I know where I'm going next, as if I'm following the argument logically, perhaps, and providing the evidence for it as I am going along.

(Continued)

Table 9.2   (Continued)

I   *So, how did your plan help that process?*

S   I suppose it was a bit like a map, which I could almost see in my mind; I could see how the various parts fitted together and so I could follow the links between them as I was writing. And the evidence I had in my notes seemed to be pulled in when I thought about the next step.

I   *And how well did you feel you had understood the topic in the end?*

S   I felt I understood it. There was quite a lot of information to bring in. I remember I had to sit down and think about the structure, really quite carefully, because there were so many points to bring in. I remember thinking I wasn't quite sure how it had gone when I gave it in, because I wasn't sure how well I had constructed it, whether I was putting everything in the right place.

I   *Can you remember these essays quite well after you've written them – does it stay in your mind?*

S   Yes, the general points stay and the actual details, once you read through them, they all come flooding back, as it were. The general arguments that I included tend to be remembered. But I always find when I'm revising that I still have to sit down and read through them.

Source: From a study described by Entwistle, 1995.

an understanding of the topic had been developed. This example illustrates a logical progression in the interview, and the search for more explanation or for reasons why a strategy was used. Some students need to be led through their experience of studying even more explicitly, being less forthcoming than this student; others may not have been monitoring their processes of studying, and so cannot describe them at all clearly.

Even with an informal discussion with a student it is better to record it, so that comments can be considered later. But when they are part of a more formal investigation, interviews will have to be recorded and transcribed. The transcripts then allow the students' comments to be systematically analysed. Typically about 30 students would be chosen so that they cover a good range of ability. In phenomenography the aim is to establish the main ways in which students differ in their responses, while grouping together similar comments. By reading the transcripts several times, similarities emerge as *categories of description*. Each of these is clarified during the repeated readings, until it corresponds closely to what the students have been saying. In reporting the findings several interview extracts are needed to make the meaning of each category explicit (Entwistle, 1997: 132–3). Finally, the researcher tries to establish any relationships between the categories that may help to explain their meaning more clearly (Marton & Booth, 1997). Sometimes the categories form a 'nested hierarchy', with each successive category containing more of the aspects found in the ultimate one. Such progressions were seen earlier in the descriptions of conceptions of knowledge and learning in Figure 3.1 and approaches to teaching in Figure 5.1.

▶ **Investigating the effectiveness of teaching**

As already mentioned, the ETL project used two questionnaires: one of these was given at the start of a course unit to discover students' aspirations and the approaches to studying adopted previously. Towards the end of the unit a second questionnaire was used to explore the approaches students had used on that unit, their experiences of the teaching and their self-ratings on what they had learned. We were interested in relating changes in approaches to studying to perceptions of the teaching experienced. Scores from the inventories, along with comments made by groups of students in interviews, were analysed and then discussed with course teams to see what 'fine-tuning' in the teaching could be arranged for next time.

The Subject Area Reports for the four subject areas in the project provide detailed results, but Table 9.3 provides an example of one analysis from the report on electronic engineering. It illustrates, in a simplified way, how we compared the effectiveness of three specific course units. In all these three settings experienced teachers had taught the same topic area (analogue electronics) using similar teaching methods (lectures, assignments of circuit problems and tutorial support in large groups of varying sizes). In spite of this

Table 9.3   Percentage agreement with items from students in three course units

Course unit (Numbers of students)		Percentage agreement with items		
		A (94)	**B** (68)	**C** (54)
Aspirations before the unit				
I want to study the subject in depth		87.2	77.9	61.1
I sometimes wonder why I ever came here		5.2	14.7	29.6
Approaches to studying *(before and during the unit)*				
I usually set out to understand	*Before*	95.6	87.5	81.2
(Deep approach)	*During*	**72.1**	**82.5**	**75.0**
Trouble making sense of things	*Before*	25.0	40.0	43.7
(Surface approach)	*During*	**61.8**	**55.0**	**34.4**
Generally put a lot of effort in	*Before*	60.3	77.5	53.1
(Effort)	*During*	**51.5**	**60.0**	**40.6**
Systematic and organized study	*Before*	65.9	62.5	46.9
(Study organization)	*During*	**44.1**	**47.5**	**50.0**
Experiences of the teaching–learning environment				
Easy pace in lectures		25.3	46.9	72.5
Amount of work required was easy		33.3	34.7	52.5
Teaching fitted in with learning		72.0	67.3	97.5
Most of material was interesting		45.3	34.7	82.5
Plenty of examples were provided		66.7	51.0	95.0
Staff were patient in explaining		81.3	81.6	92.5
Feedback given made things clearer		63.7	30.6	47.5

Note: The wording of the items has been abbreviated.

similarity in teaching methods, students' experiences of that teaching and its apparent effects on their approaches to learning proved to be different. In the study itself the analysis was based on scale scores, but here individual items are used to show the pattern of findings.

The percentage agreement of students with statements about their aspirations can be found in the top half of the table, which also compares the approaches to learning adopted before the unit began with those used during the unit. The lower half presents the perceptions of teaching at the end of those same units (for details of the full analysis, see Entwistle, Nisbet & Bromage, 2005: 28).

In Unit A, the students' aspirations showed an intention to study the subject in depth, but during the unit the percentage of the students 'setting out to understand' (deep approach) dropped markedly. Students in Units A and B reported increasing difficulty in 'making sense of things', indicating more of a surface approach. In contrast with the other two classes, a much larger proportion of students in Unit C were 'wondering why they ever came here'. The percentages of these students showing 'deep' responses decreased slightly during the unit, but the initially high proportion of surface approaches dropped markedly, indicating an improved overall way of studying. Compared with students in both the other units, however, their level of effort was substantially lower, perhaps due to their more negative feelings about the university.

Possible reasons for the changes in approaches to learning can be inferred from students' reactions to the teaching. In Units A and B, where the percentages indicating a deep approach had decreased, a majority of students had found difficulty in both the pace of lectures and the amount of work required; they also said that the content was not particularly interesting. In contrast, the students in Unit C, who showed decreases in the surface approach, showed much more favourable reactions to almost all aspects of the teaching, with the exception of feedback. But their lack of effort still counted against them. In all three units staff were seen as being patient in explaining difficulties in the set work but, while feedback was appreciated in Unit A, there was substantial dissatisfaction with it in Unit B.

The percentage response to items in the questionnaire cannot show any causal relationship between the approaches and the perceptions of teaching but, in the group interviews, students expressed general and often strong agreement about the effects of the teaching on their learning. Typical comments for each of the three units are shown in Table 9.4.

Analyses of the questionnaire responses drew lecturers' attention to possible areas of difficulty, while discussions with groups of students made clear the reasons for their concern and suggested ways of improving the situation. In everyday teaching, however, it would rarely be possible to do such detailed analyses; the general approach could be followed, however, given automated ways of collecting the data and analysing them.

While Tables 9.3 and 9.4 were based on just three course units, similar analyses were carried out in all 25 settings in the ETL project. Table 9.5 shows some of the relationships found from the sample of 1950 students who completed both questionnaires. This table shows general patterns of relationship through the inter-correlations between students' aspirations and approaches on the one hand, and the demands they felt and their experiences of teaching–learning environment, on the other.

Although a perfect relationship would show a correlation of 1.0, much lower values are inevitable when using responses to self-rating questions. With such a large sample, most of the correlations are statistically significant, but here what concerns us most is the

Table 9.4   Comments from students in the three course units compared in Table 9.3

Course A	These lectures were ... the most difficult part of the course in the second year. ... During the autumn term I honestly didn't really grasp what was going on. ... I'd been putting in as much effort into analogue as ... other courses, but it really needed special attention; I probably should have given it more at the start of the year. ... The way [the lecturer] explained it, I never really could relate the circuit to his diagrams or to the voltages that he was telling us that were there. ... At the beginning I was all at sea, sort of too much information at one time. ... I just think that we were given too many different concepts at one time. ... It seemed that once we'd gone over one specific network, we weren't really given enough time to absorb the information before we were given another one, and the difficulty level increased as you went onwards.
Course B	[There were] no tutorial solutions. We were refused any. I think our lecturer's opposed to giving solutions actually because he thinks we'll just learn it [parrot fashion]. ... Even worked examples that weren't from the tutorials [would help], so [even if] we're not given tutorial solutions, we can still see how to implement things, not just being taught theory and expected to figure out how to do it. ... When you got help it was fine, ... [but] there's only one tutor per tutorial group, and there are several people asking questions at the same time. He can't get round you all, so I find that a bit of a waste of that hour.
Course C	The lecturer (this year) is really good. ... When you've got a good lecturer who is trying to actually make you learn, rather than just make you pass, I think that's good. ... He's taken time in the lectures to actually tell us ... what we can achieve from [analogue]. ... And his enthusiasm for us to do well makes you more enthusiastic about everything. ... He'd [explain] why you were trying to learn something, trying to make sure that everyone understood in the class, rather than ... [us just] memorizing it. ... I think he's trying to get into our heads that we actually need to <u>know</u> it. ... He understands that ... there are people that are not going to study until two weeks before the exam, and there are people who study all the way through. And he can cater for that. ... He's not always on your back, but he lets you know, you've <u>got</u> to understand.

pattern of relationships before and during the course. Aspirations refer to a time before the unit started, as do the first set of approaches; the demands and experiences students experienced could only have influenced the approaches during the unit and the perceived achievements. So what did we find?

- Not surprisingly, having a deep interest in the subject produced nothing but positive correlations with good experiences on the course unit, while those associated with 'alienation' from the university experience were all slightly negative.

Table 9.5 Correlations of experiences of teaching with study strategies and outcomes

Perceptions of teaching	Aspirations		Prior approaches			Approaches during			Achievements	
	Depth	Alienation	Deep	Surface	Organized	Deep	Surface	Organized	Know	Grades
Easiness of demands made in the course unit										
Prior knowledge required	.06	–.03	.08	–.11	.04	.14	–.21	.07	.19	.24
Pace introducing material	.01	–.03	.06	–.06	.05	.19	–.26	.16	.26	.32
Academic difficulty	.06	–.05	.10	–.09	.03	.18	–.23	.12	.24	.33
Workload required	.01	–.06	.03	–.04	.04	.06	–.14	.08	.12	.25
Experiences of the teaching–learning environment										
Congruence and coherence	.08	–.17	.21	–.21	.14	.32	–.38	.25	.45	.28
Teaching for understanding	.19	–.13	.37	–.16	.16	.52	–.33	.28	.46	.27
Staff enthusiasm and support	.09	–.12	.18	–.12	.12	.28	–.20	.21	.34	.19
Constructive feedback	.10	–.12	.24	–.12	.15	.36	–.27	.26	.44	.29
Support from other students	.08	–.14	.14	–.05	.13	.22	–.08	.19	.22	.07
Enjoyment and interest	.23	–.18	.26	–.16	.18	.39	–.39	.29	.48	.39

Note: Total sample (N = 1950)

The two indicators of 'aspirations' are equivalent to those shown in Table 9.3.

'Know' is a self-rating on the knowledge acquired, while 'Grades' is a self-rating on grades actually obtained.

The bold figures draw attention to aspects more closely related to the development of understanding.

- Perceived demands, with the exception of 'workload', showed similar patterns of relationship. Before the course, correlations with 'prior knowledge', 'pace' and 'difficulty' were low, as expected, but those with 'approaches' and 'achievements' during the course increased, with the exception of 'organized effort'. Being partly a study habit, this last aspect is less susceptible to change. The only substantial correlation with workload was the self-rating of grades awarded.
- The existence of substantial relationships between approaches to studying before the unit began and the experiences of teaching during the course indicates that established approaches influence how the teaching is subsequently perceived. But the much higher correlations of all the experiences of teaching, and most of the demands, with approaches during the course and with learning outcomes, indicate stronger influences of teaching on student learning. These findings confirm the existence of a two-way relationship between approaches and experiences of teaching (Richardson, 2007). 'Teaching for understanding' showed its highest correlation with the deep approach (0.52), while four of the 'experiences' factors had correlations of over 0.4 with perceived improvements in knowledge and ways of thinking.

This analysis shows the potential value of conceptually based inventories in indicating both approaches to studying and perceptions of the teaching–learning environment. Other examples of similar analyses can be found elsewhere (Entwistle, McCune & Hounsell, 2003; Hounsell & Hounsell, 2007). By using this technique for evaluating their own courses, university teachers can see for themselves how their teaching is affecting their students' learning, and if need be, modify their approaches accordingly. However, the research described earlier in the book suggests additional ways of developing teaching.

▶ Encouraging teaching development

In this book we have been suggesting ways of thinking about the effects of teaching on learning that can guide practices across subject areas, according to the *inner logic of the subject and its pedagogy*. Although there are necessarily different methods of teaching across disciplines, the general aims of university teachers have much in common. They want their students to develop distinctive *ways of thinking and practising* and to acquire a *disposition to understand*. This idea goes beyond a deep approach by including a continuing willingness to direct effort towards understanding, and an alertness to whatever might contribute to deepening it further. The academic understanding that students develop has to be expressed in terms of accepted knowledge and the conventions used in describing it. But the activity of organizing understanding in one's own way remains crucial, if it is to become firmly rooted and, above all, easy to use in the future. That future perspective becomes increasingly important as students move out into a world of *supercomplexity*.

Figure 9.1 helps us to think back at the form of understanding we would like our students to achieve and to consider some of the ways of teaching we met earlier that are most likely to help them to achieve it.

As we saw in Chapter 4, students preparing for final exams tended to develop an integrative form of understanding, pulling together several threads of knowledge and weaving them into their own way of thinking about a topic. As a consequence of that

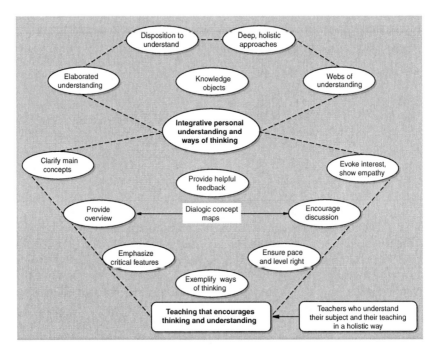

Figure 9.1 Critical features of teaching for integrative personal understanding

effort, some students reported experiencing a *knowledge object* that enabled them to visualize the main aspects of a topic within a tightly organized whole. This representation also provided logical pathways that could be used in explaining their understanding during the exam.

The holistic quality of this experience suggests the importance of teachers stressing the interconnections that exist within a topic. Some lecturers are much better at using overviews than others, as we saw in Chapter 5, but this capacity can be, and ought to be, developed. In Part 3, and again in discussing the heuristic model, we saw some of the aspects of teaching that seem likely to encourage students to develop deep approaches and a continuing disposition to understand for themselves. The importance of clarifying the nature of concepts was seen in the work on threshold concepts (Davies & Mangan, 2008), while Marton's ideas on variation theory showed the value of focusing on critical features (Marton, 2007). Providing an overview and encouraging students to consider their current understanding was prominent in the ongoing research into dialogic concept maps (Hay, in press), a technique that also encourages students to develop a dialogue, both internally and with others, as a way of bringing together ideas from many sources that could enhance their existing understanding. But this process also depends on teachers providing useful and timely feedback on assignments and assessments. Students are helped to adopt the appropriate academic discourse in their explanations through teachers thinking out loud, while lecturers need to judge the pace and level of their presentations carefully to make understanding possible, as we saw earlier in this chapter. Finally, we saw in Chapter 5, and again in Chapter 7, how strongly interest and empathy affect the quality of learning, making it both effective and congenial. All of these aspects need to be borne in mind in university teaching, but how else can it be developed?

From what we saw earlier, a close look at the nature of knowledge within the discipline offers a fruitful starting point for teaching development. As Prosser and his collaborators noted in relation to a holistic, student-oriented approach to teaching:

A major implication of [our] work is that, if we want to change and develop the ways in which teachers approach their teaching and help their students to learn, we need to help them to think carefully about what they are teaching and how it relates to, and coheres with, the field as a whole. This is a particularly important issue for teachers new to teaching, or teaching a particular topic for the first time.

(Prosser et al., 2005: 153)

They also suggested that looking for *threshold concepts* could prove valuable in encouraging staff to explore the nature of knowledge in their subject, an idea that was taken further by O'Brien (2008a). She asked several lecturers to select a topic they had found to work as a threshold in opening up the subject for students, and then to discuss that topic, and how they taught it, with a colleague who had similar expertise. O'Brien found that this interplay of ideas had proved valuable for each of the teachers as they explored the nature of knowledge within the discipline and how those ideas could be taught more imaginatively.

As a method of enhancing practice, this peer-to-peer pedagogic discussion has potential for engaging teachers in deep, supported deliberations about what they will teach, how students may learn and why one approach may be more effective than another. Appropriately focused, such discussions can orient teachers to the specific challenges and issues that the subject matter holds for learning.

(O'Brien, 2008b: 217)

Effective *teaching for understanding* depends, above all, on teaching being seen not just from the perspective of the subject specialist but also from that of the student. In other words, the teacher has to imagine what it is like not to understand, and then consider what steps are needed to help students to achieve their own understanding. This, in turn, depends on knowing what learning processes and strategies are necessary for a deep approach in the topic being taught. As we suggested earlier, interviewing a few students along the lines suggested in Table 9.2 and Appendix A, and seeing at first hand the differences between deep and surface approaches among students, can act as a *threshold experience* for university teachers as they come to see teaching and learning in a different way (Entwistle, 2008). Many of the courses now being taught as initial training for lecturers stress this perspective (Prosser & Trigwell, 1999; Biggs, 2007), helping academics to recognize that their influence as teachers goes beyond making the subject accessible. Their teaching also influences how students think about the subject and, importantly, also affects their views about the nature of learning in general and how they go about their studying (Meyer, 2005).

In all these different ways university teachers are being encouraged to take account of students' experiences of learning, but even teaching for understanding will only be effective if constructive and timely feedback is provided and if assessment necessarily involves a demonstration of understanding. In other words, the responsibility of a course team in planning and organizing a course extends to the whole teaching–learning environment, by ensuring that each element of it, as far as possible, supports the main aims of the course.

One of the difficulties for educational developers has been the negative attitude of some experienced academics to the whole notion of teaching development. This has arisen, in part, from past experiences that failed to take account of the distinctive nature of their academic discipline. Currently, staff vary in what they expect educational development to deliver, some seeing it as being a training in specific teaching techniques, such as using audio-visual equipment or incorporating elements of e-learning into their teaching. That training is important, of course, but other staff already recognize that teaching development has a broader horizon, one which helps academics to develop a more sophisticated conception of the relationship between teaching and learning, and so has a more fundamental and lasting influence on their work (Åkerlind, 2005).

> It is possible to help university teachers to recognize the value of such pedagogical training, but its effects depend on providing opportunities for intensive reflection on the implications of the research findings in relation to their own university experience and that of their colleagues.
>
> If pedagogical training does not offer opportunities for reflection and conceptual change, but focuses on changing the teaching strategies of teachers, it is likely to affect teaching only at a superficial level. Learning new teaching 'tricks' is likely to be of limited usefulness if there is a lack of pedagogical knowledge or if the teacher's intention and purpose is not to improve teaching to promote the quality of students' learning outcomes, but to improve teaching for the teacher's own comfort.
>
> (Postareff, 2007: 61)

▶ The scholarship of teaching

This broader form of professional development for teachers has been underpinned by the notion of a *scholarship of teaching*, an idea coming from Ernest Boyer of the Carnegie Foundation for the Advancement of Teaching in the USA.

> The most important obligation now confronting colleges and universities is to break out of the tired old teaching versus research debate and define, in more creative ways, what it means to be a scholar.
>
> (Boyer, 1990: xii)

He suggested that if we consider scholarship in relation to the role of the academic, four distinct forms are noticeable: the scholarship of *discovery* that adds to the corpus of established knowledge; of *integration*, which involves making new interconnections and interpretations from pre-existing sources; of *application* that depends on engagement with the world outside and leads to an integration of theory with practice; and the *scholarship of teaching*, which he saw as demanding the same habits of mind as the other forms. Lee Shulman and his colleagues at the Carnegie Foundation (Huber & Hutchings, 2005) and other researchers (Kreber, 2002; Brew, 2006) have extended this idea and described it as a *scholarship of teaching and learning*.

The scholarship of teaching and learning focuses on a conception of teaching ... not just as a technique ... but an enactment of our understanding of a disciplinary, inter-disciplinary or professional field and what it means to know it deeply. It follows, then, that teaching needs to be reconnected to scholarship and to the scholarly communities through habits of documentation, exchange, and peer review, ... [as] catalysts for ... developments in peer collaboration and review of teaching.

(Hutchings, Babb & Bjork, 2002: 2–3)

[It] is characterized by

- Deep knowledge of the subject or discipline being taught;
- Pedagogical knowledge specific to the discipline, as well as general pedagogical knowledge;
- Reflectivity;
- Sharing and peer review.

Being reflective involves informing oneself about what is already known about the particular issues relating to teaching and learning within one's own discipline, or within the context of other disciplines, and exploring how this existing information relates to one's own experiences and findings. The chief purpose of reflection is [that] it makes our work evidence-based. Through reflection we find out whether what we assume to be true about teaching and learning is indeed valid knowledge. ... Eventually, scholars of teaching share the insights gained ... [either *formally*] ... or *informally* through discussion groups, mentoring others or institutional newsletters.

(Kreber, 2005: 2)

While this level of involvement with teaching will be welcomed by some academics, others will find that the demands of their research and entrepreneurial activities limit their opportunities to share or publish their ideas about teaching. Nevertheless reflecting on the inner logic of the subject and its pedagogy is an essential requirement for developing effective and imaginative teaching at university.

Helping academics to change their way of thinking about teaching and learning, however, also depends on supportive leaders within a department and on the institutional environment in general. While university management continues to be driven by a business model and its associated terminology, and while quality assurance follows that same line by measuring productivity rather than teaching quality, there will remain a mismatch between the aims of teaching espoused by academics and the rhetoric of business plans and products coming from management. As Elton (1999) argued:

The process of change must be initiated from both 'bottom up' and 'top down', with 'the bottom' having the knowledge and 'the top' the power. ... 'The top' must use its power, not overtly or directly, but to facilitate the work from 'the bottom' and to provide conditions under which it can prosper.

(Elton, 1999: 215)

In addition, there needs to be at least a translation process to make business rhetoric engage more directly with the continuing aims of university education and with the activities of outstanding university teachers, and a light touch in quality assurance procedures that actively encourages more imaginative ways of thinking about teaching and allows them to flourish.

▶ References

Åkerlind, G. S. (2005). 'Academic Growth and Development – How do University Academics Experience it?', *Higher Education*, 50, 1–32.

Biggs, J. B. (2007). *Teaching for Quality Learning at University*. Buckingham: SRHE and Open University Press.

Boyer, E. (1990). *Scholarship Reconsidered*. Washington, DC: Carnegie Foundation.

Brew, A. (2006). *Research and Teaching: Beyond the Divide*. Basingstoke: Palgrave Macmillan.

Bruce, C. & Gerber, R. (eds) (1997). 'Special Issue on Phenomenography in Higher Education', *Higher Education Research and Development*, 16, 2 (whole issue).

Davies, P. & Mangan, J. (2008). 'Embedding Threshold Concepts: From Theory to Pedagogical Principles to Learning Activities', in R. Land, J. H. F. Meyer & J. Smith (eds) *Threshold Concepts within the Disciplines* (pp. 37–50). Rotterdam: Sense Publishers.

Elton, L. (1999). 'New Ways of Learning in Higher Education: Managing the Change', *Tertiary Education and Management*, 5, 207–25.

Entwistle, N. J. (1995). 'Frameworks for Understanding as Experienced in Essay Writing and in Preparing for Examinations', *Educational Psychologist*, 30, 47–54.

Entwistle, N. J. (1997). 'Phenomenography in Higher Education', *Higher Education Research and Development*, 16, 127–34.

Entwistle, N. J. (2008). 'Threshold Concepts and Transformative Ways of Thinking within Research into Higher Education', in R. Land, J. H. F. Meyer & J. Smith (eds) *Threshold Concepts within the Disciplines* (pp. 21–35). Rotterdam, Netherlands: Sense Publishers.

Entwistle, N. J., & McCune, V. (2004). 'The Conceptual Bases of Study Strategy Inventories', *Educational Psychology Review*, 16, 325–46.

Entwistle, N. J., McCune, V. & Hounsell, J. (2003). 'Investigating Ways of Enhancing University Teaching–Learning Environments: Measuring Students' Approaches to Studying and Perceptions of Teaching', in De Corte, L. Verschaffel, N. J. Entwistle & J. van Merrienboer (eds) *Unravelling Basic Components and Dimensions of Powerful Learning Environments* (pp. 89–108) Oxford: Elsevier Science.

Entwistle, N. J., Nisbet, J. B. & Bromage, A. (2005). *ETL Project Subject Overview Report: Electronic Engineering*, available at http://www.etl.tla.ed.ac.uk/publications.html.

Hay (in press). 'Facilitating Personal Understanding in Higher Education: The Role of Dialogic Concept-Mapping,' *Psychology Journal (of Greece)*.

Hounsell, D. J. & Hounsell, J. (2007). 'Teaching–Learning Environments in Contemporary Mass Higher Education', in N. J. Entwistle & P. D. Tomlinson (eds) *Student Learning and University Teaching*. British Journal of Educational Psychology, Monograph Series II: Psychological Aspects of Education – Current Trends (pp. 91–112). Leicester: British Psychological Society.

Huber, M. & Hutchings, P. (2005). *The Advancements of Learning: Building the Teaching Commons*. The Carnegie Foundation Report on the Scholarship of Teaching and Learning. San Francisco: Jossey-Bass.

Hutchings, P., Babb, M. & Bjork, C. (2002). *The Scholarship of Teaching and Learning in Higher Education: An Annotated Bibliography*, available at http://www.carnegiefoundation.org/dynamic/downloads/file_1_196.pdf.

Kreber, C. (2002). 'Controversy and Consensus on the Scholarship of Teaching', *Studies in Higher Education*, 27, 151–67.

Kreber, C. (2005). 'The Scholarship of Teaching and Learning', Edinburgh: Teaching, Learning and Assessment Centre, University of Edinburgh. Available at www.tla.ed.ac.uk.

Marton, F. (1997). 'Towards a Pedagogical Theory of Learning', in N. J. Entwistle & P. D. Tomlinson (eds) *Student Learning and University Teaching*. British Journal of Educational Psychology, Monograph Series II: Psychological Aspects of Education – Current Trends (pp. 19–30). Leicester: British Psychological Society.

Marton, F. & Booth, S. (2007). *Learning and Awareness*. Mahwah, NJ: Lawrence Erlbaum.

Meyer, J. H. F. (2005). 'Closing the Gap between Educational Research and Educational Development: A Model of Engagement', in C. Rust (ed.) *Improving Student Learning 12: Diversity and Inclusivity* (pp. 360–76). Oxford: Oxford Centre for Staff and Learning Development, Oxford Brookes University.

O'Brien, M. (2008a). 'Threshold Concepts for University Teaching and Learning: A Study of Troublesome Knowledge and Transformative Thinking in the Teaching of Threshold Concepts', in J. H. F. Meyer, R. Land & J. Smith (eds) *Threshold Concepts in the Disciplines* (pp. 289–306). Netherlands: Sense Publishers.

O'Brien, M. (2008b). *Teaching as Translation: An Investigation of University Teachers' Pedagogical Content Knowledge, Reasoning and Intention*. Doctoral thesis, School of Education and Professional Studies, Griffith University, Australia.

Parpala, A., Lindblom-Ylänne, S., Komulainen, E., Hirsto, L. & Litmanen, T. (in press). 'Students' Perceptions of the Teaching–Learning Environment, Approaches to Learning, and their Relationship, among First- and Third-Year Students', *Studies in Higher Education*.

Postareff, L. (2007). *Teaching in Higher Education: From Content-Focused to Learning-Focused Approaches to Teaching*. Department of Education, Research Report 214. Helsinki: University of Helsinki.

Prosser, M., Martin, E., Trigwell, K., Ramsden, P. & Lueckenhausen, G. (2005). 'Academics' Experiences of Understanding of their Subject Matter and the Relationship of this to their Experiences of Teaching and Learning', *Instructional Science*, 33, 137–57.

Prosser, M. & Trigwell, K. (1999). *Understanding Learning and Teaching: The Experience of Higher Education*. Buckingham: Open University Press.

Richardson, J. T. E. (2005). 'Student Perceptions of Academic Quality and Approaches to Studying in Distance Education', *British Educational Research Journal*, 31, 1–21.

Richardson, J. T. E. (2007). 'Variations in Student Learning and Perceptions of Academic Quality', in N. J. Entwistle & P. D. Tomlinson (eds) *Student Learning and University Teaching*. British Journal of Educational Psychology, Monograph Series II: Psychological Aspects of Education – Current Trends (pp. 61–72). Leicester: British Psychological Society.

Appendix A Example of a Typical Student Interview Schedule

This example comes from the study mentioned in Chapters 4 and 9, which was designed to investigate the 'knowledge objects' developed by some students in the process of writing essays in economic history and also being used in examinations later on. Like most of the interviews used in student learning research, these interviews focused on a specific piece of work, before asking more general questions. Students had been asked to bring the essay with them. The intention was to encourage them to describe how they went about writing that specific essay, and to focus on their experiences of developing an understanding of the topic. This semi-structured interview schedule was designed to provide a logical path for the student, even though that order was used flexibly so that the students could describe their own approach more freely. The schedule reminded the interviewer of the main aspects and ensured that data could be collected about the study's specific research questions. But the interview also involved following up, in as much detail as possible, any interesting, unanticipated aspects raised by the student. This illustration can be readily adapted to explore the ways of studying in other subject areas or with a different purpose.

▶ Introduction

Purpose of the interview.

▶ Background information

To indicate which courses/modules are being taken and why they were chosen.

▶ Title

What was the title of this essay? Why did you choose this title?
What does the title mean? Is there anything significant about the wording?

▶ Preparation

How did you go about preparing for the essay?
Was there a particular book or article you relied on? Why was that?
Tell me about the notes you made. In what detail? Was this typical?

▶ Organizing the material

When you have all the notes, what do you do next?
When you are highlighting or marking important parts, what are you looking for?
When you came to arrange these notes, how did you decide the best order to put them in?
Is that the usual way you structure an essay? Why do you use this way (different ways)?
Did you prepare a specific essay plan, or did you just write it? Is that your usual approach?

▶ Writing the essay

How does your plan (or idea of the form the essay will take) affect the way you write?
How conscious are you of the structure of the essay as you are writing? How does it feel?
How do you draw into your essay the evidence or details you need?
How easy did you find the writing? Is that your usual experience?
In what ways, if any, did you revise the draft?
In the source material, did you come across contrasting views?
If so, how did you deal with these in your essay?

▶ Understanding of the content

How well did you feel you had understood the topic you had written about?
To what extent can you remember the content of the essay now?
  [At this stage, if necessary, encourage the student to look over essay again]
What do you now see to be the most important things you were trying to say?
When I asked you what you remembered, how did you get a 'handle' on it?
When you came to think about it, what were you using? [title, essay plan, conclusion or anything else?]
Have you got a good visual memory? A photographic memory? In what detail can you see things? Is it <u>really</u> 'seeing'? Or are you building up that picture more by logic?
Going back to the essay now, how did you try to explain what was meant by the title? Is that the way you would usually do it?
In what ways, if any, does this essay fit in with other things you have been studying? Did you think about any of these links, as you were preparing for the essay or writing it?

Any other aspects not otherwise covered that are important about your ways of essay writing.

Short Revised Experiences of Teaching and Learning Questionnaire

Based on the work of the ETL project team within the
Teaching and Learning Research Programme of the ESRC

This questionnaire is an abbreviated version of the ones used in the ETL project and has been specially prepared for this book. It can be used for monitoring teaching and learning, and also for carrying out small-scale investigations. For major studies, however, the original versions are more appropriate (see website). A downloadable version of this questionnaire can be used without charge and can be found on the project website (see below).

▶ Scoring procedure

For most of the items in the questionnaires, students respond on a 1–5 scale (5=high). The exception is the item asking about students' self-rating which has a 1–9 scale. In the project, the questionnaires were machine readable, allowing the data to be transferred directly to a statistical analysis program. Most universities now have this facility, but the questionnaire has to be formatted for the specific machine.

Scores on each scale are produced by adding together the responses on the items in that scale and then dividing the total by the number of items to create a score on the 1–5 scale. Scoring can be carried out by computer, using a program such as SPSS. Each item is set as a variable and then a scale total is produced by creating a new variable by summing the items.

The questionnaire can also be set up online, allowing it to be filled in, marked and analysed, so as to provide students with a profile of their responses and an interpretation of it, and easy feedback for staff. This development was not, however, possible within the time frame and resources of the ETL project. If profiles of scores on approaches to studying are given to students, it should be done cautiously, given that this is an abbreviated version of a longer instrument, and that there is a danger of students then labelling themselves as 'deep' or 'surface', and so becoming either overconfident about their subsequent success or unnecessarily anxious about the inevitability of poor results. Instead, students need to see their profile as a way of helping them to think more consciously and critically about their studying, and so find ways to improve it.

The profiles of scores on approaches to studying can be used either with individual students or as an indication of how students using different approaches have reacted to the teaching provided. It is also revealing to look at the frequency distributions of individual items in the last three sections, as these may provide specific information of possible difficulties.

Further Information about the original questionnaires, and papers describing some of the studies using them, can be found at the project website, http://www.etl.tla.ed.ac.uk/publications.html.

KEY TO SCALES AND ITEMS

▶ 1 Approaches to learning and studying

Deep approach

1. I've tried to find better ways of tracking down relevant information in this subject.
4. In making sense of new ideas, I have often related them to practical or real life contexts.
6. Ideas I've come across in my academic reading often set me off on long chains of thought.
7. I've looked at evidence carefully to reach my own conclusion about what I'm studying.
9. It has been important for me to follow the argument, or to see the reasons behind things.
12. In reading for this course, I've tried to find out for myself exactly what the author means.

Surface approach

3. Much of what I've learned seems no more than lots of unrelated bits and pieces in my mind.
8. I've often had trouble in making sense of the things I have to remember.
11. I don't think through topics for myself, I just rely on what we're taught.
13. I've just been going through the motions of studying without seeing where I'm going.

Organized effort

2. I have generally put a lot of effort into my studying.
5. On the whole, I've been quite systematic and organized in my studying.
10. I've organized my study time carefully to make the best use of it.
14. I've carefully prioritized my time to make sure I can fit everything in.

Lack of purpose

15. When I look back, I sometimes wonder why I ever decided to come here.

▶ 2 Experiences of teaching and learning

Congruence and coherence

1. It was clear to me what I was supposed to learn in this course.
2. The topics seemed to follow each other in a way that made sense to me.
3. What we were taught seemed to match what we were supposed to learn.

Teaching for understanding

4. This unit has given me a sense of what goes on 'behind the scenes' in this subject area.
5. The teaching in this course helped me to think about the evidence underpinning different views.
6. This course encouraged me to relate what I learned to issues in the wider world.

Staff enthusiasm and support

7. Staff tried to share their enthusiasm about the subject with us.
8. Staff were patient in explaining things which seemed difficult to grasp.
9. Students' views were valued in this course.

Constructive feedback

10. The feedback given on my work helped me to improve my ways of learning and studying.
11. The feedback given on my set work helped to clarify things I hadn't fully understood.

Support from other students

12. Students supported each other and tried to give help when it was needed.
13. Talking with other students helped me to develop my understanding.

Interest and enjoyment

14. I found most of what I learned in this course unit really interesting.
15. I enjoyed being involved in this course unit.

▶ 3 Demands made by course *(Scored as **perceived easiness**)*

Prior knowledge	a	What I was expected to know to begin with.
Pace	b	The rate at which new material was introduced
Academic difficulty	c	The ideas and problems I had to deal with
	d	The skills or technical procedures needed in this subject
Workload	e	The amount of work I was expected to do
Generic skills	f	Working with other students
	g	Organizing and being responsible for my own learning
	h	Communicating knowledge and ideas effectively
Information skills	i	Tracking down information for myself
	j	Information technology/computing skills (e.g. WWW, e-mail, word processing)

▶ 4 What was learned from the course

Knowledge and subject-specific skills	a	Knowledge and understanding about the topics covered
	b	Ability to think about ideas or to solve problems
	c	Skills or technical procedures specific to the subject.
Generic skills	d	Ability to work with other students
	e	Organizing and being responsible for my own learning
	f	Ability to communicate knowledge and ideas effectively
Information skills	g	Ability to track down information in the subject area
	h	Information technology/computing skills (e.g. WWW, e-mail, word processing)

▶ Evidence of item consistency within the scales
(Cronbach alpha values)

Approaches to studying	*alpha*	Experiences of teaching	*alpha*
Deep approach	0.75	Congruence and coherence	0.72
Surface approach	0.68	Teaching for understanding	0.67
Organized effort	0.84	Staff enthusiasm and support	0.71
		Constructive feedback	0.77
		Support from other students	0.73
		Interest and relevance	0.83

Source: From a sample of 1950 students who completed both the questionnaires in the ETL project.
Note: Generally, with scales of this kind alpha values grater than 0.70 would be considered to be good, while those above 0.65 would certainly be acceptable.

Item factor structure
(SPSS, maximum likelihood factor analysis to obtain oblique factors with Oblimin, Kaiser Normalization; N = 1950)

	Factors		
Approaches to studying	I	II	III
Deep approach			
1. ... better ways of tracking down relevant information in this subject.	.60		
4. In making sense of new ideas, I've often related them to ... real life.	.43		
6. Ideas I've come across ... often set me off on long chains of thought.	.61		
7. I've looked at evidence carefully to reach my own conclusion.	.68		
9. It has been important for me to follow the argument, or to see ...	.45		
12. ... I've tried to find out for myself exactly what the author means.	.68		
Surface approach			
3. Much of what I've learned seems ... unrelated bits and pieces ...		.67	
8. I've often had trouble in making sense of the things I have to remember.		.52	
11. I don't think through topics for myself, I just rely on what we're taught.		.50	
13. I've just been going through the motions of studying.		.57	
Organized effort			
2. I have generally put a lot of effort into my studying.			.61
5. On the whole, I've been quite systematic and organized in my studying.			.74
10. I've organized my study time carefully to make the best use of it.			.86
14. I've carefully prioritized my time to make sure I can fit everything in.			.78
Lack of purpose			
15. When I look back, I sometimes wonder why I ever decided to come here (additional item not included in this analysis).			

Correlations between factors

	Deep	*Surface*	*Org Effort*
Deep	—		
Surface	−.33	—	
Organized effort	.37	−.15	—

Note: N = 1950. Loadings below 0.3 have been omitted. Three factors explained 55% of the variance, while four factors accounted for 61%. The normal eigen value criterion for this analysis would suggest the extraction of a fourth factor, but this was conceptually a component of the deep approach, more concerned with intention than process. In some analyses, the surface factor broke into two, separating the items related to fragmentation and rote learning, and those suggesting 'going through the motions'.

Experiences of Teaching	Factors					
	I	**II**	**III**	**IV**	**V**	**VI**
Congruence and coherence						
1. It was clear to me what I was supposed to learn.	.82					
2. The topics ... follow each other in a way that made sense.	.63					
3. What we were taught ... matched what we were supposed to learn.	.54					
Teaching for understanding						
4. ... given me a sense of what goes on 'behind the scenes'.		.58				
5. [The teaching] helped me to think about the evidence ...		.77				
6. ... encouraged me to relate what I learned to issues in the wider world.		.51				
Staff enthusiasm and support						
7. Staff tried to share their enthusiasm about the subject with us.			.56			
8. Staff were patient in explaining things ... difficult to grasp.			.76			
9. Students' views were valued in this course.			.49			
Constructive feedback						
10. The feedback ... helped me to improve my ways of learning.				1.05		
11. The feedback ... helped to clarify things I hadn't fully understood.				.56		
Support from other students						
12. Students supported each other and tried to give help ...					.90	
13. Talking with other students helped me to develop my understanding.					.64	
Interest and enjoyment						
14. I found ... what I learned in this course really interesting.						1.02
15. I enjoyed being involved in this course.						.53

Correlations between factors	Factors					
	Congr	**TfU**	**Staff**	**Fdbk**	**Stud**	**Int**
Congruence and coherence	. –					
Teaching for understanding	.46	. –				
Staff enthusiasm and support	.43	.50	. –			
Constructive feedback	.26	.42	.48	. –		
Support from other students	.17	.20	.34	.21	. –	
Interest and enjoyment	.27	.21	.42	.44	.53	. –

Note: N = 1950. Loadings below 0.3 have been omitted. Six factors have consistently provided the most satisfactory solution and here explained 71% of the variance, which is substantial when analysing individual items.

▶ Experiences of Teaching and Learning Questionnaire

This questionnaire has been designed to allow you to describe, in a systematic way, your reactions to the course you have been studying and how you have gone about learning it. We will be asking you a series of questions, some of which overlap so as to provide good overall coverage of different experiences. Most of the items are based on comments made by other students. Please respond truthfully, so that your answers will describe your **actual** ways of studying, and work your way through the questionnaire quite **quickly.** It is important that you respond to **every** item, even if that means using the 'unsure' category. Your answers will be **confidential.** Please put a cross in the appropriate box to indicate how strongly you agree with each of the following statements.

Name or identifying number (if required) _____

Year of course _____ Course unit _____

Degree _____

---

1   Approaches to learning and studying

This section asks about in the ways you have been going about studying in this particular course. The responses in this section mean:

  ✓ = agree   ✓? = agree somewhat   ✗? = disagree somewhat   ✗ = disagree

Try not to use **??** = unsure unless you really have to, or if it cannot apply to you or your course unit.

	✓	✓?	??	✗?	✗
1. I've tried to find better ways of tracking down relevant information in this subject.	5	4	3	2	1
2. I have generally put a lot of effort into my studying.	5	4	3	2	1
3. Much of what I've learned seems no more than lots of unrelated bits and pieces in my mind.	5	4	3	2	1
4. In making sense of new ideas, I have often related them to practical or real life contexts.	5	4	3	2	1
5. On the whole, I've been quite systematic and organized in my studying.	5	4	3	2	1
6. Ideas I've come across in my academic reading often set me off on long chains of thought.	5	4	3	2	1
7. I've looked at evidence carefully to reach my own conclusion about what I'm studying.	5	4	3	2	1
8. I've often had trouble in making sense of the things I have to remember.	5	4	3	2	1
9. It has been important for me to follow the argument, or to see the reasons behind things.	5	4	3	2	1
10. I've organized my study time carefully to make the best use of it.	5	4	3	2	1

(*Continued*)

11. I don't think through topics for myself, I just rely on what we're taught.	5	4	3	2	1
12. In reading for this course, I've tried to find out for myself exactly what the author means.	5	4	3	2	1
13. I've just been going through the motions of studying without seeing where I'm going.	5	4	3	2	1
14. I've carefully prioritized my time to make sure I can fit everything in.	5	4	3	2	1
15. When I look back, I sometimes wonder why I ever decided to come here.	5	4	3	2	1

2   Experiences of teaching and learning in this course

We would also like to know about your experiences of teaching and learning in this particular course. Try to avoid using **??** (unsure).

	✓	✓?	??	✗?	✗
Congruence and coherence in the course unit as a whole					
1. It was clear to me what I was supposed to learn in this course unit.	5	4	3	2	1
2. The topics seemed to follow each other in a way that made sense to me.	5	4	3	2	1
3. What we were taught seemed to match what we were supposed to learn.	5	4	3	2	1
Teaching for understanding					
4. This unit has given me a sense of what goes on 'behind the scenes' in this subject area.	5	4	3	2	1
5. The teaching in this course helped me to think about the evidence underpinning different views.	5	4	3	2	1
6. This course encouraged me to relate what I learned to issues in the wider world.	5	4	3	2	1
Staff enthusiasm and support					
7. Staff tried to share their enthusiasm about the subject with us.	5	4	3	2	1
8. Staff were patient in explaining things which seemed difficult to grasp.	5	4	3	2	1
9. Students' views were valued in this course.	5	4	3	2	1
Constructive feedback					
10. The feedback given on my work helped me to improve my ways of learning and studying.	5	4	3	2	1
11. The feedback given on my set work helped to clarify things I hadn't fully understood.	5	4	3	2	1
Support from other students					
12. Students supported each other and tried to give help when it was needed.	5	4	3	2	1
13. Talking with other students helped me to develop my understanding.	5	4	3	2	1
Interest and enjoyment generated by the course					
14. I found most of what I learned in this course really interesting.	5	4	3	2	1
15. I enjoyed being involved in this course.	5	4	3	2	1

3 Demands made by the course unit

In this section, please tell us how **easy** or **difficult** you found various aspects of **this course**.

✓ = *very easy*   ✓? = *fairly easy*   ?? = *unsure/not applicable*   ×? = *fairly difficult*   × = *very difficult*

	✓	✓?	??	×?	×
a. What I was expected to know to begin with.	5	4	3	2	1
b. The rate at which new material was introduced.	5	4	3	2	1
c. The ideas and problems I had to deal with.	5	4	3	2	1
d. The skills or technical procedures needed in this subject.	5	4	3	2	1
e. The amount of work I was expected to do.	5	4	3	2	1
f. Working with other students.	5	4	3	2	1
g. Organizing and being responsible for my own learning.	5	4	3	2	1
h. Communicating knowledge and ideas effectively.	5	4	3	2	1
i Tracking down information for myself.	5	4	3	2	1
j. Information technology/computing skills (e.g. WWW, e-mail, word processing).	5	4	3	2	1

4 What you learned from this course unit

Now we would like to know how much you feel you have gained from studying **this course**.

✓ = *a lot*   ✓? = *quite a lot*   ?? = *unsure/not applicable*   ×? = *not much*   × = *very little*

	✓	✓?	??	×?	×
a. Knowledge and understanding about the topics covered.	5	4	3	2	1
b. Ability to think about ideas or to solve problems.	5	4	3	2	1
c. Skills or technical procedures specific to the subject.	5	4	3	2	1
d. Ability to work with other students.	5	4	3	2	1
e. Organizing and being responsible for my own learning.	5	4	3	2	1
f. Ability to communicate knowledge and ideas effectively.	5	4	3	2	1
g. Ability to track down information in this subject area.	5	4	3	2	1
h. Information technology/computing skills (e.g. WWW, e-mail, word processing).	5	4	3	2	1

Finally, how well do you think you're doing in this course as a whole?
Please try to rate yourself **objectively**, based on any marks, grades or comments you have been given.

very well	well	quite well	about average	not so well	rather badly	badly
9	8	7	6	5	4	3	2	1

Please check back to make sure that you have answered every question.

If you have any other comments or suggestions about this course or about your own ways of studying, please add them below.

Thank you very much for spending time completing this questionnaire.
It is much appreciated.

Short Revised Experiences of Teaching and Learning Questionnaire (SRETLQ) Developed by the ETL project team within the Teaching and Learning Research Programme of the ESRC (2009)

http://www.etl.tla.ed.ac.uk/

Index